T0296904

Crafting Wearables

Blending Technology with Fashion

Sibel Deren Guler
with
Madeline Gannon
Kate Sicchio

Apress®

Crafting Wearables: Blending Technology with Fashion

Sibel Deren Guler
Brooklyn, New York, USA

Madeline Gannon
Pittsburgh, Pennsylvania, USA

Kate Sicchio
Brooklyn, New York, USA

ISBN-13 (pbk): 978-1-4842-1807-5
DOI 10.1007/978-1-4842-1808-2

ISBN-13 (electronic): 978-1-4842-1808-2

Library of Congress Control Number: 2016949367

Managing Director: Welmoed Spahr
Lead Editor: Jonathan Gennick
Development Editor: Douglas Pundick and Matthew Moodie
Technical Reviewer: Lyn Hoge
Editorial Board: Steve Anglin, Pramila Balen, Laura Berendson, Aaron Black, Louise Corrigan, Jonathan Gennick,
    Robert Hutchinson, Celestin Suresh John, Nikhil Karkal, James Markham, Susan McDermott, Matthew Moodie,
    Ben Renow-Clarke, Gwenan Spearing
Coordinating Editor: Jill Balzano
Copy Editor: Tiffany Taylor
Compositor: SPi Global
Indexer: SPi Global
Artist: SPi Global
Cover Designer: Anna Ishchenko

Distributed to the book trade worldwide by Springer Science+Business Media New York, 233 Spring Street, 6th Floor, New York, NY 10013. Phone 1-800-SPRINGER, fax (201) 348-4505, e-mail orders-ny@springer-sbm.com, or visit www.springer.com. Apress Media, LLC is a California LLC and the sole member (owner) is Springer Science + Business Media Finance Inc (SSBM Finance Inc). SSBM Finance Inc is a Delaware corporation.

For information on translations, please e-mail rights@apress.com, or visit www.apress.com.

Apress and friends of ED books may be purchased in bulk for academic, corporate, or promotional use. eBook versions and licenses are also available for most titles. For more information, reference our Special Bulk Sales–eBook Licensing web page at www.apress.com/bulk-sales.

Any source code or other supplementary materials referenced by the author in this text is available to readers at www.apress.com. For detailed information about how to locate your book's source code, go to www.apress.com/source-code/.

Printed on acid-free paper

This book is dedicated to my grandmothers, who taught me the importance of learning how to do things myself, and exposed me to the magical world of textiles and fashion.

Contents at a Glance

About the Author xvii

About the Technical Reviewer xix

Acknowledgments xxi

Introduction xxiii

■Part I: What Are Wearables? 1

■Chapter 1: A Brief History of Wearables 3

■Chapter 2: Wearable Fictions 11

■Part II: Methods and Techniques 21

■Chapter 3: From Textiles to Wearables 23

■Chapter 4: Cutting and Sewing 33

■Chapter 5: Making Electronics Sewable 45

■Chapter 6: Soft Circuits 59

■Chapter 7: Materials That Matter 73

■Chapter 8: Digital Design for Wearables 85

■Chapter 9: Digital Fabrication for Wearables 99

■Chapter 10: Designing for the Body, on the Body 111

■Part III: Fashion and Product 119

■Chapter 11: Wearable Wellness 121

■Chapter 12: Beauty Tech 133

■Chapter 13: Superhumans and Cyborgs 145

■**Chapter 14: Activated Garments**.. **161**

■**Chapter 15: Wearable Costumes** **175**

■**Chapter 16: Speculations on Wearable Futures**................................. **183**

■**Appendix: Cyborg "Fingercaps" and Resources**................................. **197**

Index... **209**

Contents

About the Author xvii

About the Technical Reviewer xix

Acknowledgments xxi

Introduction xxiii

■Part I: What Are Wearables? 1

■Chapter 1: A Brief History of Wearables 3

Overview 3

Wearables to Help You Win 5

Wearables and the Arts 6

New Ideas and New Tools 7

Wearable Eyewear 7

Wearables in Research 9

Summary 10

■Chapter 2: Wearable Fictions 11

Sci-fi Prophecies 11

Bionics and Biomimetics 12

Diegetic Prototypes 12

Minority Report 12

Back to the Future 13

Star Trek 15

Superheroes and Super-Wearables 16

Batman's Batsuit 16

Iron Man's Exoskeleton 17

Wonder Woman's Bracelets 17

007's Bag of Tricks 17

Summary 19

■Part II: Methods and Techniques 21

■Chapter 3: From Textiles to Wearables 23

Textile Manufacturing 23

Raw Materials 23

From Fiber to Fabric 24

Economic and Social Implications 25

Fashion Design 25

Textiles and Education 28

Sewing as a Class 28

Higher Education: Tech vs. Textiles 29

Sewing for Engineers 30

Electronics in Clothing 30

Project Jacquard 30

Intel's Smart Fashion 32

Summary 32

■Chapter 4: Cutting and Sewing 33

A Sewing Kit 33

Additional Materials 36

Stitches and Seams 36

Running Stitch 37

Whipstitch 38

Sewing a Button 39

Cutting fabric 40

Making a Pillow 40

Following a Pattern 42

Using a Sewing Machine 43

Summary 44

■Chapter 5: Making Electronics Sewable.. 45

Circuits and Power 45

What Is a Circuit? 45

Power Sources...49

Series vs. Parallel 50

How to Sew a Light Circuit 50

Custom-Made Kits 54

LilyPad 54

Flora...55

Aniomagic 56

Fabrickit...56

Teknikio 57

Summary 58

■Chapter 6: Soft Circuits 59

Crafting Circuits...59

Designing a Soft Switch 61

Creating a Printed Circuit Shirt..65

Assembling an E-textiles Toolkit 66

Summary 72

■Chapter 7: Materials That Matter 73

Thread as Wire 73

Conductive Ribbon and Tape 74

Conductive Fabric..75

Homemade Bend Sensor 77

Chromatic 78

    Thermochromatic 79

    Photochromatism 79

Shape Changing 80

    Shape Memory Polymer 81

    Shape Memory Alloy 81

    Polymorph 81

Glowing Materials 82

    Electroluminescent Wire 82

    Optical Fibers 82

Quantum Tunneling Composite 83

Protective Materials 83

    Schoeller Textiles 83

    GORE 84

    X-Bionic 84

Summary 84

■Chapter 8: Digital Design for Wearables 85

Software for Digital Design 85

    2D Design Tools 85

    3D Design Tools 86

Customizing Your Tools 88

    Digitizing the Body 88

    Parametric Design 94

Summary 97

■Chapter 9: Digital Fabrication for Wearables 99

Lasering 99

    Laser Cutting 100

    Laser Textures 101

    Laser Welding 101

3D Printing 102

Flexible Filaments...103

4D Printing..105

Printed Casting 106

Digitized Machines 107

Digital Knitting..107

Digital Embroidery...107

SoftWear Automation...108

Maker and Machine..109

Summary...109

■Chapter 10: Designing for the Body, on the Body 111

Skin-Centric Interfaces 112

Sensing the Body 113

3D Modeling Back End 114

Fabrication-Aware Design 114

Intuitive Gestures, Precise Geometry 115

Physical Artifacts...116

Future Applications 117

Summary...117

■Part III: Fashion and Product..119

■Chapter 11: Wearable Wellness 121

Fitness Trackers 121

Smart Clothing 123

Techstyles..123

Fit Like a Glove 124

Wearable Baby Monitors..124

Bracing Yourself 125

For Better Posture 126

Concept Products 127

Posture Suspenders Project 127

Summary 131

■ **Chapter 12: Beauty Tech** **133**

The Beauty Technologist 133

    Hairware 133

    More than Makeup 134

    Beauty Tech Nails 136

Living Makeup 137

Dermatology and Technology 138

Conductive Tattoos 140

DIY LED Tattoo Project 140

    Design and Sketch 141

    Steps to Make a Temporary Light Tattoo 142

Summary 143

■ **Chapter 13: Superhumans and Cyborgs** **145**

Cyborgs and Bionics 145

    Cyborgs for Art 146

    Cyborg Research 148

    Bodyhacking 149

Cyborg-Themed Products 151

    To Better See You With 152

    To Better Hear You With 153

Medical Bionics 154

    Brain-Computer Interface 154

    Prosthetics 156

Summary 159

■Chapter 14: Activated Garments 161

Fashion for Safety 161

To Safely Reach Your Destination 162

No Contact Jacket 163

Fashion for Privacy 163

Emotional Style 164

Social Body Lab 164

HugShirt 165

No(where)Now(here) 166

Studio XO 167

Chromat 167

Environmentally Reactive 169

Sparkle Booties 169

Dissolving Clothes 170

Wearable Façade 170

Garments as Interfaces 170

Digitizing Shoes 170

Nudgeables Accessory Kit 171

TshirtOS 171

M-Dress 172

Mirror Handbag 172

Illuminated Garments 172

Summary 173

■Chapter 15: Wearable Costumes 175

What Kinds of Wearables Are Found in Performance? 176

Sensing Performers 176

Actuation, Haptics, and Performance 178

Energy Harvesting 180

Technology vs. Performance 181

How to Design Wearable Sensors for Performance 181

    1. Choose a Sensor 181

    2. Design for the Body 181

    3. Decide What the Sensor Will Control 181

    4. Devising and Choreographing the Sensor 182

    5. Repeating Is Necessary 182

Summary 182

■ **Chapter 16: Speculations on Wearable Futures** **183**

Fashion Pioneers 183

    Hussein Chalayan 183

    Iris van Herpen 185

Future Fabric and Fabrication 186

    Spray-On Clothes 187

    Catalytic Clothing 188

    BioCouture 188

    Mediated Matter 189

Future Retail 189

    Lifestyles and Experiences 190

    Analog to Digital 192

Culture and Society 193

    Costs and Benefits 193

    Privacy Concerns 193

    Social Robotics 194

Summary 195

■ **Appendix: Cyborg "Fingercaps" and Resources** **197**

Recipe for Cyborg Fingercaps 198

Additional Resources 203

    Chapter 1: A Brief History of Wearables 203

    Chapter 2: Wearable Fictions 203

    Chapter 3: From Textiles to Wearables 203

Chapter 4: Cutting and Sewing 203

Chapter 5: Making Electronics Sewable 204

Chapter 6: Soft Circuits 204

Chapter 7: Materials That Matter 204

Chapter 8: Digital Design for Wearables 204

Chapter 9: Digital Fabrication for Wearables 205

Chapter 10: Designing for the Body, on the Body 205

Chapter 11: Wearable Wellness 205

Chapter 12: Beauty Tech 205

Chapter 13: Superhumans and Cyborgs 206

Chapter 14: Activated Garments 206

Chapter 15: Wearable Costumes 206

Chapter 16: Speculations on Wearable Futures 207

Index **209**

About the Author

Sibel Deren Guler is a researcher, designer, and educator based in New York. She develops technology that uses interactivity and computation to explore nature and create playful experiences. Designing accessible tools to improve the quality of life and empower the user is her key motivator. She has led interactive projects and workshops around the world. She has been exploring wearable technology for several years through personal research and collaboration. She is the creator of a series of toolkits under the brand Teknikio that teach you how to embed electronics into different materials. Teknikio works to fill the gap in hands-on science and engineering products for children, especially young girls. Guler has a personal interest in textiles that she credits to her mother and grandmothers, who are incredible seamstresses. She is a co-founder of the Fat Cat Fab Lab and adjuncts at Parsons the New School for Design.

About the Technical Reviewer

Lyn Hoge has been a dance teacher, costumer, and choreographer for over 40 years. She has designed and created costumes for musicals, plays, and various types of dance concerts. These include everything from simple costume plays like *Our Town* to elaborate and quirky versions of *The Rocky Horror Picture Show*. She has also created unique and functional designs for dancers in contemporary and historical styles of dance for concerts. In the past couple of years, she has been delving into the world of wearable tech and is writing about her experiences as a teacher and a student. Lyn has a BA in dance and has studied at UCLA, UCI, and several private studios.

Acknowledgments

Writing this book has been a whirlwind journey that has taught me so much, I can still hardly believe it all came together!

I would like to thank the wonderful team at Apress, without whom this book would not exist. Thanks to Jonathan Gennick, who saw the potential in the proposal and pushed the idea for this book forward; Lyne Hoge and Douglas Pundick, who made sure all the images and explanations in this book flow together to create a better experience for the reader; and Jill Balzano, who helped keep us on track and always understood when we missed a deadline or needed some extra time for image permissions. And to Tiffany Taylor for copy-editing.

I would also like to thank all the designers who dedicated the time to let me pick their brains and ask them the same questions they get asked in every interview. They helped transform and expand my perspective on wearables to make this book more thorough and complete. Thanks to Yolita Nugent, for her insight and wonderful recommendations on what areas of body technologies to explore; and Sylvia Stein, Madison Maxey, Chris Pin, and other designers and friends who helped point me in the right direction during my research about textiles and manufacturing. Thanks to all the companies and designers who granted permission for their images of their work to be featured in this book; I hope that together we will be able to reach an even wider audience and expose your talent and ideas.

A special thanks to my guest authors Madeline Gannon and Kate Sicchio, who have shared their expertise to make this book more complete and more interesting. They have helped me with many aspects of the book beyond the chapters they wrote, from helping me figure how to structure chapters to helping me choose appropriate images. On that note, I'd like to thank my friends and family, who have been extremely supportive throughout this process and have helped me keep other commitments afloat. I definitely had to be very protective of my spare time to (try to) meet all of my deadlines, and I greatly appreciate all the support and encouragement I received. A special thanks to my amazing mother, (also a talented seamstress) who always encourages me to keep going. And to my dad who once told me "I think you should write a book", here it is.

Introduction

A ring on your finger vibrates, a bracelet is illuminated with soft white lights that begin to cycle on and off in a repeating pattern, and your shirt begins to tighten around your body. Your clothes and accessories have come to life and seem to have a mind of their own. Although this may seem like a description of a scene from a science fiction story, many of these devices already exist and are being adopted by people all over the world. Doctors use them to monitor their patients, dancers use them to add expression to their performances, and educators use them to teach concepts of engineering; the applications span industries and communities worldwide.

A *wearable*, in its simplest form, is defined as an item or object that is suitable for wearing. Clothes, jewelry, armor, watches, glasses, and shoes all fit within this category. However, over the past few decades, this term has taken on a more specific connotation, referring explicitly to wearable technology. *Wearable technology* is defined as any wearable that incorporates electronics either as an accessory or as part of an item of clothing. The electronics may collect information, or they may just feature lights and speakers that are prewired to turn on in a sequence when connected to a power source. *Wearable computing* is a specific subset of wearable technology that refers to computational or sensory devices. Often these devices are miniature forms of a device that exists in non-wearable form. This book explores the evolution of different types of wearable technology within the larger world of textiles and fashion.

Wearable technologies propose completely new solutions and features to address connectivity, security, and health. The most obvious of these is that they allow for a more intimate and personal connection with the user. Although the ring, bracelet, and shirt described earlier may seem disruptive or intrusive, they are intrusive in a personal sense. Other people may not notice that your bracelet is flashing, and they won't be able to tell that your ring is vibrating or that your shirt is being stretched. These are all hidden, almost secret interactions that are directed only at the user. Unlike a loud cellphone ringtone, which could disrupt a whole lecture hall or movie theater, a gentle vibration or glow on the finger is barely noticeable. However, these new interactions and associations will ultimately breed a new set of gestures and reactions to our environments. Once we are trained to associate the sound of a bell with an incoming message, or a slight tapping on the shoulder with a reminder to straighten up, we may be augmenting our senses to a point that we expect the world to be equipped with these electronic devices. We may respond to them more intensely then we do to our primitive human instincts associated with nature.

Wearables have attracted experts from fashion, engineering, education, and several other fields to work together. The interdisciplinary nature of wearable devices serves as a unique platform for people to share skills in craft, science, design, and more. Interestingly, an important invention in the field of textiles—the Jacquard head by Joseph Marie Jacquard (circa 1801)—was the first binary information processor. At any given point, the thread in a woven fabric can be in one of two states or positions: on the face of the fabric or on the back. Pattern cards were punched or cut according to the required fabric design. A hole in the card signified that the thread would appear on the face of the fabric, whereas a blank meant the end would be left down and appear on the back of the fabric. The Jacquard head was used on weaving looms or machines to raise and lower the warp threads to form desired patterns based on the lifting plan or program embedded in the cards. Thus the Jacquard mechanism set the stage for modern-day binary information processing.

Tech companies such as Google are partnering with Levi's and other fashion companies to create clothing that is embedded with interfaces and sensors. With this collaboration, Levi's can focus on creating a comfortable and stylish item, and Google can focus on giving it function and supporting the technology. Each company is able to focus on its strengths in the collaboration, but a certain amount of training and learning is necessary for fluid communication. Software engineers at Google studied traditional methods of textile manufacturing to gain an understanding of what is possible in order to better communicate their idea to designers at Levi's. Similarly, designers at Levi's needed to learn the basics of electronics and tactile interfaces to understand how to work with them and what considerations they must factor into their designs.

This book gives examples of these types of collaborations while guiding you through common methodologies from both a textiles and technology perspective.

Book Overview

This book is divided into three parts. The first part sets the stage by providing some foundational knowledge of the history of wearables. The second part discusses techniques for crafting wearables, from a simple sewable circuit to a complex digital interface. The third part takes a look at the use of wearables in various industries and reviews some inspirational products and projects.

Part 1 of the book walks you through the factual and fictional evolution of wearable computing. Chapter 1 discusses the intersection of textiles and technology from the earliest known forms of wearable computational devices and the integration of automated and robotic techniques in the textile industry. Chapter 2 provides an overview of the influence that science fiction and other forms of narrative media have had on the wearable industry. In particular, it looks at how some popular fictional props have set the stage for the introduction of certain technologies.

Part 2 of the book includes the bulk of the "wearable recipes," showcasing some of the methods and techniques used by hobbyists and professionals as they pertain to the research and development of wearables. We begin by looking at the current state of textile manufacturing and follow with a crash course in basic sewing and pattern-making techniques. The next few chapters include tutorials for sewing circuits and creating textile "soft" sensors. We then introduce some common tools and materials used by e-textile artists and designers with reviews and recommendations for various applications. The last few chapters in this section look at new interfaces and tools for wearables and how they are changing and improving current manufacturing methods.

Part 3 focuses on real-world applications and provides an in-depth look at popular wearable products and high-tech fashion. We examine various products, from medical devices to augmented-reality glasses and consider their usability and potential scalability. This section includes some design thinking exercises to help guide you through your personal evaluation of the devices described. We then explore some more experimental approaches to wearables involving the application of electronics directly to the skin and the idea of superhuman powers. This leads into a catalogue of wearables that have been incorporated in high fashion and costumes for performance. The final few chapters of part 3 explore the cultural significance of the projects and products mentioned and speculate on future trends and implications.

This book will leave you with a comprehensive general knowledge of the state of wearables in different industries, including a well-curated list of example projects and resources. It will serve as a wonderful launching pad for your personal journey into the world e-textiles.

PART I

■ ■ ■

What Are Wearables?

CHAPTER 1

A Brief History of Wearables

The motivation for designing and making wearables has always been quite simple: to provide convenience for the wearer. As the world becomes more connected, our attention is increasingly divided. Clothing and accessories, when chosen carefully, can provide comfort and relief. For example, by adding more function to an outfit, you can consolidate the number of objects you need and make yourself more efficient when mobile. The ability to access e-mail or schedule an appointment on the go opens up new possibilities for where and how you can work. This chapter looks at the evolution of some of the earliest wearable technologies and the role they have played in fashion, technology, and society.

Overview

Before mobile phones became a widespread handheld accessory, many people wore a watch to tell the time. The history of the common wristwatch began in the 1500s, when the watch was redesigned to use simple springs as opposed to bulky, heavy weights, allowing the device to shrink considerably in size. German inventor Peter Henlein began developing small watches that hung from a chain around the neck and could be worn as a necklace. Then, in the late 1600s, the waistcoat became a fashionable item, and men began carrying watches in the pocket of their coat, leading to the popularization of pocket watches. Wristwatches appeared around the same time, but they were almost exclusively worn by women and marketed as bracelets.

The watch further evolved over time, becoming smaller and more accurate. In 1904, aviator Alberto Santos-Dumont commissioned the famous jeweler Cartier to create a timepiece that could be worn around his wrist, allowing him to keep his hands free for piloting. This proved to be a convenient place to wear a watch, and many soldiers began wearing watches to help synchronize time during war.

© Sibel Deren Guler, Madeline Gannon, and Kate Sicchio 2016
S. D. Guler et al., *Crafting Wearables*, DOI 10.1007/978-1-4842-1808-2_1

Figure 1-1. *Clock-watch made by Peter Henlein in the 16th century*

The wristwatch became widespread as a wearable after the World War I and continues to be redesigned and readapted today. The first mechanical digital watch was designed in the 1920s, and this technology was widely used until 1969, when quartz watches were introduced; the new technology greatly improved the accuracy of watches and reduced the maintenance required. In 1972, the Hamilton Pulsar electronic digital watch hit the market. In 1976, the company took the watch further, using new LCD display technology, and sold the first calculator watch. The calculator watch was redesigned by Casio in 1980 and became wildly popular as an iconic nerd accessory. In 1982, Seiko took the watch to a new level with a television watch, featuring a miniature blue LCD screen. Although the watch had to be tethered to another piece that housed the TV tuning system, it was impressive.

Over time, the price of manufacturing a digital watch decreased significantly, and companies began to add more features such as Nintendo games and address books. In 1994, Timex added a critical feature: the ability to communicate with another digital device. Using an optical sensor embedded in the watch, the Link-150 could transmit data to a PC. Other notable developments included the Casio camera watch, released in 2000, which housed a tiny functional digital camera; and the Seiko e-ink watch, released in 2010, which was the first smart watches with an interactive e-ink display. Today, companies like Apple, Samsung, and Google continue to develop watches, adding more and more functionality to the small, wearable wristband.

Although a bit smaller and arguably less commonly worn, the ring has also been used as a computational device for centuries. In the 17th century, the Qing Dynasty of China created the first smart ring in the form of an abacus embedded in a metal ring that was worn on a finger. The size of the abacus was 1 cm by 1/2 cm, and it contained seven rods with seven beads on each rod that could be moved back and forth using a small tool such as a hairpin. It is believed that the ring was used by traders who needed to make quick calculations while traveling from port to port.

The ring has been designed with other computational features over time. The Swiss ring watch appeared in 1890s as a fanciful jewelry item. Today, companies like Ringly continue to expand on the capabilities of the ring by embedding electronic interfaces and communication systems.

Another interesting wearable device is the hearing aid. The first hearing aid, also called an *ear trumpet*, was invented in the 17th century; and the first electronic hearing aid was developed in the 1890s after the invention of the telephone. Digital hearing aids hit the market in 1898. They continue to be redesigned and to shrink in size with each new version.

Wearables to Help You Win

In 1961, two mathematicians, Edward O. Thorpe and Claude Shannon, built a shoe that helped them cheat at roulette. Their idea was to hide a timing device in the shoe, which could fairly accurately predict which number the roulette ball would land on. Radio waves were used to communicate this number to the wearer of the shoe via an earpiece, allowing him to make a well-informed bet. When tested by the inventors, the gadget increased the odds of winning by 44%. However, when Thorpe and Shannon took their gadget to the casino to test it, they experienced several hardware problems and were not able to double their money as planned.

Although primitive, the invention tackled many challenges that designers of wearables are still trying to overcome today. Designing truly personal communication between the device and the wearer was one aspect of the project that took a lot of experimentation and consideration; encasing the hardware in such a way that it could withstand the wear and tear of an active person was another.

In 1972, Alan Lewis, a theoretical physicist, tackled the same problem using a computer hidden in a camera case. A few years later, in 1978, a group of mathematicians formed a group called the Eudaemons. Their objective was to create a device that would similarly help them beat roulette, and then to use the money to fund a scientific community. In the end, they also chose to conceal the computational device in a shoe. The data was input by the user by tapping a switch under the big toe in the shoe; the signal was then relayed to an output system, which was hidden in the player's shirt. The input came from three solenoids that vibrated in a certain pattern, informing the user which of the eight octants of the roulette wheel to bet on. The "shoe computer" is shown in Figure 1-2.

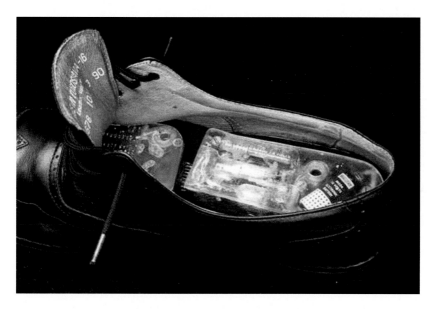

Figure 1-2. *The Eudaumons' shoe computer (courtesy of Steve Mann)*

The group took the device to Las Vegas in 1978 and reported a profit of 44% for every dollar. Unfortunately, like Thorpe and Shannon, they experienced hardware problems, the most severe being that the insulation rubbed off on the wires and the wearer experienced several electric shocks from the solenoids, burning a hole in her skin. In the end, they won approximately $10,000 and accomplished their goal of statistically predicting where the ball would land on the wheel based on input data. However, the risks involved drew the group apart, and they disbanded shortly after the trip. Their work is thought of as a precursor to data science and predictive analysis.

Wearables and the Arts

Theodore Dubois, professor of harmony at the Conservatoire in Paris, debuted his electric ballet *La Farandole* in 1883. In the ballet, dancers wore electric lights on their foreheads; batteries were concealed in the recesses of their clothing. When the dancers touched a button on their belt, the lights illuminated. The technology used in the batteries was featured in electronic journals from the time. Figure 1-3 is from an article in *The Electrician* describing the battery.

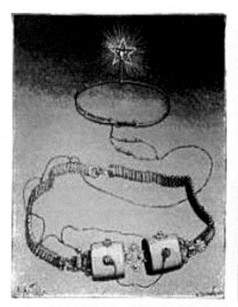 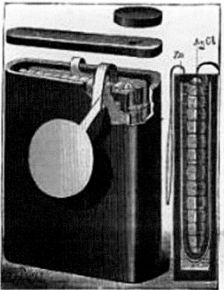

Fig 1.- ELECTRIC DIADEM AND BELT USED IN THE BALLET OF THE FARANDOLE IN PARIS.

Fig. 2.- BATTERY USED WITH THE ELECTRIC DIADEM.

Figure 1-3. *Image of a wearable electric headband from La Farandole*

One year later, in 1884, the *New York Times* published an article about a new phenomenon: the Electric Girl Lighting Company. It was said that the company rented out "illuminated girls" who would wait on homeowners while wearing filament lamps of "fifty candle power." The girls would sit either by the door or in the hall to guide guests through the house while lighting their way in the night. In the story, the cost of hiring a girl is said to be less than the combined costs of running an electric lamp and hiring a servant, thus providing the perfect replacement for both services. The *Times* article made the prediction that "in a very short time private houses will be lighted by girls, instead of stationary electric lights." The article also claimed that the creation of "Electric Girls" was almost as important as the invention of electricity. Historians believe that this story was in fact a spoof, based on the inconsistencies of many facts in the article. Perhaps the idea was inspired by Dubois' ballet and other events at the time, but no real record of the company has ever been found. Additionally, the writer for the *New York Times* published the article under a fake name, giving reason to doubt its validity. But regardless of whether the girls existed, the article shows that hiring a human lamp, so to speak, was plausible at the time—so much so that the idea was able to slip by the editor and make it into print. You will see more of these fictitious stories and their influence in the next chapter.

Back to actual historic inventions and gadgets: in 1907, German inventor and amateur photographer Julius Neubronner patented what may have been the first wearable camera. He strapped a small wooden camera to a pigeon to take aerial photographs. His tiny lightweight camera featured a timer mechanism so that it could capture a single image. Although his work won him many photography awards, the expenses involved made it an unsustainable pursuit.

In 1968, the Museum of Contemporary Craft in New York City held a monumental exhibit called *Body Covering* centered around forms for covering the body using new technology. The exhibit featured an array of wearable projects, from astronaut suits to clothing that could heat and cool itself and light up. The exhibit included the work of Diana Dew, who created a line of electroluminescent party dresses that could light up and produce siren noises. The work in *Body Covering* is particularly impressive because the designers and artists did not have specialized tools for activating their creations. They had to creatively repurpose raw materials and readily available electronics, and then embed them into clothes and accessories. Fashion designers and artists continue to experiment with embedding electronics, pushing the limits of fabric craft and engineering. Chapter 14 takes a closer look at these projects.

New Ideas and New Tools

In 1985, Harry Wainwright created a sweatshirt embedded with fiber-optic lights and a microprocessor that could control the pattern of the lights and display frames of a full-color cartoon animation on the surface of the fabric. Ten years later, in 1995, he invented a machine specifically designed to weave fiber optics into fabric. In 1997, he developed this into the first CNC machine that can embed fiber optics into any flexible material. He holds over a dozen patents based on light displays and machinery and has created custom apparel and toys for Disney, Mattel, Britney Spears, Sony, and more. Although Wainwright's work is primarily used for entertainment, he has also developed educational kits. He still consults, designs, and teaches workshops on the subject at his studio in Monessen, Pennsylvania.

Over time, textiles artists and engineers have worked together to create highly specialized tools and methods for wearables. A new genre of technology has emerged, commonly referred to as *computational craft*. In 2006, Leah Buechly coined the term *e-textile construction kit* and introduced the LilyPad Arduino, an electronic kit featuring the popular microcontroller platform that enabled people to build interactive fashion using fabric-mounted boards. The project was further developed in collaboration with popular hobby electronics company SparkFun Electronics and became commercially available in late 2007. The spirit of creating an easy-to-use platform for artists and designers to attach and program electronics on clothing has been carried on by several designers. Chapter 4 takes a closer look at some of these.

Wearable Eyewear

The first set of eyeglasses was created for Emperor Nero (who ruled from 54-68 A.D.). Eyeglass were purely analog tools for centuries until Hubert Upton created what may have been the first a pair of augmented reality glasses in 1967. Upton, an engineer at Bell Helicopter, conceived a device as a personal project that would help hearing-impaired people visualize sounds. His original design included a microphone that analyzed sounds via a portable wearable computer and sent a signal to a small fiber optic LED embedded in the glasses. Depending on the tone, the light would change color and project straight out into the wearer's field of vision. Upton surmised that if the light aligned with a speaker's lips, the deaf person would have an easier time with lip reading. Unfortunately, this was never truly realized, and the technology was repurposed for the military such that instead of translating sound into color, the light projected lines in front of pilots to give them direction while flying a plane through difficult areas or landing at night.

Wearables have shown great potential in helping the impaired. In 1977, C. C. Collins, a researcher at the Smith-Kettlewell Institute of Visual Sciences, developed a five-pound, wearable, head-mounted camera for the visually impaired. Collins used the now-popular technique of haptic tactile feedback and converted a 1,024-point image from the camera into a 10-inch square tactile grid on a wearable vest.

Many of these devices can be readapted to either augment or improve the senses, although some experimenters are focused more on augmenting perception. In 1981, Steven Mann, then in high school, fastened a 6502-based multimedia computer with text, graphics, and multimedia capability, as well as video capability, to his backpack. Mann is known as the father of wearable computing and the first person to call himself a cyborg. Since 1989, he has been wearing a computerized eyewear system that he builds and rebuilds himself. Figure 1-4 provides a snapshot of the evolution of his glasses over the years. Mann has invented countless wearable computational perception devices throughout his career, most notably the wireless webcam.

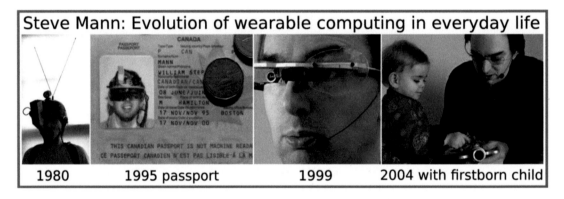

Figure 1-4. Steve Mann's wearable computer inventions (courtesy of Steve Mann)

In 1987, Reflection Technology released the Private Eye shown in Figure 1-5. It was a commercial wearable television display that could be handheld or worn over the center of one eye. It weighed less than two ounces, and the 1.2 inch × 3.2 inch display had a resolution comparable to that of a personal computer screen at the time: 720 × 280 pixels. Additionally, it drew only 1/2 watt and could be battery powered. The Private Eye was used in many wearable computer projects, including these two:

- *VuMan 1,* a project developed at Carnegie Mellon University, allowed the user to virtually maneuver through the blueprints of a house using three input buttons. The project was redeveloped through six generations from 1991–1995. Version 2 included a cursor that allowed the user to select items from a map or database, and version 3 was upgraded to include features like memory and power management.

- The *Lizzy,* developed at the MIT Media Lab by Thad Starner and Doug Platt in 1993, began as a research project to develop a wearable platform that could be used for general-purpose computing applications. It was created as an open source project with an assembly guide, in the hopes that many other people would adapt and repurpose it for their needs. Starner has continued to wear a customized computer system since he created Lizzy, updating the parts with new technologies and features over the years, and he currently leads Google's Project Glass.

Both of these projects are arguably a few decades ahead of their time and are still inspiring researchers today.

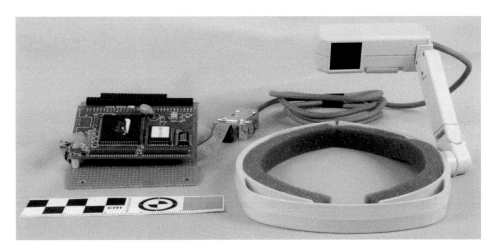

Figure 1-5. *Private Eye wearable headset (photo by Tavenner M. Hall, from Meeting the Challenge: The Path Towards a Consumer Wearable Computer)*

Wearables in Research

In 1996, the Department of Defense organized a workshop titled "Wearables in 2005" and brought industrial, university, and military visionaries together to work on the common theme of delivering computing to individuals. One notable project funded by DARPA is the *Wearable Motherboard,* also called the *Smart Shirt,* developed at Georgia Tech. An image of the shirt is shown in Figure 1-6. The Smart Shirt was developed under the paradigm "the fabric is the computer," and it brought engineering, textiles, and medical applications together. The Smart Shirt is recognized as the first "intelligent" garment, because it was the first wearable integrated information infrastructure; the group called it Personalized Mobile Information Processing (PMIP). It used optical fiber embedded in the fabric to detect bullet wounds and used embedded sensors to monitor heart rate and other vital signs during combat. As the project continued, it was developed less as a military-specific garment and more for civilians, because it featured so many new opportunities in the medical realm to monitor vital signs. The group continued to redesign and develop the architecture and textiles in an attempt to achieve their goal of creating a wearable processing system that could be reached "anywhere, anytime, and by anyone."

9

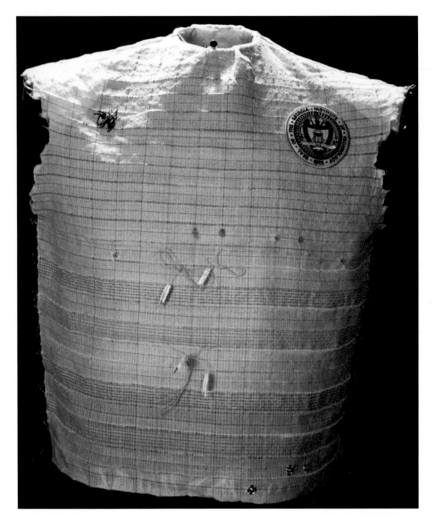

Figure 1-6. *The Wearable Motherboard (image courtesy of Sundaresan Jayaraman)*

Summary

Several important milestones were not reviewed in this chapter but are mentioned in the chapters to come as you look at more specific developments in wearables. The examples in this chapter were chosen to give a general idea of how a wearable gadget can evolve over time, adapting to new technological advances and cultural needs. For example, researchers may find they need to shift their focus to continue to fund and support their project, as in the case of Upton's augmented-reality glasses. New tools are designed for manufacturing and experimenting as interest in and demand for wearable technology increases. The next chapter takes a closer look at cultural interest in wearables and examines some fictional stories that have inspired and motivated these technologies.

CHAPTER 2

■ ■ ■

Wearable Fictions

Wearables often seem like something out of a *science fiction* (sci-fi) movie, made for another world or another time. Sometimes that's because they really *are* something out of a science fiction movie. Sci-fi is a genre of fiction that is based on imaginary concepts such as futuristic worlds and technology, parallel universes, and extraterrestrial life. It is a subgenre of *speculative fiction*, which refers more broadly to stories that involve elements of imaginary or speculative concepts as opposed to those of reality and everyday life.

The wearables field has been linked to speculative ideas, sci-fi books and films, and other imaginary media for decades. Most superheroes and villains are equipped with a magical gadget, cape, or shoes that enhance their superpowers. Sometimes the magic is embedded in the wearable, leaving us to believe that anyone with a particular hat or cloak could be transformed into a wizard. Other times the wearable simply enhances these powers, making them seem more far-fetched for everyday use. This chapter traces the evolution of fictitious wearables, connecting them to inventions and ideas that actually exist today.

Sci-fi Prophecies

Sci-fi is not only responsible to introducing us to crazy fashion styles and superpowers; many of the terms and concepts used to describe wearable gadgets and devices come from sci-fi stories. The term *cyborg* was coined in 1960 by Manfred Clynes and Nathan Kline in a story they wrote called "Cyborgs and Space." In the story, the cyborg is a human being who is augmented with technological "attachments." Today the term is defined as a person who is dependent on a mechanical or electronic device.

Neuromancer, written by William Gibson in 1984, founded the genre of *cyberpunk*. Cyberpunk is a subgenre of sci-fi in which the story takes place in a dystopian futuristic world similar to Earth. The plot usually involves a conflict between a corporation and rebellious hacker. Cyberpunk characters are generally augmented with computer implants, and there is often an underground world of computer hackers. In *Neuromancer*, one of the main protagonists has undergone surgical alterations and wears inset glasses with an alphanumeric readout, which has been tied to the origin of the concept for Google Glass.

Another famous sci-fi novel, *Fahrenheit 451*, written by Ray Bradbury in 1953, describes a futuristic world where people live under a government who has outlawed written word and instructs firemen to burn any existing books. In the book, Bradbury describes "little Seashells, the thimble radios tamped tight, and an electronic ocean of sound" in the ears of the characters. Bradbury is credited with forecasting the invention of headphones, along with many other gadgets and cultural norms of the today's world, like large flatscreen TVs.

© Sibel Deren Guler, Madeline Gannon, and Kate Sicchio 2016
S. D. Guler et al., *Crafting Wearables*, DOI 10.1007/978-1-4842-1808-2_2

11

Bionics and Biomimetics

Bionics are technologies that are built and designed based on biological systems in nature. Although the term was coin in 1958 by medical doctor Jack Steele, it was popularized in 1970 after the launch of several sci-fi books and television series. A bionic limb, also called a *prosthetic*, is one that has been replaced by an artificial limb that is electronically or mechanically powered. Bionic limbs have featured in many pieces of fiction since the 1960s and 70s, including *The Six Million Dollar Man*, the Borg of *Star Trek*, and Darth Vader. In the 1970s show *The Bionic Woman*, the main character has been fitted with several bionic parts after suffering from a traumatic parachute-landing accident. She is given a pair of bionic legs that can propel her at speeds of more than 60 mph and a bionic arm that can bend steel, along with other supernatural substitutes.

Bionic engineering has been used in the development of ultrasound imaging, cybernetics, fabric that mimics the way pinecones adapt to temperature, and more. *Biomimetics* is closely related to bionics and refers to models, systems, and elements of nature that are adapted and imitated to solve complex human problems.

Diegetic Prototypes

One of my favorite design exercises is to try to invent for an imaginary world. I find designing for the present and near future limiting in many ways; it steers you toward something practical—something that seems attainable. When you remove those requirements, you have the freedom to speculate even deeper and invent scenarios, cultures, and designs for a world that may not ever exist. Depending on the time period, planet, and dimension of your alternate and imaginary world, the clothing, spacesuits, and communication devices will be radically different from your everyday world and what you are familiar with, at least for now.

Diegetic prototype is a term introduced by Julian Bleecker of the Near Future Laboratory, which he defines as "ways in which cinematic depictions of future technologies demonstrate to large public audiences a technology's need, viability and benevolence." These depictions, or props, are fictional to the audience but completely real to the characters in the story. Diegetic prototypes are crucial to the development of a fictional world, because they help guide the audience through the sensory experience of what it is like to exist in that world. Watching characters interact with these objects makes it easier to put yourself in the world and imagine how you too could use these devices. Some of these props are believable because they could conceivably really exist in the near future, and others are extremely specific to the scenario in the story. For example, the earpiece in the movie *Her* basically already exists as a Bluetooth headset. It is a bit bulkier and does not have such a developed operating system (OS), but the concept is relatable to the majority of the audience.

Minority Report

Minority Report, a 2002 film based on Phillip K. Dick's short story with the same title, depicts a future high-tech crime unit in which police are able to predict a murder before it even happens. Although many different aspects of the movie have come true, such as advertising based on facial recognition, let's focus on the wearables. In the movie, the main character constantly uses projected touchscreen interfaces with special gloves that allow him to control the content that is displayed. The system recognizes various gestures as input, many of which are similar to the gestural interfaces used today with touchscreen phones and tablets.

Pranav Mistry of the Fluid Interfaces group at the MIT Media Lab recently released the SixthSense project, shown in Figure 2-1. The project consists of "a wearable gestural interface that augments the physical world around us with digital information and lets us use natural hand gestures to interact with that information." SixthSense consists of a pocket projector that projects visual information on surfaces, walls, and physical objects, and a camera that recognizes and tracks the user's hand gestures and physical objects using a computer-vision algorithm. This means any surface can be instantly transformed into an interface.

Figure 2-1. *A demo of inventor Pranav Mistry using his creation, SixthSense*

The user wears colored markers on their hands, which are encoded in the system to trigger specific actions in response to different gestures. SixthSense also recognizes when the user draws icons or symbols in the air with an index finger and processes them as interaction instructions. For example, drawing a magnifying glass symbol opens the Map application. The group has posted instructions on how to make your own SixthSense system for approximately $350 at `https://code.google.com/p/sixthsense/`. Several other research groups in industry and academia are working on similar systems of touchscreen interactions that don't actually involve touching, referred to as *ultrahaptic technology*.

Back to the Future

Back to the Future (1985) is a sci-fi adventure film about a teenager named Marty McFly who travels 30 years into the future in a flying car to save his family. It was the highest-grossing film of the year and has won countless awards, including being named the American Film Institute's 10th best sci-fi film.

■ **Note**   The date that McFly travels into the future (October 21, 2015, "Back to the Future Day") happened to be the week before I began writing this chapter!

In case you have not already seen the film several times (it is often shown on cable television), it features many speculative elements of this future world. In addition to flying cars and futuristic Pepsi cans, some of these elements are of the wearable genre and were recently invented as real products:

- *Smart watches*: In the film, the teenagers in the future world are all wearing smart watches on their wrists that can predict the weather "down to the tick." Today, the Apple Watch and other smart watches offer different applications capable of forecasting the weather and loading calendar appointments, along with many other features. Additionally, advancements in weather technology have led to developments like AccuWeather's new application called MinuteCast, which can give hyper-local, minute-by-minute precipitation forecasts.

- *TV glasses*: Members of the future family wear TV glasses at the dinner table. With these glasses, they can make and answer calls and watch television. Everyone is consumed their own world; Marty Jr. even complains that he can only watch two channels at a time with his glasses. TV glasses, known today as *augmented-reality glasses*, have also become a reality. With Google's Google Glass and Sony's Glastron, you can make and receive calls, check e-mail, and enter a fully augmented reality. Today's society is similarly consumed with electronics. Even if people are not wearing TV glasses, most cafes are full of people staring at their phones, reading articles or watching videos and tuning out their environment.

- *Power laces*: Who wouldn't want a pair of shoes that can tie themselves? In the movie, Marty wears a pair of Nike sneakers called Nike Air Mag with laces that automatically tighten around his ankle. Nike released a pair of Air Mags in 2011 that look identical to those in the movie but lacked the critical power-lacing feature. Four years later, the company successfully created a pair of self-lacing shoes that automatically tie themselves. In addition to being extremely iconic, Nike believes the shoes will be advantageous to athletes who already wear ankle-support braces, because the built-in ankle strap system helps to secure the ankle in place. A pair of the shoes was sent to actor Michael J. Fox, who plays Marty in the film. The shoes will sold commercially starting in 2016. The Nike shoes are shown in Figure 2-2.

Figure 2-2. *Nike's Power Lace shoes lacing up (top), and tied and lit up (bottom) (© Nike)*

Star Trek

Star Trek, one of the most popular sci-fi TV and movie series, has acquired an enormous following over the years, commonly referred to as *Trekkies*. Being called a Trekkie may seem unfashionable, but on the contrary, Trekkies have insight into many future trends. Several wearable concepts are familiar from the show, and their function and potential impact on society are very noticeable. Following are some notable props from the show:

- *Communicators*: If you have watched a few episodes of the original series, you probably recall a small flip-phone-like device that characters carried with them. Called *communicators*, these wearable devices were used to place calls to other characters. For example, Captain Kirk often used his communicator to call Spock and ask him to look up important scientific information. Nowadays, communicators have become a widespread device, commonly referred to as a smartphone.

- *Geordi's VISOR*: Geordi is a memorable character on *Star Trek: The Next Generation* who had an iconic eye visor. Geordi was blind, but after a special surgery, he was able to see through the electromagnetic spectrum with the aid of his Visual Instrument and Sensory Organ Replacement (VISOR). In 2005, a team of scientists at Stanford successfully implemented a similar bionic eye. They implanted a small chip behind the retina of a blind rat, which resulted and the rats then successfully passed a vision test. This technology is similar to the VISOR because the patient first receives the implant and then uses a special pair of glasses that have an embedded video camera. A small computer processes the light that enters the camera and wirelessly broadcasts it as an infrared LED image on the inside of the glasses. These images are reflected into the chip implanted behind the retina, where they stimulate photodiodes. The photodiodes replicate lost retinal cells and change the light into electrical signals, which send nerve pulses to the brain.

- *Tricorder*: Tricorders were small portable devices that the crew used to measure things like oxygen levels and detect diseases. Mr. Spock often carried his tricorder over his shoulder. The tricorder was used to gather an initial analysis of the conditions of a new environment and thus warn the crew about anything potentially harmful or dangerous. Various versions of the tricorder exist today, from wearable air-quality monitoring devices to wearable medical devices that can monitor various functions of the wearer's heart. NASA uses a device called the LOCAD onboard the International Space Station, which can measure microorganisms such as E. coli, fungi, and salmonella.

Superheroes and Super-Wearables

The follow-up discussion after a sci-fi superhero book or film often involves a conversation of how amazing it would be if their super-wearables actually existed. For example, Harry Potter's famous invisibility cloak makes him invisible to the outside world and is a popular wish-list item for almost anyone familiar with the story. This section highlights some superpowers that are now attainable (or nearly so) with the help of high-tech wearable devices.

Batman's Batsuit

Batman is one of the most relatable superheroes, because he is just an ordinary guy who protects the world from impending dangers. Hypothetically, anyone with a Batsuit could become Batman; the tricky part is getting the Batsuit. You might be pleased to know that this is no longer wishful thinking: the Unified Weapons Master (UWM) suit, developed by Chiron Global, features capabilities quite similar to those of the Batsuit.

The suit, intended to be worn by weapons-based martial arts fighters (such as sword fencers), incorporates a patented intelligent armor and scoring system. The UWM software measure the forces and location of impacts on the armor from attacks and processes a score based on the damage that would have resulted had the fighter not been wearing the suit. The suit's helmet is embedded with cameras and microphones that allow spectators to see and hear the battle from the fighter's perspective. Additionally, the suit is equipped with biometric data-sensing capabilities that measure the fighter's heart rate and body temperature.

Iron Man's Exoskeleton

Iron Man, a.k.a. Tony Stark, is another superhero who gets most of his superpowers from his amazing outer armor, which has evolved with each chapter of the story. The suits are made from extremely strong fictional materials and reinforced by a force field. They feature embedded weapon systems, flight abilities and jetpacks, communication sensors and systems, and more. The most unique aspects of Iron Man's suits are the *repulsors* and the *unibeam*. The repulsors emit a blast of charged particles referred to as a *force beam*; the unibeam can divert power from an attack to Iron Man's chest. The suits are extremely self-sufficient and can be powered by alternative energies such as solar and wind. The construction of the armor is also very interesting and adds to its resilience. Stark designs the suits to self-compose using an automated system of bacteria that consume specific metals and then die, leaving small granules of metal "cells" behind. These cells are the basis of the suit and supply energy and computing power to the armor. They also have the ability to fold in on themselves, allowing the suit to contract and expand.

The U.S. army's Tactical Assault Light Operator Suit (TALOS) is almost as strong and powerful as Iron Man's suit. The suit is actually composed of a "liquid armor" that can solidify instantly, shielding the soldier from attack. The project, which is an initiative of the United States Special Operations Command, began in 2013 and is led by a team of researchers from 56 corporations, 16 government agencies, 13 universities, and 10 national laboratories.

The team is working to equip the final suit with the following key features:

- Comfortable and flexible, conforming to the body

- Embedded with sensors that provide cues to the soldier via a next-generation antenna that includes dynamic tuning, the Future Interoperable Radio Enclosure (FIRE), and a tactical radio sleeve for cell phones

- Ability to reapply energy to enhance efficiency of motion and reduce impact load by weight distribution through the body (a bit like a unibeam)

- A powered cooling vest to sustain body temperature and a biosensor-equipped combat shirt that can monitor a soldier's physiological status

Several other new technologies and features are being developed for the suit. Although it may not be nearly as advanced as the latest edition of Iron Man's suit, it is expected to be similar to the early Iron Man Mark I suit. The team aims to have the project completed by 2018.

Wonder Woman's Bracelets

Wonder Woman is armed with a pair of special metal bracelets, also known as the Bracelets of Submission. They are indestructible and can absorb the impact of incoming attacks such as bullets, fire, and energy blasts. Slamming the bracelets together creates a wave of concussive force, strong enough to make other superheroes' ears bleed (even Superman!).

Will.i.am's Puls bracelets are not advanced enough to shield off attacks, but they can certainly make enough noise to make your ears bleed. These wearable bracelets are embedded with functions like WiFi, Bluetooth, a pedometer, GPS, as well as really loud speakers. Experts expect to see a lot of similar bracelets might appear in the near future.

007's Bag of Tricks

James Bond has been an immensely popular fictional character for more than 50 years. Bond, also known by the code name 007, is the beloved superstar intelligence agent of the Secret Intelligence Service MI6. Originally developed as a books series by Ian Fleming, more than 40 Bond books and 25 movies have been made. The Bond stories always feature futuristic vehicles and gadgets that help Bond save the day. He uses more than 200 gadgets throughout the series, a nearly complete list of which can be found on the Wikipedia page: `https://en.wikipedia.org/wiki/List_of_James_Bond_gadgets`.

Several of these gadgets now actually exist, some as spy accessories and others embedded in popular devices. Following is a list of a few of these wearable gadgets that are now available as consumer items:

- The homing beacons featured in *Goldfinger* (1964) are extremely useful for Bond's mission. One beacon enables Bond to track the villain he is after; the other, Bond carries in his shoe to help MI6 track him. A new technology called the Digital Angel chip consists of a tiny sensor that measures biometric data like body temperature. It wirelessly transmits this information and GPS location to an antenna. The device was designed for medical applications and can be implanted just under the skin, to help doctors track their patients. It can also be used in gadgets like electronic collars for pets, to help monitor their behavior.

- Bond's Seiko wristwatch in *For Your Eyes Only* (1981) contains a two-way radio transmitter for voice communication and can receive digital message readouts. This is only one feature of the smart watches that have been coming to the market recently. Smart watches like the Apple Watch can receive messages, control nearby devices via Bluetooth, track your location, and much more. What seemed extremely futuristic and novel to an audience of the 1980s is much less impressive to us today.

- The polarizing glasses in *A View to a Kill* (1985) allow Bond to see through tinted glass. Several other Bond movies feature X-ray glasses that enable him to see through clothes, containers, and more. Evena Medical developed a pair of glasses called *Eyes-On* that allows doctors to see through a patient's skin (see Figure 2-3). Using a multispectral lighting technique, the doctor can see the veins under the skin! Another device that features X-ray vision is the Golden-i headset by Kopin. The headset uses infrared technology to see through walls and other objects. Carmaker Mini is developing a pair of smart goggles for drivers, which project information and images in front of the driver. The glasses can communicate with cameras placed around the car, enabling the driver to see through and around the car. Although these technologies are still primitive and expensive, they show that X-ray spyglasses may not be far off.

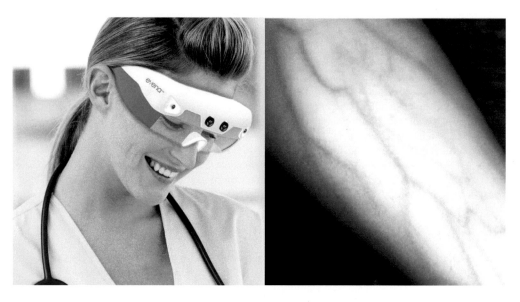

Figure 2-3. *Evena Eyes-On glasses (left), and veins in an arm as seen through the glasses (right) (© Evena Medical)*

- Bond wears a miniature ring camera in *A View to a Kill* (1985). These days, you can purchase a camera hidden in a keychain on the Internet for less than $10. More expensive spy cameras are embedded in eyeglasses, watches, pendants, and other wearables. Concepts for a ring camera have been featured in many design awards, but the real gadget remains fictional.

Summary

The stories and concepts mentioned in this chapter are just a small percentage of the hundreds of fictional props that have inspired the creation of actual products, many of them wearable. The next time you watch a science fiction film or read a book, pay attention to the devices the characters use, especially in older stories. You may find that some of the futuristic objects in these stories have already passed and are archaic to a modern audience, whereas others are extremely similar to something you can buy at a convenience store today.

This first part of the book has given some background about how the concept of wearables has developed through both fact and fiction. The next part looks at different techniques for designing and creating wearables, and how they are (and aren't) adapting and evolving with new technologies.

PART II

Methods and Techniques

CHAPTER 3

■ ■ ■

From Textiles to Wearables

In order to understand how electronic devices can be embedded into clothing, let's first review current and past textile and manufacturing techniques. Textiles is a billion-dollar global industry, and the top three exporters of textiles are China, India, and Italy. Most clothing is produced at a mass scale to reduce cost and speed up the manufacturing process: it is much easier to set up a machine to make 1,000 shirts at once then it is to run a machine 1,000 times to make each shirt. Additionally, most consumers prefer clothing that is affordable and of good quality. A subset of people give a higher priority to ethical manufacturing processes and unique designs. These products usually come from smaller-scale, boutique manufacturers where the facilities are set up to make a few articles of clothing at a time. This greatly affects the price of the product, because more labor and time are needed to produce it; thus this subset of consumers are wealthier and the product is not accessible to a diverse group.

This chapter follows the process of clothing manufacturing from fiber to garment and explains how electronics can be inserted into these processes. These techniques are still being explored on a small, semi-private scale, but some companies are making great strides to formulate ways to implement them on a larger scale.

Textile Manufacturing

A *textile* is a flexible material composed of a network of natural or artificial fibers. Textiles are also referred to as *fabric* and *cloth*. Although all three of these terms have the same meaning, they can have subtle differences depending on the context. For example, *cloth* is often used to refer to a textile that has been finished, such as a tablecloth.

Raw Materials

Textile manufacturing begins with the cultivation of fiber. The most common natural fiber is cotton. In 2007, the global cotton yield reached 25 million tons, and cotton was cultivated in more than 50 countries. Other common natural fibers include the following:

- *Flax*: Cultivated from a flax plant. The best grades are used to make linen.

- *Jute*: Cultivated from the Corchorus plant and often used to make rope and rugs.

- *Hemp*: Harvested from the Cannabis plant and often used to make dresses, sacks, and rope.

- *Wool*: Comes from domesticated sheep and often used for warm clothing.

- *Silk*: A valuable, strong protein fiber harvested from silkworms and often used in scarves and high-end apparel.

© Sibel Deren Guler, Madeline Gannon, and Kate Sicchio 2016
S. D. Guler et al., *Crafting Wearables*, DOI 10.1007/978-1-4842-1808-2_3

Wool and silk are *protein fibers*, meaning they are cultivated from an animal. Protein fibers are generally more valuable.

Synthetic fibers are made from polymers that are synthesized from raw materials such as petroleum. The materials are polymerized into a long chemical bond; different chemical compounds yield different types of fibers. The most commonly used synthetic fibers are nylon, polyester, and acrylic. Synthetic fibers offer advantages over natural fibers because they are more durable and can readily soak up different dyes. They are also preferred because they can also be designed to have properties such as stretch, waterproofing, and stain resistance. Some particularly interesting synthetic fabrics are discussed in Chapter 7.

From Fiber to Fabric

The fibers go through a series of steps known as the *preparatory processes* to prepare them for the next part of the process: spinning. During these processes, the fibers are made into *rovings*, which are bundles of fiber. *Spinning* is when the roving is twisted into a yarn or thread and spun onto a bobbin. This can be done with natural or artificial fibers, and there are different spinning techniques for each. Finally, the spun threads are woven into flat fabric using a loom. Modern engineering advances have increased the efficiency and accuracy of looms, although it is still necessary for a skilled weaver to watch over them in case something goes wrong—the slightest impurity in the fibers can cause the loom to jam and stop. The number of looms a weaver supervises varies from 1 to 100.

During the weaving process, patterns can be woven into the fabric, or they can be transferred onto it later with dye or printed during the finishing process. For example, Figure 3-1 shows textile artists demonstrating *ikat* weaving. Weaving is another multistep process, and I will not go into great detail. The basic steps involve washing, bleaching, singeing, smoothing, shrinking, and dyeing or printing. Several other steps may be involved, depending on the textile and desired outcome.

Figure 3-1. *Textile artists demonstrating double ikat weaving at the 2002 Smithsonian Folklife Festival (photo by Mary Martin, courtesy of the Smithsonian Institute)*

Other methods for making textiles include knitting, crocheting, knotting, and felting. There are large-scale mechanical machines that can perform all of these processes, some of which are becoming digitized. These are discussed in Chapter 9.

Finally, the fabric is ready to be cut, embellished, and sewn, as explained on a do-it-yourself level in Chapter 4. This has been a very abbreviated introduction to the textile manufacturing process—it is actually quite complex and takes several months or even years from start to end.

Economic and Social Implications

Although growing cotton provides jobs to millions of people, it is expensive to sustain. Cotton is classified based on how it is grown: organically or genetically modified. Cotton needs to be farmed intensively and uses large amount of water, fertilizer, and insecticide. For example, in India, 5% of the land is used to grow cotton, and this 5% is responsible for 55% of the pesticides in the country.

Harvesting the fibers is not the only costly part of the process. The finishing processes mentioned earlier, such as washing, bleaching, and printing, all consume large amounts of water, electricity, and time. Additionally, factory conditions in the textiles world often violate labor rights. Workers are sometimes forced to work long hours in poor conditions and paid extremely low wages. A simple Internet search for "textile factory fraud and disaster" yields many heartbreaking stories and facts.

Many top fashion brands take advantage of countries where labor is cheaper and have their manufacturing done abroad to drive down the price of production. This in turn creates new problems; the brand does not have tight control over the products, and they become easier to copy, leading to many *knock-offs*. Additionally, companies now have to budget for transportation costs (shipping and duty taxes), which sometimes can be more than the labor savings.

Furthermore, the urgency to take manufacturing abroad hurts the economy and job market at home. Many clothing manufacturers in the United States were forced to shut down in the 1990s when companies started to take manufacturing abroad, resulting in more job losses in the textile and apparel industries than in every other type of manufacturing. Studies show that between 2000 and 2011, an average of 17 factories per day closed up shop. However, some of these companies are realizing their mistakes and working to bring production back to the United States. These companies are investing in new technologies to streamline the process at home, resulting in less production time and lower labor costs per garment.

Fashion Design

Another important field in wearables is *fashion design*. Fashion design, also called apparel design, is a separate field from textiles and is defined as the application of design to clothing or accessories. Fashion designers use textiles created by textile designers to create clothing and other wearables. Their process involves an entirely different set of steps, which I briefly describe here. Fashion design is a very detailed process and can be explored in more details through books and courses specific to the subject. The following steps serve as a basic tutorial of how a fashion designer goes from concept to finished product or collection:

1. *Fashion forecast*: The designer must explore upcoming trends for the season to predict the future landscape of fashion.

2. *Conceptualization*: The designer collects all of these trends and chooses a focus or a theme. This could be based on an event or emotion. These ideas are usually collected on a board of images called a *mood board*. The mood board features images that are pertinent to the overall theme of the collection; this can range from pictures of an environment the clothing would be made for to emotional expressions the clothing might create, such as comfort or power. Nowadays it is easy to create a mood board online using a service like Pinterest.

3. *Illustration and silhouette*: This is when the actual sketching and drawing occur. The concept is manifested in a series of drawings of the different elements of the collection on a series of silhouettes. Although most designers do this by hand, computer-aided software techniques are becoming more popular. These are discussed in Chapter 8.

4. *Color, fabric, and trim selection*: The designer selects the fabrics and trims that will be part of this collection. They choose fabric based on properties like weight, strength, and texture. After the types of fabric are decided, the color palette is determined. Colors are chosen based on the mood board and other factors such as the season and forecasted trends.

5. *Technical design*: A technical sketch is needed to move into production. This is like a blueprint for the piece, with instructions on how it is made; detailing all measurements, seams, trim placements, and so on. A mock-up of the garment is made from muslin, based on this sketch, and fitted onto a mannequin. The garment is adjusted and redesigned until it resembles the desired look.

6. *Patterns*: The final step in the development process is making a pattern from the technical design. Patterns can be made by hand or digitally with pattern-making software. Several versions of the pattern may be made, for use in house and otherwise. Patterns must be adjusted according to factory guidelines when sent into production. Which may feature different notations from the designer's version. An example of a pattern is shown in Figure 3-2. Chapter 4 explains how to interpret a pattern. A good pattern is the ultimate key to a well-fitting garment.

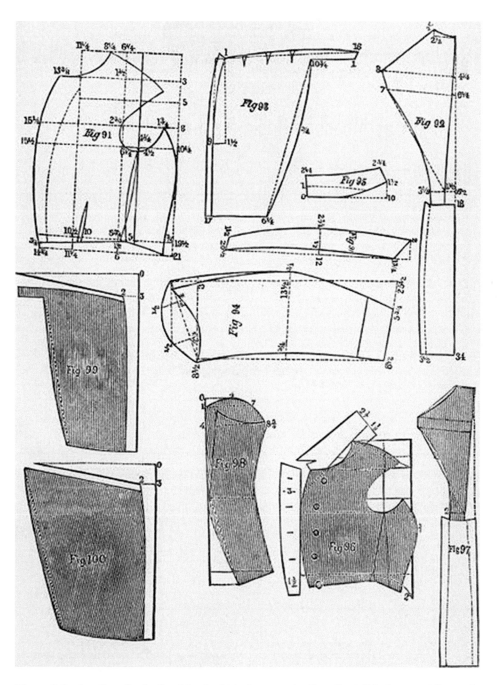

Figure 3-2. *A pattern for the front, back, skirt, sleeve, and collar of a stylish dress-coat (image from the Encyclopedia of Scientific Tailor Principles by D.C. Christner, 1880)*

7. *Style selection and feasibility*: Finally, the collection is assessed based on financial and production feasibility. These are determined by the goals and budget of the brand for this particular collection. The number of pieces in the collection can depend on many factors, such as the intended distribution process and target audience. There may be a variety of high-end and low-end pieces in the collection, or they may all be on one end of the style spectrum. After the costs and manufacturing methods are optimized, the first set of samples is made and presented to buyers, retailers, and other influencers of the brand.

Textiles and Education

This section explains the various roles of textiles and sewing in education and highlight new efforts to blend electronics with textiles as an educational tool.

Sewing as a Class

When I was in middle school, the entire grade had to take sewing class. We collectively made a quilt (each student made a patch) that was donated to the local children's hospital. When I reached high school, sewing was a popular elective class. Nowadays, when I go into a school or museum to teach a wearables workshop, I know not to assume that students have had the same exposure to sewing that I did. In fact, I am surprised when more than one student knows how to sew. This goes for 4th graders, high schoolers, and even college students who have never threaded a needle. Although you can probably get by without this skill, basic stitching does not take that much time to learn and definitely pays off in the long run.

■ **Note**   Don't worry if you're in the camp of those who never learned how to sew. The next two chapters walk you through basic sewing techniques and teach you how to sew a simple light circuit!

Figure 3-3 shows a high school girl learning how to sew a light circuit in a workshop that I taught while researching ways to engage girls with engineering and science. There were 12 girls total in this workshop, and only 2 or 3 of them knew how to sew before starting their project.

Figure 3-3. *Consent wearable designed by a Washington Irving Campus student during a sex education "Wearing Consent" after-school program (April 2015; photo by Norene Leddy)*

The question of why sewing is no longer being taught in schools or offered as an elective is more complicated then it may seem. The digital divide in education has been a key issue in many learning standards and systems. Schools and other educational venues all over the world are working hard to ensure that their students do not fall behind, because computer literacy is becoming a critical skill of the future workforce. Unfortunately, this often means reviewing budgets and making cuts to curricula that do not fit with these project future values, in order to make room for new technology, and sewing is often one of the first to go.

However, research is proving that blending electronics with technology is extremely valuable as an educational tool. Some researchers have developed their own toolkits for this purpose (myself included), as discussed in Chapter 5. Sewing as an entry to electronics makes the concepts more accessible and less abstract.

Higher Education: Tech vs. Textiles

Higher education in the fashion and textile industry faces the opposite problem. Many programs are set in their ways, using traditional drafting and cutting methods rather than embracing the new technologies and software that are available. Most curricula focus on these foundational methods rather than new interdisciplinary techniques. Before students can experience these new methods, teachers need to become familiar and comfortable with them. Although some schools are working to solve this problem by bringing in technology experts and providing faculty training, many programs are not showing any progress. This is, of course, a multifaceted issue that must be considered by the administration and board of the department of the institution before more modern techniques are introduced and enforced.

Sewing for Engineers

Yet another area to be explored is the value of using textiles in engineering classrooms at the university level. As the next section demonstrates, many breakthroughs and innovations in textile manufacturing have resulted from the collaboration of engineers with textile and apparel designers. Additionally, exposure to the process of textile design and materials of textiles is valuable for engineers, regardless of whether they pursue fashion later in their career. Working with fabric and thread presents new and interesting challenges. It is a hands-on experience—not too different than other traditional hands-on projects in the engineering classroom—that forces you to think of a simple circuit in an entirely different way, for an entirely different application. Chapter 5 explains the nuances and intricacies of designing a circuit that is sewable.

Electronics in Clothing

At this point, you can probably see why weaving electronics into clothing is not as simple as it may sound. Not only do the electronics have to be small, lightweight, and flexible like fiber, but they also need to be formed into the fabric at an early stage to be durable. This involves retrofitting several different machines and processes.

Harry Wainwright, who invented a machine for weaving fiber optic fibers into fabric, was mentioned in Chapter 1. Wainwright's process is a good case study, because it shows how he went from an idea to designing his own processes and tools for mass production. Let's look at other projects that are taking on electronics textile manufacturing at this level.

Project Jacquard

Google's Advanced Technologies and Products (ATAP) team is working to integrate electronics into clothing in a new way. The goal of the project is to make any piece of fabric into an interface. By weaving with conductive yarns and thread, the team, led by Ivan Poupyrev, believes they can integrate touch sensors and more right into clothes, car seats, curtains, and everything else. An example of what this interface would look like on fabric, and how you would interact with it, is shown in Figure 3-4. As Poupyrev explained in an interview with *Wired*, "If you can weave the sensor into the textile, as a material you're moving away from the electronics. You're making the basic materials of the world around us interactive."

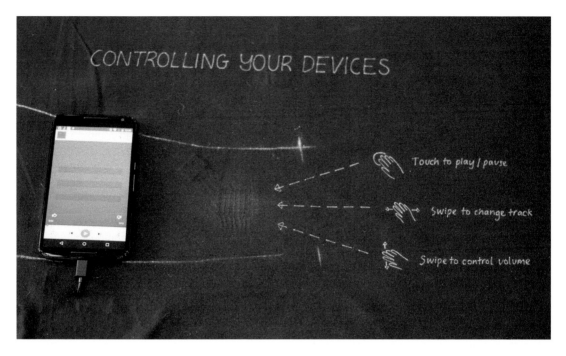

Figure 3-4. *A prototype of a Project Jacquard interface on denim (photo by Maurizio Pesce, licensed under CC BY 2.0)*

Like Wainwright, ATAP is not inventing entirely new materials, but rather is inventing new ways to use and combine these materials. The key ingredients of these future fabric interfaces, the conductive threads and fabrics, have been around for centuries. However, embedding these materials into textile manufacturing at a mass scale is not currently possible, mostly because the tools do not exist to do so.

For Project Jacquard, Google collaborated with textiles manufacturers and fashion designers. For the first phase of the project, the team partnered with a boutique textiles manufacturing company in Japan to understand the textile process. Eventually, they were able to design a yarn based on a metallic alloy (hence conductive) that can be woven into several other fibers using a strong braiding process. The yarn can be used to make denim, silk, polyester, and even wool that is conductive and comes in any color.

Google does not intend to start a textiles manufacturing factory, or even a clothing company, for these special textiles. The ATAP team's plan is to develop software that can be used with these new wearables. They want to continue to find partners who can share their expertise and help streamline the process. Although the team is enthusiastic about embedding this technology into clothes, there are still a lot of problems to be solved that fall on the fashion-design side. For one thing, this process will completely change a manufacturing company's supply chain and add a lot of tests and processes to production. The first fashion label partner for this project is Levi's. With these challenges in mind, Levi's is excited about the potential solution, because it could really customers' relationship with clothing.

It is evident that the digital world is becoming a larger part of consumers' personal world; people are constantly connected with their smartphones and fitness trackers. Adding digital functionality into clothing could be revolutionary if done correctly. You can read the latest about Project Jacquard at `www.google.com/atap/project-jacquard`.

Intel's Smart Fashion

Google is not the only tech company aware of this trend. Intel has also been making an effort to engage in the wearables field. In 2014, it hosted a competition called Make It Wearable, where people were invited to submit a wearables concept in the form of a one-minute video. A panel of judges selected a winner, who was given seed funding and counsel to bring the idea to life.

The Intel Curie Compute Module has had a large role in this process. Curie is a complete microcomputer the size of a button, designed to make the creation of wearable devices faster, simpler, and more accessible. Additionally, Intel has been partnering with famous designers and brands to bring wearable innovations to market. In a recent collaboration with fashion label Chromat, they created apparel that forms to the human body directly. So far, they have debuted two items. The first is a sports bra that responds to changes in perspiration, respiration, and body temperature. The bra is able to vent and cool the wearer using the Curie module as the central brain of the system. The second item is a 3-D printed carbon-fiber dress that morphs based on the wearer's adrenaline levels.

Smart clothing will not only be able to extend the capabilities of smart devices and gadgets; it also will be able to respond to the human body and create a more comfortable, intimate wearable experience. As Chromat's CEO, Becca McCharen, explains in an interview with FastCoDesign, "I think in the future, everyone will have a body scan, buy the files online, and print out their garments and get something fully customizable to their form."

Although this project does not introduce a new machine or material into the manufacturing process, it is designed with future manufacturing in mind. As it becomes easier to customize clothing, it is important to speculate and prototype these customizations. What will consumers value in a custom pair of pants? Will it be the fit, the responsiveness to their emotional state, or the touch interface that connects to, or even replaces, their phone and other devices? High-tech fashion projects by Chromat and other designers are presented in Chapter 13.

Summary

This chapter has provided an overview of how most wearables are produced, from raw material to mass production. Additionally, you learned about the social and economic impact of the industry and the current state of textiles in education. The textile industry is an old and essential market with tremendous future potential. As advancements in technology lead to new consumer needs, the textile and fashion industries need to be prepared. New technologies will present many challenges to factories and companies that have invested time and money into streamlining their current processes. On the bright side, marriages between major fashion brands and technology companies will help guide this new potential market. Although textile companies may be nervous about venturing forth, many tech companies are extremely eager to see what the future of embedding electronics into clothing will bring. In the end, these wearables have to be stylish, comfortable, and affordable. To achieve these goals, the technologists will have to find fashion and textiles designers who can make this happen.

The next chapter discusses the basics of sewing and following a pattern to help guide you through the tutorials in this book. If you are already proficient with these skills, you should be able to breeze through Chapter 4.

CHAPTER 4

▪ ▪ ▪

Cutting and Sewing

This chapter serves as a crash course in sewing and working with fabric. If you have never learned how to sew or need a refresher, consider this chapter a guidebook for the projects in the remainder of the book. You will need to acquire a basic sewing set, which is described in the next section, and some fabric. These materials can be found at most craft stores or at a fabric store, if there is one local to your area. You could also cut up an old article of clothing as scrap fabric to practice with.

By the end of this chapter, you will learn how to sew different stitches, follow a pattern, and sew a button onto an article of clothing. These skills will be useful for repairing clothing, replacing a missing button, or patching a pair of pants. The chapter covers basic sewing terminology and techniques, which you can explore further in media dedicated to sewing and textile techniques.

A Sewing Kit

The first step is gathering your sewing toolbox. A simple sewing toolkit can be found in any general store, craft store, or pharmacy. Depending on the store, the kit will be more or less complete, but it will include basic tools. The sewing tools needed for the tutorials in this book are listed in Table 4-1. Some of them may require a more specialized sewing store or can be ordered online.

© Sibel Deren Guler, Madeline Gannon, and Kate Sicchio 2016
S. D. Guler et al., *Crafting Wearables*, DOI 10.1007/978-1-4842-1808-2_4

Table 4-1. Contents of a Beginner's Sewing Kit

Tool	Use
Tailor's chalk 	This soft, chalk-like material leaves traces on fabric that can gently be brushed or washed off. A thin bar of soap works as a substitute.
Colored thread 	A basic sewing kit comes with colored spools of thread. It is good to have a rainbow of colors, with more specific colors for specific jobs. For example, when mending a light gray pair of pants, you will want to find the closest shade of gray thread.
Pins and pincushion 	Pins come in many different shapes and sizes. They are used to hold fabric in a desired shape before sewing. It is also useful to have a pincushion to collect you pins and needles. You can easily make a pincushion by folding a piece of fabric into a ball shape or sewing a small pillow (as described later in this chapter).
Sewing needles 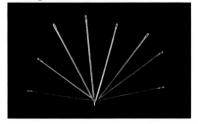	Sewing needles are the integral part of the sewing kit; they are necessary for learning how to sew. Sewing needles come in many different size and shapes particular to the fabric they need to go through. For example, embroidery needles are thicker and blunt, because they are used with thick thread to go through porous canvas. Try to find a variety pack, with several different kinds of needles.

(continued)

Table 4-1. (*continued*)

Tool	Use
Shears 	Sewing shears are different than regular scissors and an important part of your toolbox. They are designed to make long, smooth cuts in different fabrics and stay sharp for a long time. If they become dull, they should be sharpened with special sharpening instruments.
Thimble 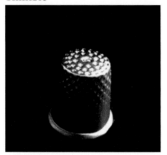	This is a useful tool when you're learning how to sew, because it can protect your fingers and help you push a needle through thick fabrics. It is worn on your thumb or index finger.
Tape measure 	This flexible ruler is great for measuring along curved edges and perimeters. Tape measures are most commonly used for taking measurements during fittings: the distance around a person's waist or chest, down a leg, and so on.
Needle threader 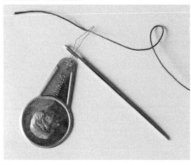	This tool is used to help thread a needle and is handy piece of a beginner toolset, especially when you are experimenting with different needles and threads.

A typical hobby sewing set may also include a few buttons, safety pins, and snaps. A more advanced set may include a seam ripper, which as its name suggests is used to rip apart seams of a piece of clothing.

Additional Materials

In addition to the tools described, there are some materials that are always good to have in your sewing kit. For starters, scrap fabric is a must. Velcro may be useful when making something where you don't want to use buttons. Similarly, a zipper is a good alternative and may be more appropriate for some projects, such as sewing a coin purse. As you explore different projects and techniques, you may also find that you need some ribbon to add to a trim, or some elastic to make a flexible waistband for a skirt or a pair of shorts. Every tailor's sewing kit is full of unique remnants from past projects that only get more interesting with time.

Another material that is good to have in stock, especially for electronics sewing projects, is *interfacing*. Interfacing is a material used to add stiffness to a fabric. As you learn in Chapter 7, some conductive fabrics are not very thick, and attaching interfacing makes them easier to work with. There are two different type of interfacing: *nonwoven interfacing* does not have a grain and works in most cases, whereas *woven interfacing* does have a grain and is preferable when using stretch fabrics. *Fusible interfacing* has one side that is fusible and another side that is smooth and not fusible. The fusible side contains a heat-activated adhesive that can be glued to the fabric using an iron; the other side can be sewn on.

Stitches and Seams

In this section, you learn how to make two basic hand stitches—running stitch and whipstitch—and how to sew on a button. These three things will take you a long way. Although they may seem simple and straightforward, they will be awkward at first; you should practice each of them until the motions feel natural. Using a thimble is optional for these tutorials, but it is common practice to wear a thimble on your finger to help push the needle through fabric.

For each of these techniques, the first step is threading a needle and knotting the thread. Threading a needle can be very frustrating, especially when you're just learning, but tools like a needle threader make it easier. One factor is the size of the *eye* of the needle. The eye is the hole on one end of the needle that the thread passes through. The larger the eye, the easier it is to thread the needle. Another factor is the thickness of the thread. The thicker the thread, the more likely that it will fray and be difficult to pass through the eye. In order to prevent the thread from fraying, I recommend that you cut the tip of the thread at an angle with your shears, to create a point. Another common practice is to wet the end so that the thread stays together. It is best to start with a shorter, more manageable amount of thread; 20–24" is a good length to work with. If the thread is very long, it is more likely to get tangled and caught while sewing.

First prepare your thread as just described. If you don't want to use a needle threader, then all you have to do is hold up your needle so you can see the eye, and pass the end of the thread through the eye.

If you'd like to use the threader, follow the steps diagrammed in Figure 4-1:

1. Take the needle in one hand and the needle threader in the other. Insert the wire loop of the needle threader through the eye of the needle. The loop is made of very thin wire that should be able to pass through the eye, even if it is small.

2. Hold the needle and the threader in one hand, making sure the loop is still sticking through the eye of the needle, and take the end of the thread in your other hand. Stick the thread through the loop of the needle threader, and fold it over to meet the remaining thread, as shown in part 3 of the diagram.

3. Keep your hand on the thread, and pull the loop of the threader completely through the eye of the needle. Now, release the thread, and pull the loose end all the way through so that there is only one strand passing through the eye.

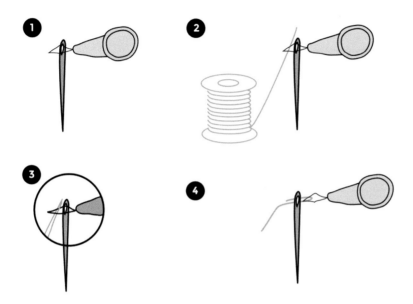

Figure 4-1. Threading a needle, steps 1–4

    4.   You must tie a knot at the other end of the thread to hold it in place. You can tie the knot on one end of the thread, or double the thread so that both ends meet, and tie a knot as shown in Figure 4-2.

Figure 4-2. Tying a knot at the end of the thread

Running Stitch

This is the most basic stitch and results in an even, straight seam. Start with a threaded needle and a piece of fabric. The steps are diagramed in Figure 4-3:

    1.   Start with the needle underneath the fabric. Poke the needle through the fabric, and pull it all the way through so that the knot is taut on one end, as shown in part 1 of the diagram.

    2.   Flip the needle, and poke it through the top of the fabric about a quarter of an inch to the right of the first hole. Pull the needle through the back of the fabric until it is taut. You've made your first stitch!

    3.   Flip the needle again, poke up through the back of the fabric about a quarter of an inch to the right of where you made the last hole, and pull the needle up through the top.

4. Continue going through the fabric, alternating sides, in a straight line until you either (almost) run out of thread or reach the end of the material. The stitch should look like part 5 of the diagram.

5. To make a knot, draw the needle through the last stitch, making a loop, stick the needle through this loop, and then pull taut, as shown in part 6. Repeat a few times until the knot feels sturdy, and then cut the thread.

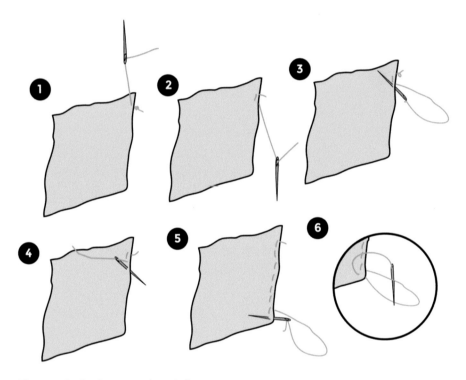

Figure 4-3. *Sewing a running stitch*

Whipstitch

Whipstitch is useful for sewing around the edge of a piece of fabric. For this tutorial, let's sew a patch onto another piece of fabric. The steps are diagramed in Figure 4-4:

1. Poke your threaded needle through the base layer fabric and then through the edge of the patch, or top layer, about a quarter of an inch from the edge of the patch. Pull the needle all the way through so that the knot is taut on the back of the bottom layer.

2. Flip the needle, and stick it over the edge of the fabric so that it only goes though the bottom layer, as shown in part 2, and pull all the way through. This should result in a stitch that is perpendicular to the edge of the patch.

3. Poke the needle up through the base fabric and patch, close to where the first stitch started, to create another perpendicular stitch next to the first one. Continue this all around the edges of the patch until it is secured to the base layer of fabric.

4. Once the patch is secure, knot and cut the thread as described in step 5 of the running stitch tutorial.

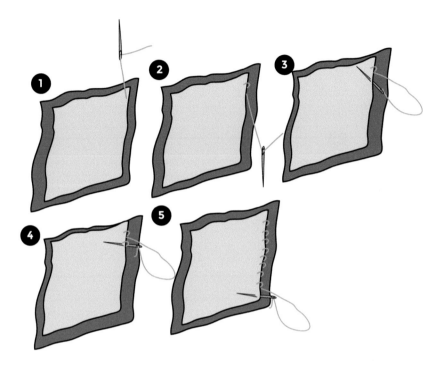

Figure 4-4. *Sewing a whipstitch*

Sewing a Button

This technique is used when you need to sew a button or snap onto a piece of fabric. Start with the threaded needle, a button, and a piece of fabric. The steps are diagramed in Figure 4-5:

1. Decide where the button will be placed on the fabric, and mark it with your tailor's chalk. Note the holes in the center of the button; there should be at least two holes, but there may be four.

2. Stick the needle through the middle of where the button will go on the fabric. Before pulling the needle through, place the button over the fabric, and pull the needle though one hole of the button as shown in part 1. Pull the needle through the fabric and the button, holding the button in place.

3. Flip the needle back toward the fabric, stick the needle through another hole on the button and the fabric, and pull it taut on the back of the fabric, as shown in part 2. If your button has four holes, try to go for the hole that is diagonal to the one you first anchored.

4. Go through each of the holes, in and out through both sides of the fabric, two or three times, until the button feels secure on the fabric; it should look like part 4.

5. When you finish sewing the button onto the fabric, pull the thread to the back side of the fabric and tie a knot as described earlier.

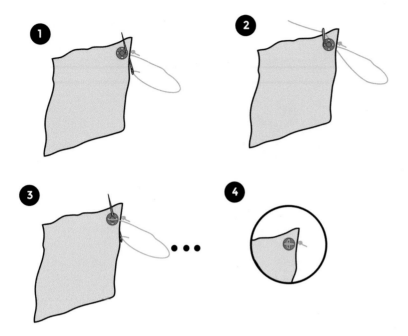

Figure 4-5. *Sewing a button*

Cutting fabric

In order to cut fabric with a smooth edge, there are some basic guidelines to follow:

- The fabric must be flat, clean, and wrinkle free, so wash and iron it if necessary.

- Place the fabric on a flat surface, and smooth it out; a large table works well.

- Draw the shape you'd like to cut with the tailor's chalk. If necessary, use a flat edge or ruler while drawing.

- Begin to cut through the fabric with your sewing shears. Open the scissors completely, and make long, fluid strokes through the fabric. Hold the scissors very steadily; a slight shake could result in an uneven cut. You can also use a rotary fabric cutter if you have one.

- If cutting a straight line, you may want to lay a ruler or other straight edge on the fabric to help guide you. One method is to line up the fabric with the edge of a surface and cut parallel to the surface.

- Do not use these scissors to cut anything other than fabric. They are designed to cut through fabric and risk falling out of alignment or becoming dull if misused.

Making a Pillow

To practice these stitches, making a simple pillow is a great first project. You need the following tools and materials:

- Some scrap fabric (or other fabric if you would like)

- Needle

- Pins
- Thread
- Scissors
- Cotton or foam to stuff the pillow

Follow these steps to make your pillow, as diagrammed in Figure 4-6:

1. Cut two square pieces of fabric equal in size out of your fabric, and thread your needle with the desired color of thread.

2. Pin all four edges of the pillow together, as shown in part 1.

3. Sew together three edges of the pillow using a running stitch, about half an inch from the edge of the fabric. Try to make your seams even.

4. Take the pins out of the fourth side of the pillow, reach in, and turn the pillow inside out to hide the seams of the three edges.

5. Stuff the pillow with the desired amount of stuffing material, and close the fourth edge with some pins.

6. For the last edge of the pillow, use a whipstitch to attach the two pieces of fabric together.

7. Congratulations! You have put together your first pillow!

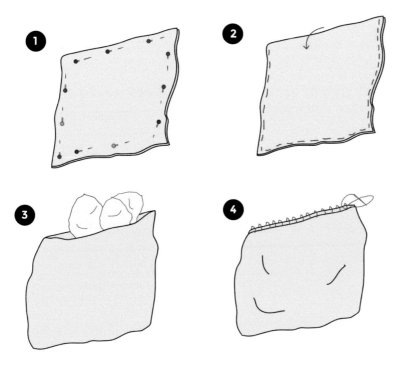

Figure 4-6. *Sewing a pillow*

Following a Pattern

After learning how to sew, cut fabric, and make a pillow, a good next project would be to make a garment from a pattern. For your first garment project, choose a simple pattern. When you find a pattern that you like, check whether there is a labeled size; if so, make sure it is your size. Some patterns have multiple sizes printed on the pattern, which can be confusing to follow. If this is the case, it may be useful to outline the size you are following with a dark- or bright-colored marker. Before making the garment out of your desired fabric, it's a good idea to make a sample, also called a *muslin*.

■ **Note**   The term *muslin* also refers to untreated cotton fabric, but for this chapter it refers to a different definition given below.

A *muslin* is a mock-up version of a pattern made from a plain fabric. Muslins are useful for making a first draft of the garment that can be revised and changed, before making the final version out of the desired fabric. Follow these steps:

1. Read the instructions printed on the pattern or on the accompanying guide. The guide includes tips on how to cut out the pattern tissue, how to construct the garment or item, the best way to select sizing, and so on.

2. Check to see if the pattern allows for seams. If it does not, you will need to add them in when cutting out the pattern later.

3. Find the *grain lines*. These are the long, straight lines on the pattern with arrowheads at one or both ends. This arrow tells you which direction the paper pattern pieces should sit with respect to the grain of the fabric. To find the grain lines of the fabric, find the *selvage edge*: this is the edge where the pattern ends and is sometimes white. The grain lines are the same direction.

4. Take note of the following markings on the pattern: notches, shortening lines, button holes, darts, and dots.

5. You are ready to cut out the pattern. The cut lines are the solid lines surrounding the dashed lines. If there are no dashed lines, this means the sewing line is not marked on the pattern; in this case, it is safe to assume that the sewing line is about half an inch inside the cut line. When cutting out the pattern, use normal paper scissors. Cut along the cutline very carefully; if you make a mistake, just try to match the cut back to the line.

6. Trace the pattern on the scrap fabric you are using to make a muslin, and cut it out of this fabric. It may help to pin the pattern to the muslin while cutting it out to hold it in place. When pinning fabric that you are going to sew, it is easiest to place the pins perpendicular to the direction the seams will go, so that you can easily sew through them.

7. Assemble the pattern from the fabric pieces according to the guide. Use pins to hold the pieces together by pinning the pattern together along the edges.

8. If you have experience with a sewing machine, you may want to use one instead of hand sewing. Otherwise it is better to hand-stitch the pieces together so that it can easily be mended. Try on the muslin and note the areas where the form is ill-fitting. Be sure to cut out the pattern from the final fabric with these changes in mind.

Using a Sewing Machine

Sewing machines are preferable for making sturdier, even stitches, and they get the job done much more quickly than sewing by hand. They can produce several different types of stitches from straight, to zigzag, to a more intricate, curvy seam. Sewing machines use a slightly different mechanism than hand sewing: for one thing, the eye of the needle is on the other end, near the sharp point. This needle does not go up through the fabric one way and down another—instead, it just pokes through the surface of the fabric at set increments. Also, there is a second spool of thread beneath the needle plate, called the *bobbin*. What happens when the needle goes under the needle plate? Refer to Figure 4-7 to see how the machine locks in each stich.

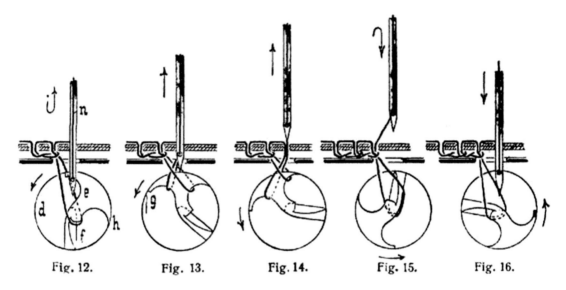

Figure 4-7. *A diagram of the stitching mechanism of a basic sewing machine (from the 1904 Lexikon der gesamten Technik (dictionary of technology) by Otto Lueger*

The needle is affixed to the needle bar and is driven up and down by a motor and gearbox. When the tip of the needle passes through the fabric, it pulls a small loop of thread through with it. A hook mechanism under the needle plate pulls this loop and wraps it around another piece of thread, which is reeled from the bobbin. The two threads interlock around the fabric, forming a stitch, and the needle is pushed up and slightly forward before it goes through the fabric again.

A basic sewing machine is fairly inexpensive and can even be found at a thrift store or a secondhand marketplace like Craigslist. When learning how to use a sewing machine, an electric pedal–powered machine is easiest. You will have to learn how to thread the machine and get a feel for the pedal power. This is perhaps the most important part, because steady control of the pedal determines the evenness of the stitch. The other important factor in evenness is the ability to hold the fabric in place and feed it through the machine. It is important to tinker a bit with the sewing machine until you really get a feel for these things before attempting a more advanced project.

Summary

After completing the tutorials in this chapter, you should have confidence in your basic sewing skills. If you are looking to take them even further, there are some resources listed in the appendix. Additionally, you have now gained perspective about what goes into assembling a wearable. Of course, when produced at a mass scale, automated machines do several of the steps covered here, but a considerable amount of work still needs to be performed by skilled workers. The next chapter provides you with a basic overview of electronics and teaches you how to combine your sewing skills with circuits to create embedded wearables.

CHAPTER 5

■ ■ ■

Making Electronics Sewable

Making electronics sewable may seem like a trivial task to the skilled crafter who is experienced in repurposing materials. Even so, learning some basic tips and tricks will help unleash your creativity. This chapter guides you through some conceptual and technical considerations when sewing with electronics.

Like most interdisciplinary fields, e-textiles is exciting because there are so many possibilities to be explored. There are techniques in textiles that can be tested with electronics, and methods in designing electronics that can be tested and adapted for wearables—not to mention the wealth of new (or, rather, unconventional) materials that can be introduced to both fields. Of course, not all translate perfectly from one field to the other, and some do not work at all. But new techniques have been invented along the way, and custom parts have been designed for new applications.

This chapter begins with an overview of circuit design. I give you a basic overview of a circuit with some considerations to keep in mind when designing a wearable circuit, especially when it comes to choosing the right power source. This is followed by a tutorial for making an LED wristband using off-the-shelf electronic components. The last section highlights some of the new techniques and custom parts that have come out of the e-textiles field in the last decade. I review five different kits that attempt to make sewing with electronics accessible and interesting to a wider audience.

Circuits and Power

This section provides an overview of basic electronics— or rather, all you need to know to get started with soft circuits. Because wearables ideally need to be lightweight, finding the right power source can be the most difficult part of designing a wearable circuit. If you are already comfortable with electronics, then most of this will seem redundant, but it may be wise to skim over it nonetheless.

What Is a Circuit?

A very simple definition of a *circuit* is a conductive path that allows electricity to travel across it. A basic circuit is composed of a power source, a conducting path, a switch, and a load. Your next question may be, what is a conductive path? A *conductor* is anything that allows electricity to flow through it. Different materials have different levels of conductivity, which is based on their chemical composition. Table 5-1 gives some everyday examples of conductive materials as well as nonconductive (or *insulating*) materials. As an exercise try to think of a few other materials that could be added to this list.

© Sibel Deren Guler, Madeline Gannon, and Kate Sicchio 2016
S. D. Guler et al., *Crafting Wearables*, DOI 10.1007/978-1-4842-1808-2_5

Table 5-1. *Examples of Conductors and Insulators*

Conductor	Insulator
Copper (as well as most metals)	Most plastic
Water	Styrofoam
Human skin	Wood (that is totally dry)
Plants	Glass

Back to the other parts of the circuit: the power, switch, and load. The *power* is the power source of the circuit, most commonly a battery, although it could also be a solar panel or other "alternative" power source. The *switch*, as you learn more about in Chapter 6, is a device that enables you to turn a circuit on and off. And the *load* is the part of the circuit that consumes the power; it is what you are turning on or off.

There are a few more terms I would like to introduce that are not tangible parts of a circuit but are equally, if not more, important to understand conceptually. The *voltage* is the difference in charge between two points on a circuit and is measured in volts. Different components require different amount of voltage to turn on. The *current* is the rate at which electrons flow through the material; it is measured in amps. Different components draw different amount of current to stay powered. Last, the *resistance* is a physical property of the material that resists the electric current and is measured in ohms. The lower the resistance, the easier it is to force electrons to leave atoms and move through the material, and the more conductive the material is. Although materials have an inherent resistance, sometimes additional resistance is needed to make sure the power is supplied at a manageable rate. For example, an LED light may only be rated to receive 20 milliamps of current, and let's say you have a wall power adaptor that supplies a constant 1 amp of current to the circuit. In order to restrict the current flowing through the LED, you can add a resistor and ensure that the LED does not burn out from a high current. The next section explains how these three values are directly related through Ohm's Law.

Figure 5-1 illustrates a basic circuit with these terms defined in the appropriate location on the diagram. As you can see, the circuit is set up as a loop, with the arrows illustrating that the current is flowing from positive to negative. This is a basic rule of circuits: electrons flow (that is, the current flows) from positive to negative. The order of components depends on what you are making: for example, if you want to limit the current to the LED with a resistor, you need to place the resistor before the LED, not after it.

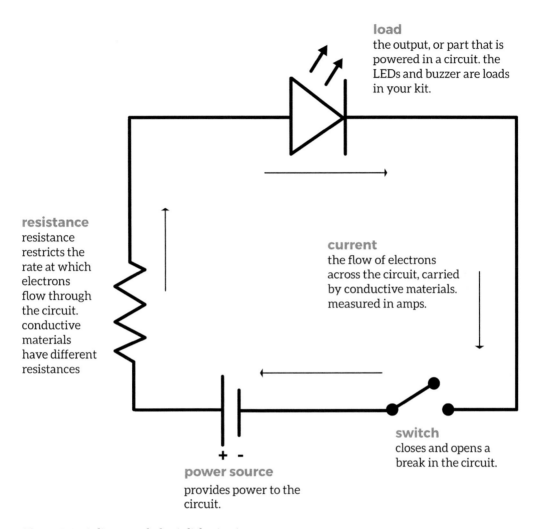

load
the output, or part that is powered in a circuit. the LEDs and buzzer are loads in your kit.

resistance
resistance restricts the rate at which electrons flow through the circuit. conductive materials have different resistances

current
the flow of electrons across the circuit, carried by conductive materials. measured in amps.

switch
closes and opens a break in the circuit.

+ -

power source
provides power to the circuit.

Figure 5-1. *A diagram of a basic light circuit*

A *short circuit* is basically equivalent to connecting from the positive end of the power source to the negative without putting anything in between. This will drain or *burn out* your battery very quickly. You should always make sure there are no short circuits in your design.

Components have two or mores leads through which they connect to the circuit. On a common through-hole LED, the two long legs are the leads. Some components have a certain *polarity*, meaning one lead is positive and one lead is negative. In this case, the component must be oriented in the circuit such that the positive aligns with positive and negative with negative. Otherwise, electricity will not flow through them, and this will cause a break in the circuit, like an open switch. Components like switches and resistors are *symmetric*, meaning they do not have a preferred direction and can be inserted into the circuit in either configuration. Pay attention to the polarity when building a circuit.

To demonstrate this, let's test the polarity of an LED. You need a through-hole LED (with two legs) and a coin-cell battery (CR2032 is preferred). Take your LED and sandwich the legs around the coin cell such that the thin edge of the coin cell is in the middle and the legs are touching the flat circular sides, as shown in Figure 5-2. There is a 50-50 chance that your LED will turn on. If it doesn't turn on the first time, keep the battery in place and flip the LED so the opposite legs are touching the sides. Why does it work in one direction and not in the other? Because the LED has a certain polarity: one leg must connect to positive and one leg must connect to negative. The battery also has a polarity: the positive side is usually labeled with an etched + mark, and the negative side is usually textured and not as smooth.

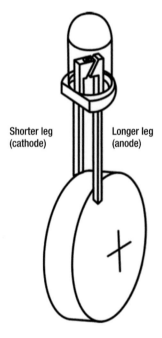

Shorter leg
(cathode)

Longer leg
(anode)

Figure 5-2. *Testing an LED*

If you hold up the LED, you will notice that one leg is slightly longer than the other. The longer leg is positive and is called the *anode*, and the shorter leg is negative and is called the *cathode*. It may take a while to remember this, but for someone who spends a lot of time tinkering with electronics, this becomes second nature.

Here is a recap of key properties of circuits that you should always keep in mind when designing and troubleshooting:

- A circuit is always a loop.

- Electricity flows from positive to negative around the loop.

- Everything in the circuit must be oriented in the same direction.

- Any time a component is put into the circuit backward, it causes a break in the circuit and may result in a short circuit or a circuit that cannot "turn on".

- If the negative and positive sides of any component or connection cross, this creates a short circuit.

Power Sources

When choosing a power source, a few factors help determine what will be appropriate. First, you must find a power source that will provide enough power to all the components in your circuit. To find out how much power each component requires, you may need to refer to the *datasheet*. The datasheet is a product-specification sheet that the manufacturer of the electronic component provides. It lists the minimum amount of volts and amps the component must use and draw, as well as other useful information like the maximum temperature it can withstand without literally burning out. For example, most LEDs draw around 3 volts, so a power source that provides anything less than 3 volts will not provide enough voltage to turn on the LED.

When researching batteries, along with the voltage, another value is listed: the *capacity* of the battery, which is measured in Ah (amp-hours). The capacity of the battery measures the rate at which the battery will discharge at the rated voltage. For example, a battery with capacity of 100 Ah can provide 5 amps over a 20-hour period. If you are powering a circuit that requires 10 amps, the battery will last only 10 hours. A common coin-cell battery usually has a capacity of only 50 mAh (that's milliamp-hours). This is why a coin cell is insufficient to power anything that requires more than 50 mA.

For most wearable and e-textile projects, the power source of choice is a battery unless the concept of the project is centered on alternative power. Another common power source for electronics that I haven't mentioned is a wall power adaptor. This is not ideal for wearable applications for the obvious reason that it requires being tethered to an outlet, thus restricting the movement of the wearable.

Batteries are divided into two classes: primary and secondary. A *primary* battery is not rechargeable, whereas a *secondary* battery *is* rechargeable. Table 5-2 provides information about common primary and secondary batteries as well as pros and cons to consider for wearable applications.

Table 5-2. *Types of Batteries for Wearable Applications*

Battery Type	Alkaline	Lithium Polymer	Coin/Button Cell	Nickel Cadmium
Description	Cylindrical or rectangular shaped, used in many electronic devices from remote controls to radios; available in 1.5–9 volts	Usually flat, rectangular, and found in cellphones and cameras. Most common voltage is 3.7–7.5 volts	Small, round batteries commonly found in toys and hearing aids. Typically comes as 1.5–3 volts	Rechargeable battery commonly used in flashlights and larger toys like remote-control helicopters
Pro	Very common and inexpensive	Rechargeable, fairly compact, has a large capacity for its size Can be salvaged from old cell phones or digital cameras	Compact, lightweight, inexpensive Comes as rechargeable and nonrechargeable	High voltage and capacity for its size Can be recharged several times
Con	Can be heavy Not rechargeable	Can be expensive if new Requires custom connections or contacts for attaching to a circuit or charger	Does not provide much power or current only works for low power projects	Expensive Needs a custom holder or contacts
Example of a circuit that would be ideal	Speaker/Sound-related circuit	Microcontroller and LED lights or buzzer	A few LED lights	Small/medium-sized fan or servo motor

Series vs. Parallel

There are two different ways to connect elements of a circuit together: connecting in *series* and in *parallel*. The components in a circuit are connected in series if the same current is travelling through them. They are connected in parallel if they have unique current values flowing through them. Figure 5-3 shows a circuit with the components connected in series vs. parallel.

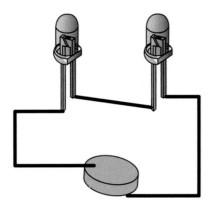 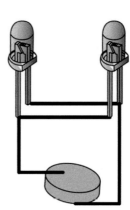

Figure 5-3. *A circuit with lights connected in series (left) and parallel right)*

To connect a circuit in series, you need to connect all the components together in one path, making one long, single loop from positive to negative. To connect a circuit in parallel, you need to create several parallel paths that each loop from positive to negative.

Now that I've explained the difference, I should explain when each is useful. In other words, when should you use a parallel circuit and when should you use circuit in series? This can be explained using the most important law of circuits: Ohm's Law. Ohm's Law states that the voltage in a circuit is the product of the current and the resistance: $V = I \times R$. Most of the time, two of these values are known, and the other can be calculated using this equation. Let's consider an example scenario for each circuit to see when it would be more useful than the other.

For the first example, suppose you want to connect a string of five LED lights together. If you connect them in series, each one will depend on the LED before it. In other words, if one LED were to burn out, all the LEDs that come after it would not get power because there would be a break in the circuit! If you connect them in parallel, each LED will independently draw power from the battery. Thus, parallel is a better configuration for this circuit.

For the second example, you want to connect two batteries in an attempt to double the voltage of the circuit. If you connect them in series, the voltage will double as needed, and the capacity will stay the same. If you connect them in parallel, the voltage will stay the same, but the capacity will double.

How to Sew a Light Circuit

The following tutorial for how to sew a light circuit uses basic materials that can be sourced from most electronics stores. I assume you have basic sewing skills like threading a needle and sewing a running stitch and therefore do not go into detail about sewing techniques. If you are not comfortable with this, you can review the tutorial in the previous chapter.

You are going to sew a light-up wristband. For this project, you need the following items:

- Needle

- Scissors

- Pliers

- Conductive thread

- LED

- Metal snap

- Felt or other scrap fabric

- Sewable battery holder for CR2032 battery

- CR2032 coin-cell battery

The metal snap will act as a switch, such that when the snap is closed, the light will turn on; and when it is open, the light will turn off. You can also use different metal enclosures to make this simple switch; several of them are mentioned in Table 6-1 in chapter 6.

Follow these steps:

1. Thread your needle with conductive thread. Depending on how big you want to make your circuit (I recommend a medium size to start), 18 inches should be plenty.

2. Find or cut out a rectangular piece of felt or other fabric about 2 inches wide and long enough so that it can comfortably wrap around your wrist.

3. This next part is an essential skill when sewing with electronics. Pull your LED's legs apart slightly. Try to make note of which leg is positive and which leg is negative. Now, take your pliers and, starting with one leg, gently curl the leg up toward the bulb in a loop shape, as shown in Figure 5-4. Do not pull too hard, or as the leg may break off. Make sure the loop is not too small (you need to sew through it later!), and make sure it is nice and tight (you may need to pinch is together or make two loops, depending on how long the leg is). Do the same with the other side. Make sure the loops are not touching each other when you are done.

Figure 5-4. *Curling the legs of the LED*

■ **Tip**   It may be easier to start from the bottom of the leg (furthest from the bulb) and wrap it around one side of the pliers while curling it up toward the bulb.

4.   Place the pieces on the felt to get an idea of how the circuit will look, as shown in Figure 5-5. Make sure you know which leg loop from the LED is positive and which is negative. If you can't remember, you can sandwich the LED around the battery and test again, as described in the previous section.

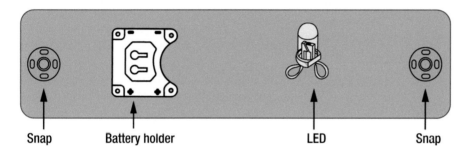

Snap   Battery holder   LED   Snap

Figure 5-5. Layout of components on wristband for light circuit

5.   You are ready to sew the circuit as shown in Figure 5-6. First connect the positives. When sewing through looped legs, make sure to go over the loop a couple of times with the thread, poking your needle through the middle of the loop on one side and down right next to the edge of the loop on the other side as illustrated in Figure 5-6. Make sure these stitches are tight; otherwise, the loops may not conduct the current from the battery.

6.   Once the positive loop is secured, sew a running stitch from the loop to the positive hole of the battery holder with the same thread. The stitches do not have to be too close together, but I recommend making them fairly tight and even.

7.   When you reach the positive hole on the battery board, poke your needle into the hole and then up right near the edge (as you did with the LED loop) a couple of times so that it is secure. Then, bring your thread to the back side of the band, and tie a knot, and cut it. It should look roughly like the illustration in Figure 5-6.

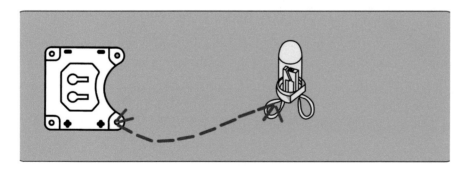

Figure 5-6. Sewing from positive to positive: steps 5–7

8. When you have reknotted your thread, you can connect the negative side of the circuit. You do not connect negative battery to negative LED directly; you use a snap in between to act as a switch for the light and a clasp for your bracelet. Start from the negative hole on the battery board, and sew to the closer edge of the bracelet. Now, sew the female snap onto the edge. Make sure the snap is facing the right way, so that it will fit with the other side when closed. To secure the snap, sew around the holes on the outer edge, like you would sew a button. Tie a knot, and cut your thread.

9. Last step! Starting with the loop of the LED light that is not secured (this should be the negative loop), sew around the loop a few times to secure it to the fabric as you did with the other side. Then, sew a running stitch away from the battery holder, toward the other end of the bracelet. When you reach the end, place the male snap on the back side of the fabric so that when you close the bracelet, the ends overlap and close the circuit. Sew the snap securely onto the fabric, and tie a knot when you are finished. You can now cut off the remaining thread.

10. To test your wristband, insert the battery (make sure it is in the correct orientation) and close the snap, as shown in Figure 5-7. The light should turn on! There you have it: a simple lightband that uses a common through-hole LED, a metal snap, and a battery board. If the LED doesn't stay on or doesn't turn on at all, refer to the troubleshooting tips that follow.

Figure 5-7. *The completed lightband*

▪ **Troubleshooting**   If the light does not turn on, first check the back side of your lightband to make sure no threads are crossing or touching in such a way that they could create a short circuit. Then make sure all the connection points with the electronics are secure. You may need to gently tug on the thread to see if it is making good contact. If the light turns on when you tug on the thread, you need to tighten these connections. If the light still doesn't turn on, make sure your LED is oriented correctly, and try a new battery. You may want to use a multimeter. If you need to take the lightband apart or remake it, don't worry—sewing with electronics can be very tricky, especially on the first try!

To add another LED to your lightband, you want to attach it in parallel. You can design your circuit to look like the example circuit in the previous section.

Custom-Made Kits

Using raw components is great for prototyping purposes, but (as you may have noticed if you completed the previous tutorial) raw components are not always very durable or aesthetically pleasing when it comes to wearable applications. For this reason, several designers and engineers have developed custom electronic boards that are meant to be embedded in fabric and thread rather than solder and wires. I mentioned a few of these kits in previous chapters, but here is a closer look at five different e-textiles kits. If you search the Internet, you can find others available, but these five have interesting back stories. The first three kits are shown in Figure 5-8.

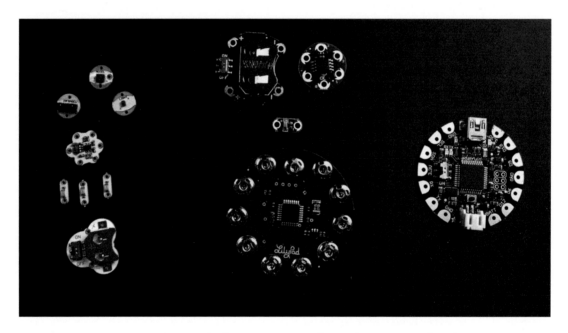

Figure 5-8. *Aniomagic Sparkle board (left), LilyPad Arduino (middle), Flora board (right)*

LilyPad

The LilyPad Arduino is the first sewable microcontroller (`www.lilypadarduino.org`). It was developed by Dr. Leah Buechley as part of her doctoral thesis at the University of Boulder. Around 2005, Dr. Buechley began experimenting with e-textiles and developed an e-textiles kit with her collaborator, Nwanua Elumeze, whom you read about later in this section. Dr. Buechley and Elumeze were testing the kits with students, and Dr. Buechley began to feel as though the kits were too limited: she wanted to give students a way to program the circuits they were building. She set out to create a fabric microcontroller using laser cut pieces of fabric and large through-hole electronics. Though the boards proved to be interesting and engaging to the students, they were hardly durable and not very user friendly. Dr. Buechley began to make improvements to the board, she experimented with ways to use smaller surface mount components on the board and realized the shape of the board was limiting her design. She tried a circular flower instead, which proved to be easier to work with and became the final shape of the board. An early prototype of the LilyPad is shown in Figure 5-9.

Figure 5-9. *Early, flexible prototype of the LilyPad Arduino (photo by Dr. Leah Buechley, licensed under CC-BY-2.0)*

Dr. Buechley continued to teach workshops using her homemade boards and found that her project was extremely successful in attracting girls to engineering. Around the same time, the now-popular Arduino board was just getting started, and a new company in Boulder called SparkFun Electronics was beginning to make and sell Arduino kits. Dr. Buechley was a frequent customer of SparkFun, and during one of her visits she began brainstorming with the founder about making her fabric microcontroller into a commercial product. By October 2007, the LilyPad Arduino was released. The LilyPad has sold more than 10,000 boards since then and continues to be a pioneer platform of DIY wearable computing.

Dr. Buechley continued developing content and new parts for the LilyPad with her research group at the MIT Media Lab called High-Low Tech. The LilyPad has several complementary input and output boards including LEDs, vibration motors, temperature sensors, and more. The group also developed a smaller version of the board called the LilyTiny, which is based on the atTiny microcontroller and suitable for smaller-scale projects. Dr. Buechley left the Media Lab in 2014 to pursue her personal design practice, but she continues to make many contributions to this field. She has coauthored two books based on the LilyPad and continues to lead workshops and inspire many with her work.

Flora

The Arduino Flora is another sewable microcontroller, designed by the founder and CEO of Adafruit Industries (a popular online hobby electronics site), Limor "Lady Ada" Fried. The Flora board is similar to the Arduino LilyPad in that it is also round and compatible with the Arduino IDE. It features 14 sewable pads and was designed to be as fabric-friendly as possible; it is the center image in Figure 5-8. The main difference between the two platforms is that the Flora is built around a different microprocessor chip and thus has built-in USB support, whereas the LilyPad does not. The native USB driver on the Flora offers a unique feature: when the board is plugged in to a computer, it can emulate a keyboard, allowing you to make a custom keyboard for your computer using soft circuits.

The pin layout of the Flora is a bit different from the LilyPad's and is designed to easily integrate with the Flora's custom accessory boards, which feature sensors and outputs that are different than those of the LilyPad line. The Flora's boards include an accelerometer, a GPS location sensor, a lux (intensity of light) sensor, and a color sensor board. Adafruit also produces its own brand of LED lightboards for the Flora, called NeoPixels. NeoPixels offer many advantages over other sewable LED boards, primarily that they are individually addressable and low power. This means that using only one pin from a microcontroller, you can chain together as many NeoPixels as you like and address each one to output a different light pattern.

Like the LilyTiny, the Flora comes in a smaller size: the mini Flora is called the Gemma board. You can find more information about the Flora and its family at www.adafruit.com/category/65. The wearables team at adafruit posts a new tutorial each week on the online Adafruit Learning System; you can find them at https://learn.adafruit.com/category/flora.

Aniomagic

Aniomagic was developed by Nwanua Elumeze as part of his doctoral thesis at the University of Boulder. Elumeze and his colleagues were investigating ways of adding "tiny bits of computation" to everyday objects to make them respond to ambient changes in the environment, such as temperature and light. The team quickly realized that the programming platforms they were utilizing were too bulky and slow for what they hoped to achieve. They wanted to create something that could be programmed on the fly. Elumeze dreamed of paintings and stockings encoded with programs that could trigger a circuit in a dress when someone passed by.

Elumeze set four goals for his project: he decided it needed to be easy to use, low-tech (for user interaction), affordable, and able to be programmed *ambiently* (meaning it can be programmed from a variety of sources without additional wires or other hardware). This resulted in the invention of the *Sparkle* board: a small, inexpensive, sewable circuit board that can be programmed with light from any graphical web browser.

The board features a sensitive light sensor that is preprogrammed to respond to certain light patterns. The light pattern can be programmed by writing a few lines of code on the web site or dragging sliders in a simple graphical interface. The interaction is simple, allowing the user to focus on the design and function of the project rather then spending time on small details of the electronics. Figure 5-8 shows the Sparkle board with four LED lightboards. Inspired by the shape of the LilyPad Arduino, the Sparkle board also features round, sewable, petal-like edges with large conductive pads.

The Aniomagic library has grown beyond these initial boards and now includes several sensor boards including touch, magnet, and sound. The team has also developed and released another series called *Chicklet*, which can be programmed via sound. Unfortunately, Elumeze decided to discontinue the Aniomagic line in July 2015. You may still be able to find a kit from a reseller (SparkFun and Maker Shed, to list a couple), and the project web site still exists at www.aniomagic.com.

Fabrickit

Fabrickit developed by Despina Papadoupolos and Zach Eveland, is a set of electronic "brick" modules designed for making wearable projects. Fabrickit combines sewing with soldering to make prototyping with electronics simple. The set consists of three different bricks, shown in Figure 5-10, and a special connector ribbon called *wire*:

- *Battery brick*: A removable and rechargeable coin-cell battery. The board has a built-in USB charging circuit and port.

- *LED brick*: Comes in two styles, one with and one without an on-board LED in the middle with solderable pads (for attaching the ribbon)

- *Snap connector brick*: Three snaps on a small board with solderable pads on the other end. There is a male snap connector and a female snap connector. The snaps provide an easy, non-permanent solution to sewing electronics, because you can snap and unsnap to make and break connections.

- *Wire*: A very clever solution to the intricacy of sewing long traces with conductive thread without crossing them. It comes as a ribbon with three parallel conductive thread columns embedded in the middle. Between each conductive column is a strand of normal ribbon, which separates and insulates the conductive threads from one another. The conductive ribbon can be sewn on with conductive thread. It can be cut to any length and then attached to the final project with hot glue or sewn on with regular thread.

Figure 5-10. *Fabrickit modules (left, courtesy of Despina Papadopoulos), Teknikio Wearable Electronics Set (right)*

Fabrickit is licensed to SparkFun Electronics and is currently distributed via the company's online store. For more information, tutorials, and resources, visit `www.fabrick.it`.

Teknikio

Teknikio began as a research project (then called Invent-abling) to find ways to engage girls in STEM (science, math, engineering, and science). After a series of initial workshops using raw materials and other e-textiles parts, I decided that these were too difficult for young children (and even adults) to use. Although the smaller boards are perfect for fashion applications, they are a bit tricky to use for educational purposes, when you are trying to point out different features of the electronics. I set out to find a way to make the parts more user-friendly and developed a series of custom circuit boards in the process. The boards feature bigger sewing pads with larger labels, making them easier for a novice user to sew through. Our mission is still focused on empowering girls, but has evolved to promote gender neutrality and dilute gender barriers. I believe that boys should also know how to fix a shirt button; they should not shy away from basic sewing skills due to gender stereotypes.

The project has evolved over time and expanded into the retail realm. We currently make two different e-textiles kits and several sewable circuit boards. Our latest addition- LED shapes experiments with the idea of not only make the LED boards easier to use, but designing the boards to have fun shapes like hearts and stars. We find that users are drawn to this new series and treat them more like sequins, than electronics. We are doing more research in this realm. The Fabtronic Sewing Set is intended to serve as an intro for teaching circuits with sewing or for the curious hobbyist who wants to try sewing LEDs lights without investing too much time or money in a more complex kit. The Wearable Electronics Set, shown in Figure 5-10, is more substantial and includes eight sewable boards, raw components, pliers, conductive fabric, thread, and a mini sewing kit. This kit was designed for someone who really wants to dig deep into the realm of analog e-textiles and try several different circuits. It can also be used in an educational setting and can be applied to several subjects including art, home ec, science, and technology. Both kits are analog but can be used with microcontrollers and most of the other platforms mentioned in this chapter. You can find more information about the kits and example projects online at `www.teknikio.com`.

Summary

You should now have a strong foundation for understanding e-textiles. If you would like a more detailed explanation of a circuit, resources are available both online and in other books dedicated to this topic. You have also completed your first e textiles project, an LED wristband! Although this may seem trivial, your experience designing and crafting this circuit will be useful in future projects. Finally, you were introduced to several custom toolsets that have been developed to make e-textiles more accessible and fabric friendly. The evolution of each of these kits leaves provide value insight into context as to the issues their designers are hoping to overcome with new tools.

Perhaps you will discover your own obstacles and solutions throughout your exploration of e-textiles. Whether you want to turn your discovery into a product or share it on an open platform is, of course, up to you. The next chapter highlights a few designers who have shared their research and experience in e-textiles and made great contributions to this open source community.

CHAPTER 6

■ ■ ■

Soft Circuits

What exactly makes a circuit soft? A *soft circuit* is any circuit that is embedded into a soft or flexible material. They are often composed of flexible conductive materials such as fabrics and threads along with discrete electronics components that are sewn in or attached by some other means. By this definition, the opposite—a non-soft or hard circuit—would apply to any circuit that is composed of hard, nonflexible materials such as plastic and metal.

Soft circuits are also called *e-textiles*, where the *e* stands for electronics. The term *e-textiles* refers to the general field of combining electronics with textiles and does not necessarily refer to something that is wearable. Although techniques used in e-textiles can be applied to wearables, they are also used in interior design and other objects. This chapter looks at some techniques used to create soft circuits and highlights designers who have made remarkable contributions to this field.

Crafting Circuits

Artists who are looking to push the boundaries of their work have been exploring the art of crafting a circuit out of nonconventional materials for many years. Similarly, scientists who want to test the usability of different materials in different contexts have conducted many experiments in this realm. Crafting circuits lends itself to various interdisciplinary practices combining art, design, and technology. By reimagining an electronic component or repurposing a raw material in a new or unconventional form, you can invent and reinvent them. This process sparks new ideas for household products, medical devices, wearables, and more.

Hannah Perner-Wilson and her collaborator, Mika Satomi, have been developing an online encyclopedia of soft-circuit designs, tips, and tricks for the do-it-yourself wearable electronics community since 2009. Their site, How to Get What You Want (`www.kobakant.at/DIY`), is an excellent resource for anyone looking to explore the intersection of sewing and electronics. As stated on the site, the project "aims to be a comprehensible, accessible and maintainable reference resource, as well as a basis for further exploration and contribution."

The site is organized the way a basic electronics store would categorize its products, and includes tutorials on how to make different actuators, sensors, and connectors. Perner-Wilson and Satomi also post reports from their experiences sourcing and using materials commonly used in the projects. The pair works under the collaborative name *Kobakant* and leads workshops around the world to teach their techniques; the workshop schedule can be found on their site. Although they do their best to help readers source materials locally, several of the projects can be purchased as kits from Perner-Wilson's Etsy store. Kobakant's portfolio includes many other projects beyond How to Get What You Want, several of which have a speculative edge, using textiles and electronics as tools for exploring future interactions.

Perner-Wilson continued this work as her masters thesis, entitled "Kit-of-No-Parts," in which she explored the intersection of craft and electronics beyond textiles. Figure 6-1 shows a collection of soft-circuit sensors she created. Her personal work can be found on her web site, `www.plusea.at`, where she documents her adventures with engraving circuits in wood carvings, embedding metals into ceramics, and more.

© Sibel Deren Guler, Madeline Gannon, and Kate Sicchio 2016
S. D. Guler et al., *Crafting Wearables*, DOI 10.1007/978-1-4842-1808-2_6

Figure 6-1. *Textile sensor database (photo by Hannah Perner-Wilson, 2009)*

Following is a list of the soft-circuit projects in Figure 6-1, including their function and materials used in the sensor. They're listed from left to right, starting with the top row:

- *Pressure sensor matrix:* Made by layering velostat between neoprene stitched with conductive thread and conductive fabric tabs

- *Sticky tape pressure sensor:* Made from tape, velostat, and conductive thread

- *Beaded tilt sensor:* Made with conductive fabric, fusible interfacing, fabric base, and a heavy metal bead string on conductive thread

- *Crocheted potentiometer:* Made from resistive yarn, nonconductive yarn, and a metal bead strung on conductive thread

- *Bend sensor:* Made by layering velostat between neoprene stitched with conductive thread and conductive fabric tabs with snaps

- *Knit stretch sensor:* Made with piezoresistive and nonconductive yarn

- *Fabric touchpad:* Made from a piece of resistive knit fabric with conductive fabric contacts fused along the edge

- *Fabric potentiometer:* Made of a resistive track from Eeontex fabric and a conductive fingertip wiper made of stretch conductive LYCRA

- *Stroke sensor:* Made by stitching conductive thread into neoprene with conductive fabric contacts on the back

I have highlighted the work of Kobakant because it offers a comprehensive and whimsical approach to soft circuits. There are several other wonderful resources available for those who are interested in researching soft-circuit techniques; they are listed in the appendix. The next section guides you through how to make a pushbutton switch using conductive fabrics.

Designing a Soft Switch

Most metal fabric closures naturally lend themselves to becoming switches. A *switch*, in its simplest form, is something that can be opened and closed or turned on and off. There are hundreds of variations on this simple mechanism, but for the sake of the tutorial, let's look at two types: the momentary switch and the toggle switch.

A *toggle switch* is a switch that holds its state. When it is put in the open position, it stays in the open position; and when it is in the off position, it stays in the off position. For example, most light switches use toggle switches to turn on when pressed or flicked and turn off when pressed or flicked again. Metal clasps and snaps commonly used in garments naturally lend themselves to being repurposed as switches. For example, a metal snap is conductive and has two parts that can click together (on) and be separated (off). Table 6-1 shows different closures that can be repurposed as switches.

Table 6-1. *Textile Closures for Making Switches*

Metal snap

Metal clasp

(*continued*)

Table 6-1. (*continued*)

Metal zipper

Conductive Velcro

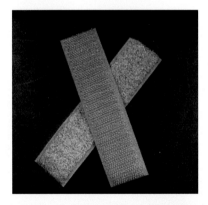

Metal grommets

The *momentary switch* is a switch that does not hold its state: in other words, it only reacts to an external force when the force is applied. A push button, for example, is often a momentary switch. When you use a remote control you are interacting with push buttons. When you press the Volume Up button, the volume does not continue to increase after you release the button; it only increases when you are pressing the button.

I will now explain how to make a textile push-button switch. For this project, you need the following items:

- Needle
- Scissors
- Conductive fabric
- Foam or other soft, springy material
- Felt or other scrap fabric
- Nonconductive thread

The construction of the switch with templates is shown in diagrams. Follow these steps to construct the button:

1. Cut out two square pieces of scrap fabric and two slightly smaller squares of conductive fabric with tabs, as shown in Figure 6-2.

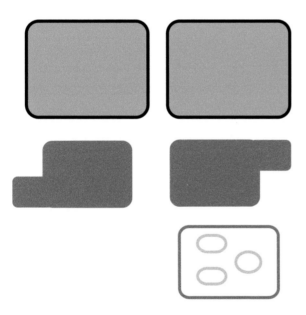

Figure 6-2. Felt (top), conductive fabric (middle), foam with holes cut out (bottom)

2. Cut out a square piece of foam or other squishy material, slightly larger than the conductive fabric but smaller than the nonconductive fabric. Poke a few large holes in the center of the foam.

3. To put the pieces together, make a sandwich with the foam in the middle, conductive fabric on both sides of it, and nonconductive fabric on the outside. Place the conductive pieces such that the tabs are sticking out on different sides, as in the diagram.

■ **Tip** To hold the conductive fabric in place, you may want to use a bit of fabric glue and tack it down onto the nonconductive fabric. You can also attach some Heat'n Bond to the fabric instead of glue. This may be a bit more involved but is more easily reversible if you need to take it apart.

---

4. Make sure the foam piece in the middle is covering the conductive fabric on both sides. Also make sure the holes are large enough that when pressed together, the two pieces of conductive fabric on either side touch. This is what will close the switch.

5. Using nonconductive thread, sew around the outer edges of the nonconductive fabric to close the button (see Figure 6-3).

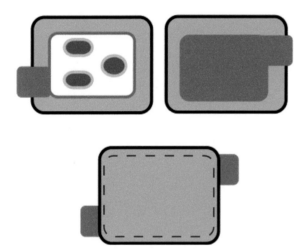

Figure 6-3. *Assembling and closing the button*

6. To test your button, you can attach it to a circuit or test for conductivity using a multimeter. If you're using a multimeter, bring the meter to the conductivity setting. Put one lead on one tab and one lead on the other. Then, press down on the padding of the button; the meter should beep when the button is pressed, signifying that the switch is closed. If you're building a circuit, you need an LED, a battery, and three alligator clips. Arrange the pieces as shown in Figure 6-4.

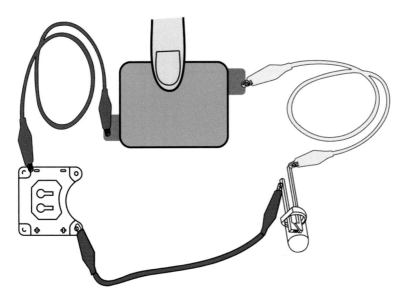

Figure 6-4. *Push-button test circuit with alligator clips and LED*

Press down on the button, and the LED should turn on!

■ **Troubleshooting**   If the button does not seem to be working, rip the seams and see if everything is in place. You may need to make the hole in the foam a bit larger, or readjust the position of the foam so that the conductive swatches do not touch when the switch is in the relaxed (unpressed) position.

Creating a Printed Circuit Shirt

Of course, not all textile circuits are made of conductive thread or fabric. Just as circuits are screen-printed onto boards, they can be printed onto fabric. By using conductive inks with traditional screen-printing tools, textile artists are able to print actual circuit traces onto fabric. Although these traces may be more visible than thin threads, they provide a simpler solution when designing a piece involving circuits with several traces. It is also possible to create sensors and other components with conductive ink. For example, a simple proximity sensor or antenna involves a coil and can be designed as a flat printed image; see Figure 6-5 for examples.

Figure 6-5. *Conductive ink designs: resistor (left), proximity sensors (middle and right)*

The screen-printing process uses a mesh-based stencil to apply ink onto a substrate such as fabric, paper, or wood. An ink-blocking stencil is "burned" onto a mesh and forms open areas that transfer ink through the mesh. A fill blade or squeegee is moved across the screen stencil, forcing ink through the mesh openings and printing the image onto the substrate. A starter screen-printing kit usually includes a tutorial on how to burn an image onto the screen and apply the ink.

For the purpose of soft circuits, the only difference in this process is the ink. You can try Bare Conductive paint, copper paint, or other metallic conductive paints. If the ink is too thin, it is recommended that you thicken it using a neutral substance that does not affect the conductivity. All inks have a different resistance, which you should research and consider when making your selection. For example, if the printed image involves a long, continuous trace of ink, the resistance will be much higher than that of a shorter trace. You can also use this effect to intentionally create resistors in your circuit by using a busy pattern to make the length of the trace longer. Additionally, the number of coats you apply can increase the conductivity; it is recommended that you apply additional coats of ink to longer traces.

The composition of the substrate you are printing on may affect the conductivity of the ink. You should always test the ink on your substrate by printing a series of lines with varying thickness before applying your design, to find the correct thickness. The image below shows images on a screen printed circuit with components attached (left), the process of screen-printing (middle), and another screen-printed conductive pattern (right).

Assembling an E-textiles Toolkit

Table 6-2 provides a suggested list of materials and tools for a beginner wearables toolbox, in addition to the sewing tools mentioned in Chapter 4. The table also includes suggestions on where to source these parts. Some of the parts are described in this chapter, and others are described in Chapter 5.

Table 6-2. *Suggested Materials and Tools for Beginning in Wearables*

Part		Sourcing	Notes
LED	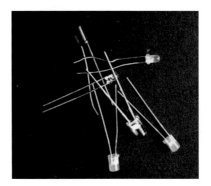	DigiKey, SparkFun, Adafruit, Micro Center	
Sewable LED		SparkFun, Adafruit, Teknikio, Micro Center	Can come as a single color or RGB LED
Conductive thread and yarn		SparkFun, Adafruit, LessEMF	Steel and silver based
Conductive fabric		SparkFun, Adafruit, LessEMF	Stretch and nonstretch

(*continued*)

Table 6-2. (*continued*)

Part		Sourcing	Notes
Fabric sensors		Less EMF, Plug and Wear	Can be woven with conductive and nonconductive threads and yarns, or bought premade
Multimeter		Amazon, SparkFun, Adafruit	For troubleshooting the circuit
Alligator clips		SparkFun, Adafruit, Micro Center	For testing a circuit before sewing
Pliers		Jo-Ann Fabric and Crafts, Michaels	For making raw components sewable

(*continued*)

Table 6-2. (*continued*)

Part		Sourcing	Notes
Sewable battery holder	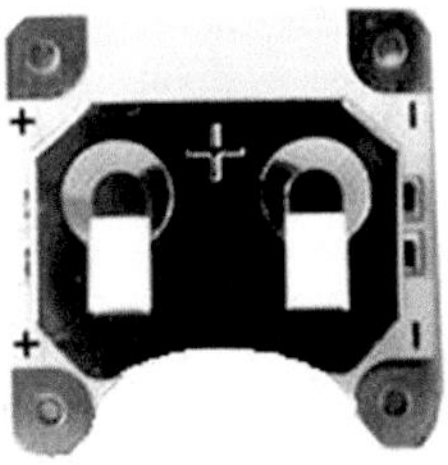	SparkFun, Teknikio, DigiKey	Provides power to e-textiles
Velostat		LessEMF	A resistive material used to make pressure and bend sensors (tutorial in the next chapter)
Heat'n Bond	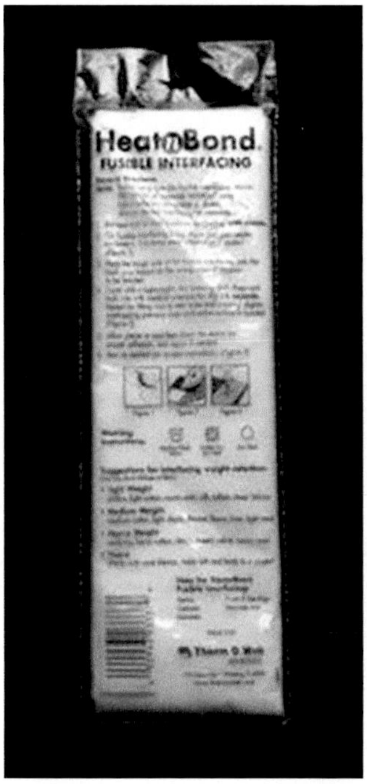	Jo-Ann Fabric and Crafts, Michaels	To attach fabrics together without sewing

(*continued*)

Table 6-2. (*continued*)

Part		Sourcing	Notes
Fabric Glue		Jo-Ann Fabric and Crafts, Michaels	To attach fabrics together without sewing
Foam and scrap fabrics		Jo-Ann Fabric and Crafts, Michaels	
Optional Parts			
Hot glue gun	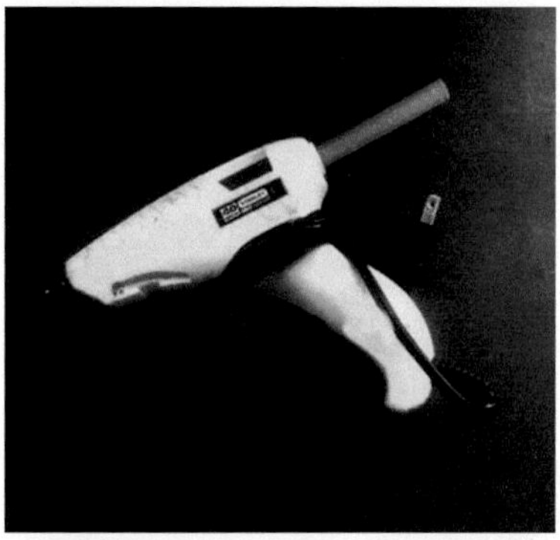	Craft store, Staples	
EL wire	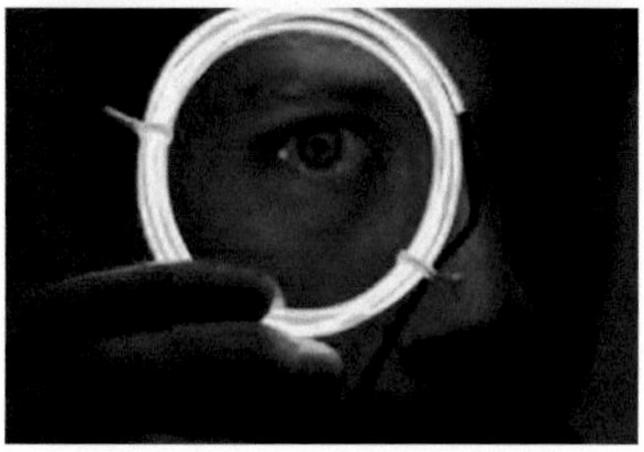	SparkFun, Amazon, Adafruit	For a nice glowing effect

(photo licensed under CC BY 2.0; taken by Flickr user thematthewknot)

(*continued*)

Table 6-2. (*continued*)

Part		Sourcing	Notes
LiPo battery	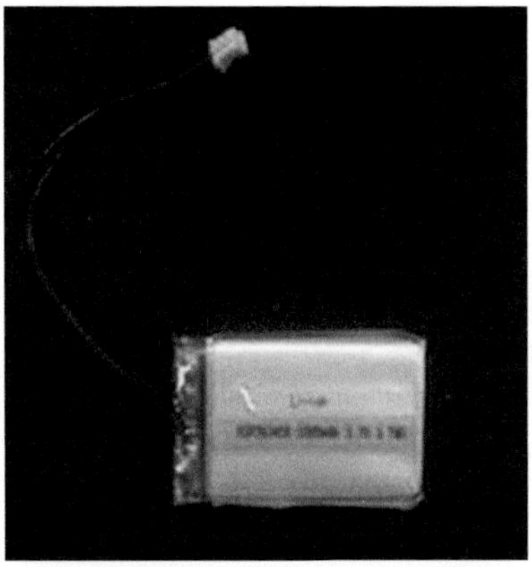	SparkFun, Adafruit, Micro Center	For multiple lights, provides more power in a compact size.
Beads, buttons, sequins	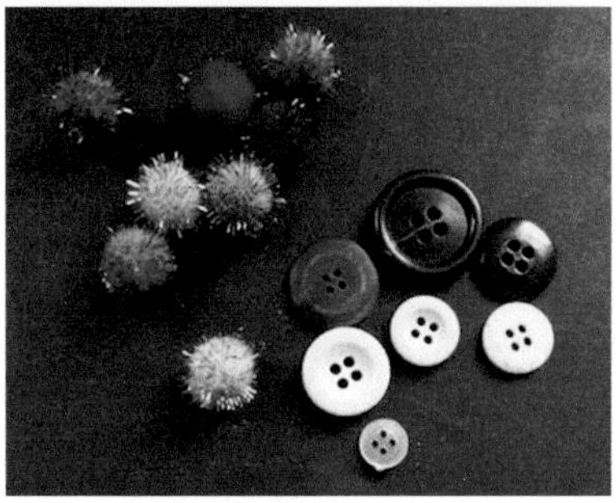	Jo-Ann Fabric and Crafts, Michaels	Metal beads can be used to make sensors; nonmetal can be used as decoration.
Conductive paint		SparkFun, Adafruit	To screen-print circuits

(*continued*)

Table 6-2. (*continued*)

Part		Sourcing	Notes
Sewable microcontroller		SparkFun, Adafruit, Micro Center	For programming: Arduino LilyPad or Flora. For plug-and-play: Aniomagic.
Sewable vibration motor		SparkFun, Teknikio	For an output other than light
Custom sewable sensor boards		SparkFun, Adafruit, Aniomagic	Commonly used with sewable microcontrollers to create more complex circuits

You may be able to source these materials from local electronics stores and other online electronics suppliers. However, the sources mentioned here are reliable in terms of quality and likelihood of having the items in stock. Additional suppliers are listed in the appendix.

Summary

You've now learned about basic sewing skills, basic circuits, and crafting sensors from raw materials. At this point, I recommend referencing the sources provided in this chapter and in the appendix and trying some different soft-circuit projects. As you explore different materials and techniques, you may design your own version of some of these projects or discover an entirely new soft circuit! In any case, I encourage you to document and share your work, both so you can review your progress and so that others can draw inspiration from your work. The collaborative and open nature of artists and designers in this field is what really makes it so wonderful to explore.

The next chapter presents some interesting smart materials that can also be embedded into wearables and soft circuits.

CHAPTER 7

■ ■ ■

Materials That Matter

Now that you are better acquainted with e-textiles and textiles, I am going to introduce a new set of materials that, in my opinion, make wearables far more interesting. For now, I will generally refer to them as *smart materials*. A smart material, in essence, is any material that has a property that changes state in reaction to an external stimuli such as temperature or light. Smart materials include piezoelectric materials, which generate voltage when pressure is applied; shape memory polymers, which change shape when they reach a certain temperature; and photoresistive materials that respond to changes in light intensity. There are many, many categories of smart materials, some of which are industry-specific.

These materials are inspirational for designers and engineers working in the wearable realm, because they provide ideas for new interactions and new possibilities. Many of these materials can be programmed to respond and react to the environment in a way that emulates natural interactions between humans (or other organisms) and their environment. Smart materials can be programmed to undergo a set amount of phase changes. For example, a shape-changing plastic could take one form when it reaches 100°C and then take another form when it reaches 150°C.

This chapter focuses on a select group of smart materials that are commonly embedded in wearables and are excellent prototyping tools for product and wearable design. I have already mentioned conductive materials, which fall under this category, but I explain in greater detail the properties of conductive thread that make it ideal for certain applications and less ideal for others.

Thread as Wire

Whenever I show someone a soft circuit for the first time, they turn it over, look at the components, and ask how the parts are connected. The answer is the special thread. The thread replaces wire or solder that normally hold components together, allowing for a more flexible and, in some ways, more durable connection. Wires can be difficult to attach to clothing and are stiff and restrictive, not to mention that they might totally clash with the design. Conductive thread, on the other hand, can be sewn into the fabric, just like any other thread, allowing for smoother integration.

There are many different types of conductive thread, varying in composition and thickness. The most common are steel- and silver-based threads, which are also the most affordable. Conductive thread can also be made from strands of copper, gold, tin, nickel, and other metals. The thread is composed of a core material such as cotton or polyester mixed with metal alloys and is not insulated, making it ideal for electronic connections.

When choosing which thread to use for a wearable project, you should take into consideration a few key factors. First, the conductivity and resistance of the thread is important. Different metals have different levels of conductivity; Table 7-1 shows a few common metals to give you an idea of how to compare them. Second, the thickness of the thread is important to consider. The two most common weights of conductive thread are two-ply and four-ply. Four-ply contains twice as much metal as two-ply but is usually significantly thicker. Steel-based threads, for example, are usually quite thick, which makes them easier to secure

© Sibel Deren Guler, Madeline Gannon, and Kate Sicchio 2016
S. D. Guler et al., *Crafting Wearables*, DOI 10.1007/978-1-4842-1808-2_7

electronic components, but they can be difficult to sew. Thicker threads also tend to fray and come apart. However, they offers some advantages over thinner coated threads, in that the steel can withstand higher temperatures, thus making it solderable. Other project-specific factors include the color of the thread, the elasticity (some threads are elastic, allowing for even more flexible connections), ability to give off heat, and so on. Third, you must consider the reaction to skin or any moisture; some metals corrode more quickly than others when exposed to skin.

Table 7-1. *Conductiveness of Common Metals*

Metal	Resistivity at 20°C (m)	Conductivity at 20°C (S/m)
Silver	1.59×10^{-8}	6.30×10^{7}
Copper	1.68×10^{-8}	5.96×10^{7}
Gold	2.44×10^{-8}	4.10×10^{7}
Nickel	6.99×10^{-8}	1.43×10^{7}
Lead	2.2×10^{-7}	4.55×10^{6}
Stainless steel	6.90×10^{-7}	1.45×10^{6}

Although some conductive threads are more durable than others, they all eventually fray over time, especially after they are washed. Some ways to reinforce the thread are to cover it with conductive glue, solder the connections (if possible), and use small pieces of conductive fabric at the connective joints. Other tricks include covering the ends of the thread with hot glue or clear nail polish to seal them together.

The thickest form of conductive thread is conductive yarn, which is similarly made by mixing metal strands with cotton and other materials. Conductive yarn is often used to make DIY textile sensors or is knit into woven wearables like gloves to create conductive touch points.

Conductive Ribbon and Tape

I mentioned conductive ribbon in the context of the Fabrickit in Chapter 6, but this is not the only use of this material or the only manufacturer. Different types of conductive ribbons and tapes are shown in Figure 7-1. Conductive thread ribbon cabling is produced in a few different varieties, depending on the intended use. The ribbon produced by Fabrickit has three conductive strands and is a steel-based blend, making is solderable.

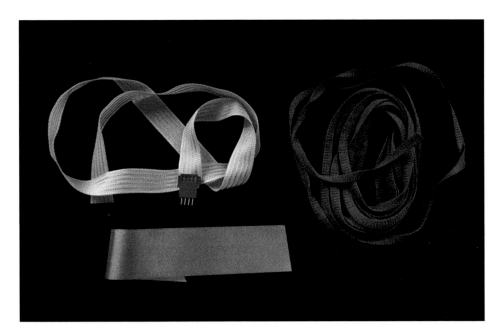

Figure 7-1. *Conductive ribbons and tapes*

Another version, produced by R4R LLC, is a flatter ribbon with four conductive silver strands. Its intended use is to be connected with flexible flat cable connectors, as shown in Figure 7-1. This makes if easy to integrate with most electronic boards. It comes in white and black and can be dyed different colors without affecting the conductivity.

AMOHR is a German company specializing in conductive tapes. It manufactures several different varieties including elastic, pressure sensitive, and a version with a heating element. Conductive heating elements are commonly used for applications like heated car seats and blankets.

Plug and Wear is an Italian textile company specializing in conductive sensors. It manufactures resistive tapes that are woven with silver thread. The company also has pressure-sensitive textiles and tutorials for creating different kinds of sensors with its fabrics.

Conductive Fabric

If you can make conductive thread, you can make conductive fabric. *Conductive fabrics* are fabrics that conduct electricity. They are made by blending or coating fabric with metal fibers. Conductive fabrics are heavily used in medical garments because metals like silver also have antibacterial properties. The composition of conductive fabric gives it different textures. There are a few major manufacturers of conductive fabric in the United States and a few in Europe, as listed in the appendix. This section highlights a selection of conductive fabrics, some of which are shown in Figure 7-2.

Figure 7-2. *A selection of conductive fabrics. From left: iron-on, stretch, nylon*

Iron-on Conductive Fabric

This fabric is coated with nickel or copper on one side and has iron-on coating on the other side. This makes it ideal for attaching to other fabric, wood, glass, or paper, using heat. It is fairly soft and can be manipulated like nonconductive fabric. The nickel may cause skin irritation.

Electrolycra

This is usually silver-plated, stretch, conductive fabric. It is very conductive and similar to ordinary LYCRA or other elastic fabric. Depending on the weave, some versions only stretch in one direction, and others stretch in both directions. The resistivity may change when stretched, depending on the blend. This is ideal for wearables that need flexibility, such as gloves and undergarments. It can be found under the brand names Electrolycra and Medtex.

Tin/Copper/Cobalt Plated

These fabrics are highly conductive and solderable due to their high temperature tolerance but cause skin irritation. They can be used in between two layers of nonconductive fabric. These fabrics can be found under the brand name Flectron.

Super-Light Mesh

This fabric is extremely thin and lightweight and is therefore very useful for wearable applications. It is woven from very thin strands of copper or silver thread or wire. This mesh is sold as a curtain material for shielding electromagnetic radiation.

Velostat

Velostat is a film made from polyolefin that is impregnated with carbon, thus making it conductive. It is most commonly used as packaging material to protect items that could be damaged by electrostatic discharge. Velostat is useful when making soft-circuit sensors because it has an interesting property: the resistivity decreases under pressure. You can use it to make your own pressure or bend sensors by sandwiching it between two conductive layers. I provide a short tutorial on how to do this in the next section.

Homemade Bend Sensor

This tutorial walks you through how to make a pressure sensor using several of the materials described in the previous section. The key element of this pressure sensor is the velostat. The resistance of velostat decreases when force, or pressure, is applied to the surface, and when you bend the sensor, this effectively puts pressure on it. To measure, or sense, pressure, you are going to measure this change in resistance. The construction of the bend sensor may seem similar to the push button you made in the previous chapter. Figure 7-3 illustrates the steps to construct the bend sensor.

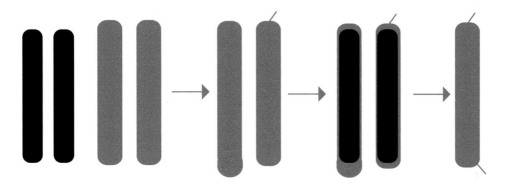

Figure 7-3. *Steps 1–4: assembling the bend sensor*

You need the following materials and tools for this project:

- Velostat
- Conductive thread
- Conductive fabric (optional)
- Neoprene or other nonconductive squishy fabric
- Scissors
- Needle

Follow these steps

1. Cut two identical rectangular shapes out of velostat. The size of the bend sensor is determined by how sensitive you want to make it. The more conductive thread you can fit under the velostat, the more sensitive your sensor will be.

2. Cut a slightly larger version of the same two shapes out of the neoprene or nonconductive fabric.

3. Thread your needle with conductive thread. You are going to sew across one side of the neoprene fabric, as in the third step shown in Figure 7-3. Start close to one end and sew all the way to the other end, using a zigzag stitch. When you get to the other end, tie a knot and leave some thread hanging past the edge. Do this to both pieces of the outer fabric. You can also sew a small tab of conductive fabric on the end, to create a larger connection pad. I have illustrated both versions in the diagram.

4. It is time to assemble you sensor! Place each strip of velostat on top of a piece of neoprene, such that the velostat is covering the stitched side. Make sure the velostat is completely covering the stitches, but leave the tabs of conductive thread or fabric at the ends exposed. Then make a sandwich with the two sides, putting the velostat in the middle. Sew around the edges of the neoprene with regular nonconductive thread to seal the sensor.

5. You can test your sensor by connecting it to a multimeter, as shown in Figure 7-4. Put a probe on each end of the bend sensor, and set the multimeter to the resistance setting, at the 2 kilohms scale. Push on the bend sensor. You should see the resistance decrease when you apply pressure or bend it. You can now connect it to a circuit in place of a bend or pressure sensor.

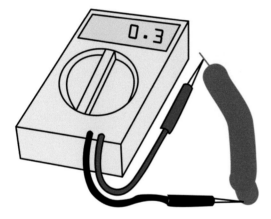

Figure 7-4. *Testing the bend sensor*

Chromatic

Chromatic materials change color in response to changes in their environment. Adding chromatic materials to wearable designs presents a range of interactions. These interactions happen automatically, in the sense that the material is preprogrammed to respond to a change in the environment instead of the user specifically.

Thermochromatic

Thermochromatic pigment changes color in response to temperature. The pigment is usually created with liquid crystal technology, which you may be familiar with from "mood rings." The liquid crystals are encapsulated within the dye. At a preprogrammed temperature, a chemical reaction causes the liquid crystals in the dye to reorient and produce a change of color. This may happen due to an increase or decrease in temperature. This technology is also used in baby bottles to detect a change in temperature. Although this pigment can be mixed with inks, it is usually used with a thin film.

Another technique for creating thermochromatic materials is with leuco dyes. Leuco dyes can acquire two different color states. In the first state the dye appears colorless, but when it reacts with heat or UV light it absorbs visible light and changes to a different color (the second color state). This type of dye is used for sun-printing and can be applied to fabrics. Hypercolor is an example of a thermochromatic fabric that is coated with leuco dye; a sample of hypercolor fabric changing color can be seen in Figure 7-5. Lumi is a company that produces a thermally reactive dye as an alternative to screen-printing. Their tagline is "print color with light."

Figure 7-5. *Hypercolor fabric turning from orange to yellow*

Photochromatism

Photochromatic materials change color in response to electromagnetic radiation such as sunlight. This is a reversible process: the color reverts back to the original state. A common application of this technology is in eyeglass lenses, where the lenses automatically darken when exposed to sunlight and clear up when in a dark environment. It is also being experimented with in fabric dyes to create patterns on fabric that change depending on the light exposure or time of day. Figure 7-6 shows apparel from the Photochromia project, by The Crated, which reveals new patterns when exposed to sunlight.

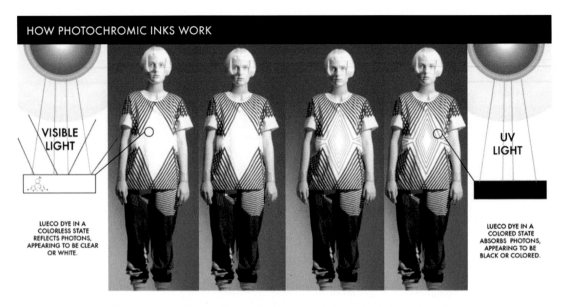

Figure 7-6. Photochromia outfit diagram by Madisson Maxey (photos by Spencer Kohn)

Shape Changing

Shape-changing materials may seem to be the most magical of the smart materials presented in the chapter. They can literally morph from one shape into another without physical manipulation by the user, as shown in Figure 7-7. I discuss three different types of shape-changing materials in this section.

Figure 7-7. SMP returning to its programmed shape when submerged in hot water

Shape Memory Polymer

A shape memory polymer (SMP) is a plastic that has the ability to return to an original state after it has been deformed. The plastic is preprogrammed during the manufacturing process to have different solid crystal states that it can take. This change is induced by external stimuli such as a change in temperature or voltage. Additionally, SMPs can have multiple states: for example, a plastic-based SMP may take one shape when it reaches one temperature and then morph into another. During the transition, the polymer becomes rubbery and elastic, and it hardens into a glassy state when the stimulant is removed and the transition is complete. The type of SMP is determined by what activates it. Following is a list of several of these types:

- Light-induced SMPs react to a change in the wavelength of light. This could be a reaction to UV light or simply a change of color.

- Thermoactive SMPs react to a change in temperature. This is similar to polymorph plastic, which is mentioned in the next section.

- Electro-active SMPs use electric current to activate the polymer. This is useful in a situation where heat is not accessible as a stimulant. Usually the material contracts or bends when exposed to the current. SRI International, a nonprofit research center, has developed a material called *electroactive polymer artificial muscle* (EPAM). As SRI explains, artificial muscle offers an alternative to the way in which many types of industrial, medical, consumer, automotive, and aerospace products are powered and operated. Additionally, EPAM is much lighter, smaller, quieter, and cheaper. It can be used in haptic displays to improve human computer interaction and flat conformal loudspeakers and could even be implanted to create active medical prosthetics.

Shape Memory Alloy

Shape memory alloys (SMAs) are similar to SMPs in that an SMA is an alloy that returns to its programmed shape when heated. SMAs can have a one-way or two-way memory effect. In the one-way effect, the material remembers a programmed shape when heated. When it is cooled, it remains in this shape until physically reformed. In the two-way effect, the alloy has two states. When it is heated, it returns to one programmed shape; and when it is cooled to a lower temperature, it takes the form of the second shape. SMAs are usually composed of a blend of metals like copper-aluminum-nickel or titanium-nickel. They tend to be quite strong and can support unusually large strains. Although SMAs are preferred for certain applications, SMPs are usually chosen over SMAs because they are less expensive to manufacture and more resilient over time. SMAs fatigue and lose their memory effect after constant use.

Nitinol, commonly referred to as *memory wire*, is an SMA that is extremely biocompatible and is often used in medical applications such as stents and orthodontic braces. It is also extremely resilient when used in eyeglass frames. Nitniol is also being used by fashion designs to activate clothing, you will read about some examples of this in Part 3 of this book.

Polymorph

Polymorphic materials have the ability to exist in more than one shape. Similar to SMPs, they react to external stimuli such as heat. Unlike SMPs, they do not remember their shape at different states; they simply become reshapeable or remoldable. Polymorph pellets are commonly sold as a prototyping/design tool under brand names like Insta-Mold and Thermoplastic. Polymorphs are a useful material when designing wearable applications because they can quickly be reformed from one solid state to another.

Glowing Materials

Although LEDs are commonly used when creating wearables, they offer very direct light that does not always suit the desired aesthetic. The glowing materials described in this section offer thin, flexible alternatives to LEDs that provide more of an ambient glow rather than a focused splash of light.

Electroluminescent Wire

Electroluminescent (EL) wire, also called *glowire,* is a material that emits light when current is passed through it or it is exposed to a strong electrical field. It is often compared to the phenomenon of bioluminescence. EL wire is composed of phosphor-coated copper at the center, surrounded by two thin conductive wires, which are encased in a clear protective sleeve and then covered in a layer of colored vinyl. The outer layers protect the center from moisture. When current flows through the copper and conductive wires at the center, the phosphor glows. EL wire comes in many different colors; the colors are set by the frequency of the applied power and the colored plastic layer.

EL wire is used in a variety of different applications including safety lighting for automobiles, light sculptures, and illuminated fabric an example of EL wire sewn onto a shirt can be seen in Figure 7-8. It is also available as a thin plastic sheet. ElastoLite is one manufacturer of these sheets and markets them as waterproof lamp sheets that can be embedded in wearable projects.

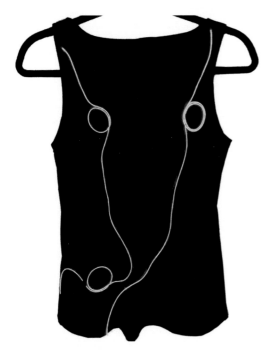

Figure 7-8. *Top for a "Tron" Halloween costume made using EL wire*

Optical Fibers

I mentioned optical fibers in Chapter 1, when discussing the work of Harry Wainwright, who has pioneered many techniques for embedding optical fibers in clothing. Extremely thin optical fibers can be woven into fabrics to illuminate them. Optical fibers are able to carry light from one source point, usually a super-bright

LED, across a very long length of fiber, creating a more distributed light than the single LED point. Fiber-optic fabric can have a starry texture when the fibers are slightly exposed and light leaks out. The fabric is used to illuminate all kinds of clothing, from hats and gloves to wedding gowns.

Quantum Tunneling Composite

Quantum tunneling composite (QTC) is a flexible polymer with extraordinary electrical properties, commonly used for pressure switching and sensing. In its normal state, it performs as an electrical insulator; but when it is deformed, it become the complete opposite and acts like an excellent conductor. It can pass very high currents even at a very small size. QTCs are composed of metal filler particles combined with an elastomeric binder, such as silicone rubber. They are a fairly new material developed in the last 20 years. Currently they are used to make a variety of textile switches and pressure sensors (QTC).

Protective Materials

Several academic and industry research groups specialize in developing new coatings and compositions of fabric to give it extraordinary functionality and efficiency. This section mentions a few particularly interesting and innovative textiles.

Schoeller Textiles

Schoeller Textiles is a Swiss company specializing in researching and developing new textiles. Many of its inventions mimic biological inventions and are very interesting for wearables. Follow are some textiles developed for protective purposes; more can be found on the company's web site (`www.schoeller-textiles.com`).

C_change

C_change is a windproof, waterproof fabric membrane that responds to changes in temperature and other factors. It was developed to mimic the fir cone, which opens and closes in response to different weather conditions. Similarly, the C_change membrane reacts to environmental conditions by opening to increase breathability or closing to trap moisture. It is advertised as having the ability to ensure a pleasant body climate in all conditions. This fabric is used for racing and extreme weather jackets by various brands.

NanoSphere

NanoSphere is a nanotech-based surface-finishing technology for fabric, which repels dirt and water from becoming absorbed. It was developed based on the natural self-cleaning effect of certain plants whose leaves are always clean because dirt cannot stick to the surface. The obvious benefit of this technology is that the fabric does not need to be washed as often as it protects itself from common stains.

INZECTIC

INZECTIC provides protection from ticks and mosquitos. When the insects come into contact with the fabric, they become immobilized and usually die. The fabric also repels mosquitos from landing on the wearer. Additionally, it is able to breathe and quickly wick moisture out of the fabric.

GORE

GORE is a research and development firm specializing in smart fabrics (www.goreprotectivefabrics.com). In addition to providing an array of windproof and waterproof fabrics that are ideal for outerwear, the company has created a contaminant-aware fabric. Although many of these fabrics are commercially available, several have been developed specifically for military use. The contaminant-aware fabric can be easily decontaminated if it is exposed to certain chemicals: regular fabrics cannot be fully cleaned after exposure to those chemicals, but GORE CHEMPAK does not absorb the chemicals in the same way and thus can be easily cleaned.

X-Bionic

X-Bionic (www.x-bionic.com) is a research center and think tank that develops revolutionary textiles, mainly used for outerwear and athletic clothing. I highlight a few of the company's materials here; they make several others that are similar to the technologies described from Schoeller and GORE.

Xitanit

Xitanit is a material that is able to absorb body heat from working muscles and then distribute and dissipate it throughout the surface. The material is extremely conductive and reflective. The conductive property allows it to quickly dissipate heat on the exterior while keeping the interior cool. Additionally, the knit structure distributes perspiration evenly across the surface.

Macrotermes

Macotermes is a cooling material that was inspired by the air-conditioning system of a termite nest. The texture of this unique fiber is modeled after the channels and porous structure on the nest's interior. It is this texture that gives the fabric special cooling properties.

BIONIC Aramid

BIONIC Aramid can withstand temperatures up to 400°C without melting! This material is based on the threads of the Golden Web Spider. This spider's threads are four times as strong as steel. Scientists modeled the chemical construction of the Aramid structure after the protein structure of the spider web. The fibers that are woven in lengthwise are different than those that are woven widthwise; this prevents the yarn from transferring heat and makes it fire resistant.

Summary

Now your wearables toolbox has expanded even further, from sewing tools and sewable electronics to include smart textiles and dyes. Entire books are dedicated to smart fabrics and are full of fascinating material that expands on what has been presented in this chapter. As a collector of interesting objects, I have acquired samples of many of these materials. I find that when thinking about a new project, it helps to experiment with a variety of tools and materials before deciding what to use in the final version. Hopefully these materials will be inspirational as you imagine what clothes and wearable devices will be made from them in the future.

The next few chapters present new fabrication techniques and software tools that have had a huge impact on the future of wearables.

CHAPTER 8

■ ■ ■

Digital Design for Wearables

Guest Chapter by Madeline Gannon

We have a long tradition—as old as human civilization itself—of crafting wearable garments and objects for the body. But it is only in the past 30 or 40 years that we have been building tools to digitize these traditionally analog practices. Although we shouldn't reject millennia of accumulated knowledge, handcrafted design processes have certain limitations that digital tools can help overcome. For example, when designing wearables that need to be custom-fitted to the body, such as prosthetics or masks, a design for one person is not easily adaptable to another; this creates a lot of redundant work when it's time to scale up production. In addition, pragmatic functions—like archiving, editing, sharing, and duplicating a wearable—are hard to do with analog design workflows. Computer-Aided Design (CAD) software, however, is incredibly useful for these processes.

This chapter goes over the benefits of using design software and highlights commonly used tool sets for digitally designing wearables. It touches on designing for fabrication and shows you ways to tailor your digital tools for more customized workflows in wearable design. If you are new to digital processes like *3D modeling*, *3D scanning*, and *parametric modeling*, keep in mind that there is a learning curve. But with a bit of patience and perseverance, integrating digital tools into your design process will enhance both your efficiency and your creativity.

Software for Digital Design

CAD tools—software for digital design—fall into two primary categories: tools for designing in two dimensions and tools for designing in three dimensions. If you are new to digital design processes, you may want to start by experimenting with two-dimensional CAD tools; these tend to be easier to learn, and they pair nicely with 2D fabrication processes. For those diving into 3D-modeling and 3D-printing wearables, this chapter has suggestions for choosing the right software for your design needs. A nearly endless number of CAD tools are available, but this section highlights specific examples that are most useful for designing and producing wearables.

2D Design Tools

The design and fabrication of clothing has traditionally existed as a *two-dimensional process*: you use 2D templates to cut out a design from a 2D sheet of fabric, which you then sew into the three-dimensional garment. Although it is perfectly adequate to do this process by hand, you can also use software to assist in the creation and execution of your design.

Graphic design software like Adobe Illustrator and CorelDRAW, and CAD software like AutoCAD and Vectorworks, provide digital canvases for drawing 2D patterns and designs. Most important, these software packages (and many others) can export your design as a *vector graphic*, which can be sent to a fabrication machine. Vector graphics are a way of representing a digital image as a series of 2D (x,y) coordinates plotted

S. D. Guler et al., *Crafting Wearables*, DOI 10.1007/978-1-4842-1808-2_8

on the screen. Because the digital image is represented as coordinates and not pixels, you can send vector graphics to all sorts of two-axes digital fabrication machines, including laser cutters, vinyl cutters, and more traditional paper printers and plotters. The next chapter goes over digital fabrication tools in more detail, but keep this in mind: if your software can export a design as a file type with the extension `.dxf`, `.dwg`, `.ai`, or `.pdf`, chances are you can send your 2D digital design to a fabrication machine.

3D Design Tools

3D modeling is a more recent addition to the wearable designer's repertoire. Commercially available software for 3D modeling is tailored toward three distinct domains: product design, computer graphics and animation, and architectural design. Notice anything missing? Currently there are no 3D-modeling tools designed specifically for fashion design or wearable design! The next section addresses this limitation; for now, let's find the best available option for the type of wearables you'll be designing.

Choosing the Right Modeling Software

Learning to 3D-model can be technically challenging and time consuming. To make things even more difficult, each 3D design tool brings its own strengths and weaknesses when it comes to geometric representation, usability, and cost. This makes learning multiple programs difficult, so it's best to start with the design tool best suited to your needs.

If you use geometric representation as a guiding criterion, designers creating wearables that are more closely related to product design, such as medical devices or shoes, should use *solid modeling* software. Examples of solid modelers include Dassault Systèmes SOLIDWORKS, Autodesk Fusion 360, and OpenSCAD. Designers creating wearables with more free-flowing, organic forms should use software that's more tailored for computer graphics, animation, and architectural design, such as Rhinoceros 3D, Blender, or Autodesk Maya.

If you use usability and cost as the guiding criteria, Blender and OpenSCAD are free, open source programs with vibrant developer communities. Autodesk products have free student software licenses, but professional licenses are costly. Rhinoceros 3D is perhaps the easiest to learn and the most extensible through its Grasshopper plug-in. Maya is perhaps the most difficult to learn, but it is also the most powerful in terms of 3D modeling.

Finally, the most tried-and-true method for choosing the right design tool for your needs is to first find work that you admire and then contact the creator to inquire about their digital design tools and workflows.

3D Modeling for 3D Printing

3D modeling can be used in every phase when designing a wearable: in the concept phase for rendering images; in the development phase for rapid prototyping and 3D printing; and in the production phase for preparing for mass production processes, like injection molding. However, the constraints and requirements of a 3D model change for each of these phases. For example, a 3D model created to look its best in a rendering may not be built properly for 3D printing. This section focuses on 3D modeling for rapid prototyping and looks specifically at how to 3D-model for 3D printing.

A 3D model needs to satisfy three basic requirements before it can be printed:

- The geometry must be a *closed solid* or a *closed mesh*.

- The geometry cannot have *self-intersecting faces*.

- The geometry must match the *minimum resolution* of a printer.

For a 3D model to be a closed solid or a closed mesh, all the faces must be joined together such that there are no holes in the mesh. Another way people describe this property is that the 3D model needs to be *watertight*. Imagine you poured water into your 3D model: would water leak out? If so, then your model has a hole that needs closing. Figure 8-1 shows a valid, closed solid model compared to an invalid 3D model with a hole.

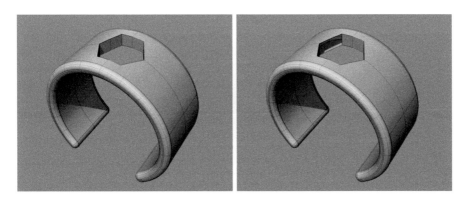

Figure 8-1. *The 3D model on the left shows a closed solid model, but the model on the right has a hole in its hexagonal cutout. This hole violates the watertight principle, which makes the model invalid for 3D printing*

3D geometry has both an *in*side and an *out*side. The mesh is *self-intersecting* when the inside of the mesh gets flipped outside. In Figure 8-2, the inside of each mesh face is colored magenta. You can tell when a 3D model is turned inside-out when these inverted magenta faces show on the outside of the 3D surface. Figure 8-2 shows a valid mesh compared to one with inverted faces.

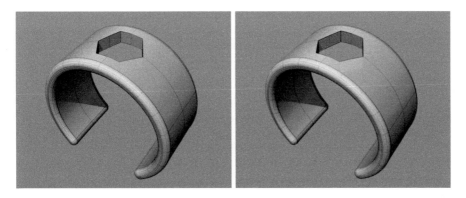

Figure 8-2. *The 3D model on the left shows a closed solid model, but the model on the right has inverted faces in its hexagonal cutout. These inside-out faces violate the self-intersecting principle, which makes the model invalid for 3D printing*

When 3D modeling for 3D printing, it's important to design for the minimum print resolution of your 3D printer. The *print resolution* of a 3D printer is the minimum size for any geometry to be printed. If you design a 3D model with features that are smaller than the minimum resolution of a printer, then those features are too small for the 3D printer to realize. Moreover, different 3D printers have different print resolutions: a standard FDM desktop 3D printer may have a print resolution of around .1 mm, whereas a higher-end SLA printer may have a resolution of 10 microns! Figure 8-3 shows a bracelet that failed during 3D printing because details in the 3D model were below the minimum print resolution of the 3D printer.

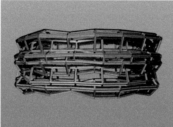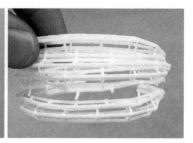

Figure 8-3. *This sequence of images shows a digital design with the corresponding physical print. A 3D print can fail or break when the 3D model has details that are below the print resolution of the 3D printer*

Customizing Your Tools

As previously mentioned, currently available 3D-modeling software is not built specifically for digitally crafting wearables; it is most commonly used for architectural, aeronautical, automotive, and product design applications. However, designing for the body has different challenges than designing a building, a boat, a car, or a gadget.

Human bodies are highly complex, highly specific physical contexts; 3D-modeling tools tend to be empty virtual spaces that ignore physical contexts. This can make it difficult to digitally design wearables that have a tailored or ergonomic fit. Moreover, every *body* is different; creating variations of a design for multiple body types can be a laborious task in current 3D-modeling software. Modifying a design to work for S, M, L, and XL sizes is not as simple as scaling a 3D model up or down.

This section looks at two strategies for customizing your 3D-modeling tools to circumvent these limitations. First, you see techniques to *digitize the body*—bringing a digital reference of the physical body into a virtual modeling environment. Next you learn about *parametric modeling* techniques—a way to rapidly iterate and build variation into a digital design. Integrating these two strategies into your 3D-modeling workflow helps to customize your tools so you can tackle the more difficult challenges for digitally designing wearables.

Digitizing the Body

Bringing a digital reference of a body into your 3D-modeling tool is one useful technique for 3D-modeling wearables. Although some modeling software has default human bodies that you can directly import into the 3D-modeling environment, these tend to be idealized forms that are mainly used as scale figures for a 3D-modeled scene. To get a more accurate representation of a body, you can *digitize*—or *3D scan*—a person's body. *3D scanning* is a process of digitally capturing the body using hardware and then using software to process and reconstruct the captured data into a 3D mesh. This mesh can then be imported into your 3D-modeling environment.

Central to 3D scanning is the idea of *resolution*. The resolution of a 3D scan is the amount of detail and geometric fidelity it has to the physical counterpart: low-resolution scans have a low amount of detail, and high-resolution scans have a high amount of detail. It's important to find the right resolution for digitizing the body: if you have too little detail in your 3D scan, a design may not accurately fit the body; if you have too much detail in your 3D scan, the file size of your 3D model may be too big for your modeling software to process. Figure 8-4 shows a full-body 3D scan that has been resampled at different resolutions.

Figure 8-4. *A full-body 3D scan that has been resampled to four different resolutions. The scan with the highest resolution (densest number of mesh faces) is in the background, and the scan with the lowest resolution (sparsest number of mesh faces) is in the foreground*

The three most useful 3D-scanning techniques for digitizing the body are *photogrammetry*, *depth cameras*, and *structured light scanning*. The process of 3D scanning may seem technologically complex, but there are a number of options with a low point of entry to get you started. For example, instead of purchasing expensive 3D-scanning hardware, you can use your smartphone camera, an inexpensive depth camera like the Microsoft Kinect, or a projector and camera to 3D-scan the body. The following sections go into detail about the advantages and limitations of each of these three digitizing techniques.

Photogrammetry

Photogrammetry is a 3D-scanning process that stitches together photographs to create a fully three-dimensional model. It works by taking a lot of photos of an object from every possible angle. The photogrammetry software then reconstructs a 3D object from these 2D images by analyzing slight differences in the light reflected off the object in each photograph.

Although these software algorithms are quite sophisticated, photogrammetry is an easy and affordable way to 3D-scan something. It requires a little planning but no special hardware. All you need is a decent cell phone camera to get started: the algorithms handle all the complicated model reconstruction, and you get back a fairly accurate digital representation of your physical capture. Figure 8-5 shows the resulting capture session from one photogrammetry app, 123D Catch. Notice how, given a set of photographs, the software is able to estimate the world position of the camera.

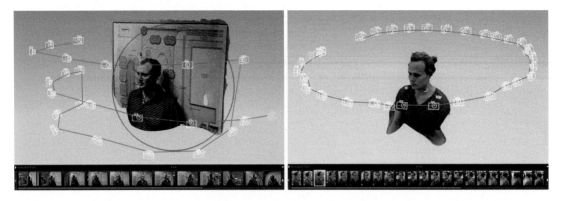

Figure 8-5. *These two screenshots show how photogrammetry software, like Autodesk's 123D Catch, constructs a 3D model from a set of photographs. (Screen captures from* www.instructables.com/id/3D-Printing-your-own-full-color-bobblehead-using-1.*)*

However, there are limitations. Photogrammetry algorithms look for *minute* changes across a large set of images, so they are very sensitive to environmental changes such as moving capture subjects or changes in lighting. Moreover, captured images need a decent amount of overlap to fully reconstruct a 3D object. This works well for small to medium-sized objects, like a toy or a vase, but can be difficult for large objects, like a human body. Also, this need for overlapping images makes it difficult to adequately capture areas with large amounts of three-dimensional change, such as hands or fingers.

For the best results, keep these requirements in mind when using photogrammetry to 3D-scan the body:

- The person being captured must remain *very* still.

- The lighting in the space where you doing the capture must remain *very* consistent.

- The images being captured must significantly overlap. Plan your capture session to reach difficult areas of the body, like the top of the head and the hands and arms.

Many programs and apps use photogrammetry for 3D scanning, but the two I recommend starting with are Autodesk's 123D Catch (free) and Agisoft's PhotoScan (free 30-day trial).

Depth Cameras

Depth cameras use various hardware and software configurations to sense the three-dimensional world, but all they follow a similar technique: project infrared (IR) light out into an environment and then sense where or when the IR light hits a surface. Depth cameras use IR light because it is invisible to the human eye: a depth camera can beam high densities of information into an environment, and you and I are none the wiser. Depth cameras reconstruct this information as depth maps, point clouds, or meshes. Figure 8-6 shows examples of point clouds captured by a Microsoft Kinect.

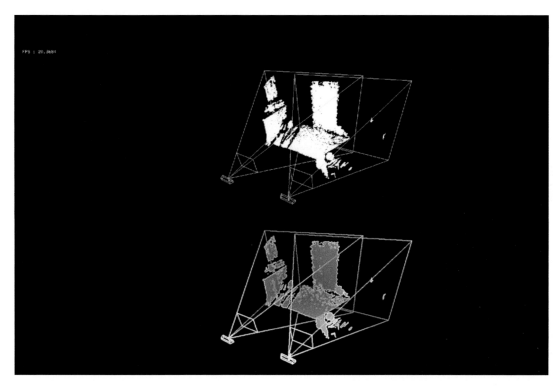

Figure 8-6. *Point clouds from a Microsoft Kinect. This raw data can be processed into refined 3D meshes using various optimization algorithms*

Different depth cameras have different resolutions (the amount of detail they can sense): low-resolution depth cameras, such as the Microsoft Kinect, tend to be cheaper, whereas high-resolution cameras, like Artec 3D hand-held scanners, tend to be more expensive and used for more specialized purposes.

3D scanning with depth cameras takes more time to master than photogrammetry, where you can use an app on your smartphone to start 3D scanning. However, depth cameras have distinct advantages that can be worth the time and monetary investment. For one thing, depth cameras are very resilient to changing lighting conditions in your capture environment. Unlike photogrammetry, these cameras use IR light, not visible light, to sense the world: if the environmental light changes in the middle of your scanning session, it won't be sensed by the depth camera, and your scan won't be ruined. With depth cameras, you can even 3D-scan a subject in a completely dark environment!

Depth cameras are also flexible and useful devices for analyzing the body. Yes, you can use them to create a static 3D scan, but you can also use depth cameras to dynamically sense how the body is moving. They give you the ability to detect and track different movements, interactions, and gestures for one or more bodies. Access to this real-time data can be invaluable when designing wearables for parts of the body that are constantly moving, like shoes and medical braces.

One of the limitations of depth cameras is that they can't scan objects or surfaces that are reflective or refractive. Depth cameras work by projecting and then sensing IR light; if you try to scan a reflective surface, like a mirror, the projected beams of IR light bounce away from the camera's IR sensor. If the projected light never returns to the sensor, then the camera can't read in the depth data. When using depth cameras to digitize the human body, this issue comes up most often when the person being scanned is wearing reflective jewelry, a watch, or glasses; but even a person with very oily or sweaty/wet skin can corrupt scan data. This can leave noticeable holes in your scan data.

Structured Light Scanning

Structured light scanning works similarly to 3D scanning with depth cameras: you project light into an environment and then sense how that light hits a surface. However, instead of using infrared light that you can't see, structured light scanning uses a standard projector and camera. *Three-phase* structured light scanning works by projected three specifically patterned calibration images onto the capture subject. Figure 8-7 shows how these 2D patterns deform when projected onto the capture subject and then generate the 3D scan.

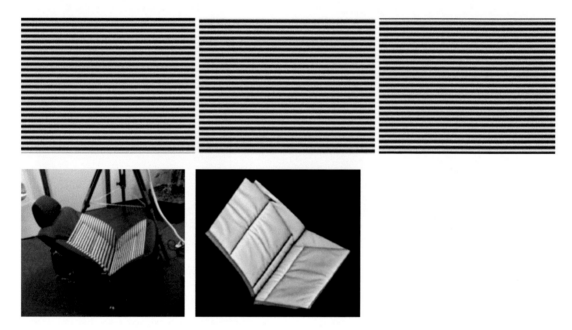

Figure 8-7. *Three-phase structured light scanning can be an economical way to get high-resolution 3D scans. The top row shows the three calibration images for three-phase scanning. The bottom row shows the calibration images projected onto a car seat and the resulting digitized surface; note the high level of detail in the wrinkles of the leather seat. (Images courtesy Wikimedia Commons, licensed under CC BY 3.0.)*

This sounds quite complicated—*and it is*—but basic structured light scanning is a very inexpensive way to get high-resolution 3D scans. All you need is a projector, a camera, and some smart software. There are open source software options, if you would like to try it yourself. I recommend this tutorial from MIT: `http://fab.cba.mit.edu/content/processes/structured_light`.

You will most commonly find structured light scanning being used to capture the bodies of actors for films. In this scenario, highly specialized stages filled with DSLR cameras and programmable LED lights sequentially bounce light off the capture subject. One spectacular example is *Light Stage V* from the University of Southern California's Institute for Creative Technologies. Light Stage V is a geodesic dome with 156 programmable LED lights. As the LED lights are sequenced on and off, a high-speed camera captures the light bouncing off the capture subject at 24 times per second. A high-speed structured light projector adds dynamic geometry information onto this reflectance data. What results is an extremely high-detail 3D scan—down to the pores of the skin. For more technical details and images, see `http://gl.ict.usc.edu/Research/DigitalEmily/`.

Table 8-1 summarizes this section in a simple, easy-to-read form. As you decide which digitizing technique to use, keep in mind the constraints of your capture subject, capture environment, and project budget.

Table 8-1. *Summary of the Benefits and Tradeoffs for Each Technique That Digitizes the Body*

Technique	Pros	Cons	Level
Photogrammetry	Easy to learn and use	Subjects must remain very still	Beginner
	Inexpensive	Lighting must remain very consistent	
	Can capture full 3D objects	Not good for capturing details like hands or fingers	
Depth camera	Scan quality independent of lighting conditions	Not good for capturing reflective surfaces	Intermediate
	Many moderately priced hardware solutions		
Structured light	Extremely high-detail scans	Expensive, large setup	Advanced
		Complex software solutions	

Case Study: Open Fit Lab

One great example of how digitizing the body can change the way you design and construct wearables is the *Open Fit Lab*. The Open Fit Lab is an initiative by Lisa Kori Chung and Kyle McDonald to bring new software techniques to traditional clothing construction. In this case, they are using a depth camera and custom software to automatically generate patterns for tailored pants.

To create these digital pants patterns, the Open Fit software uses a Microsoft Kinect to scan a person's legs and extract specific body dimensions. These dimensions, such the *crotch length*, *hip-to-floor* height, and *thigh*, *calf*, and *ankle* widths, then update a generic pants pattern to fit this specific body. The newly generated 2D pattern is projected onto a bolt a fabric, and tailors mark up, cut out, and sew together the customized pants. Figure 8-8 shows the process from software interface to physical fabrication.

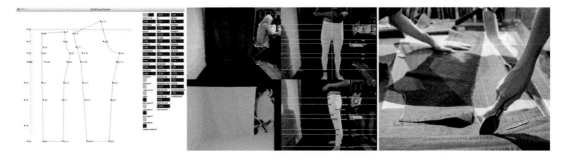

Figure 8-8. *The Open Fit workflow begins with a parametric pattern generator. The pattern generator is updated by real-time readings from a person's body. The updated pattern is projected at a 1:1 scale onto fabric for final construction. (Images courtesy of Lisa Kori and Kyle McDonald, Open Fit Lab.)*

The Open Fit workflow elegantly balances digital/physical processes in digitally generating patterns and facilitating analog fabrication. However, the digital workflow does not necessarily need to stop at the design phase: these digital patterns could also be cut using a 2D-fabrication machine. The digital files generated by the Open Fit software are the same kinds of files a laser cutter or CNC drag knife uses to cut out a design from fabric. Admittedly, this is not a necessary step. But it is a great example to illustrate how easily digital design and fabrication processes link together. As you are engulfed in the process of digital design, keep in mind how your digital design will eventually come out of the computer and into the physical world.

Parametric Design

Now that you have brought the human body as a digital canvas into your 3D modeling environment, you have a great starting point for designing wearables. But these modeling environments have one more limitation that can make your design and production processes cumbersome: 3D models are very hard to adapt.

When you digitally create a wearable design using existing CAD environments, it is 3D-modeled as a single, static object. However, wearables rarely ever exist as a single static version: a single design might need multiple formal adaptations to fit different body types, fabrication techniques, or even aesthetic sensibilities. This is where parametric design can help.

Parametric design is a technique for embedding variation directly into your design. One parametric object that you may encounter daily is the disposable coffee cup. This cup has *fixed variables* that don't change, like the diameter of its top and bottom rims, and it has *open variables* that do change, such as its height and volume. The relationship between the height and volume of the coffee cup is its defining *parameter*. Changing one variable of a parameter affects the others: tweaking the height of the cup modifies the overall volume of coffee that it can hold, for example. With parametric modeling, the effort you put into building the original model gives you instant variation without the need to reconstruct any geometry. As in the cup example, the design effort to create a 12-ounce cup also lets you generate 16 oz cups, 20 oz cups, or even 23.57 oz cups.

For wearables, parametric modeling is exceptionally helpful for *iterating*, *customizing*, and *personalizing* a design. Basing the 3D model of a wearable on parameters lets you rapidly iterate through a wide range of options during the design phase. A designer can explore formal and functional changes just by tweaking a few variables. Figure 8-9 shows a parametric bracelet being modified by the designer. The parametric model is dynamically transformed by simply shifting the values of a few variables.

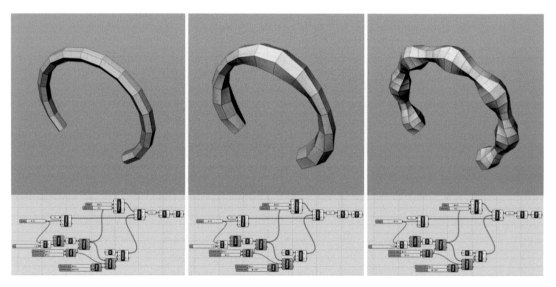

Figure 8-9. *The design of this bracelet can be rapidly explored using parametric modeling. Just tweaking the radius and twist of each bracelet segment generates many variations on a single form*

Once the design of a wearable is finalized, you can use the same techniques to customize and adapt the overall design to multiple body types. Figure 8-10 shows the parametric bracelet in a variety of sizes. Each variation keeps the same aesthetic and fabrication constraints of the original model but is sized to fit a different wrist diameter.

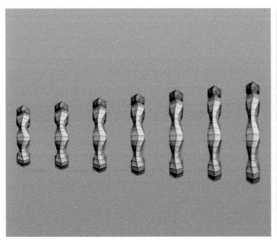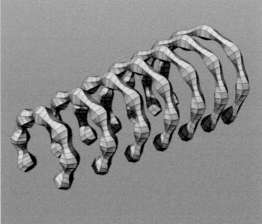

Figure 8-10. Adapting a wearable design to fit many body types is streamlined using parametric modeling techniques. When this example bracelet is sized up and down, the fabrication properties (such as wall thickness) are preserved

In the previous two examples, all the changes in the parametric model result from tweaking one or two numeric values. Parametric models abstract the formal behaviors of a design down to interdependent numbers. These numbers don't need to be arbitrary values; they can be very specific data for personalizing a design to an individual. The bracelets in Figure 8-11, for example, are personalized with the individual's Twitter data. The overall aesthetic, design, and fabrication constraints are consistent, but the data gathered from each individual person generates a unique form.

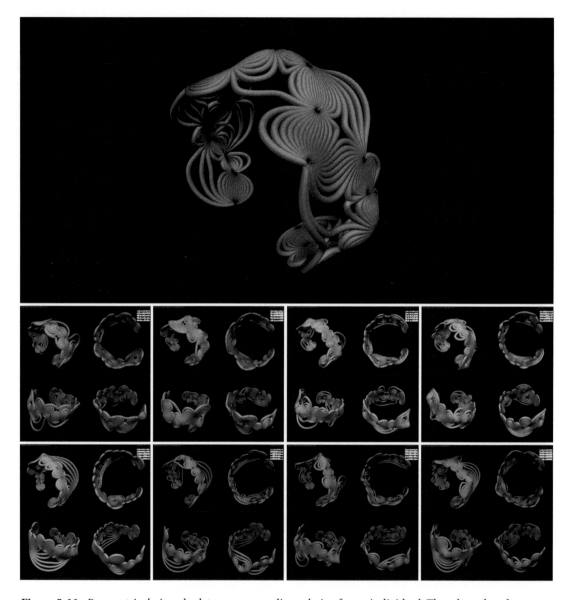

Figure 8-11. Parametric design also lets you personalize a design for an individual. These bracelets share aesthetic values but integrate an individual's Twitter data to generate uniquely distinct forms

Tools for Parametric Modeling

Most 3D modeling environments use back-ends or plug-ins that support parametric design. They can be *scripted* (where you write code to build the model) or *visual* (where you construct code through a drag-and-drop interface). The principles behind both kinds are the same: they offer back-door access to the geometry functions that the program uses. Table 8-2 shows three of the most commonly used tools for parametric modeling in existing CAD software.

Table 8-2. *Features of Three Parametric Modeling Tools*

Interface	Modeling Software	Features
Grasshopper	Rhinoceros 3D	Visual programming Language
		Easier to learn
		Helpful online community
MEL Script	Maya 3D	Proprietary scripting language
		Access to powerful geometry and physics libraries
Python	Blender 3D	Commonly used scripting language
		Free and open source
		Helpful online community

If you have programming experience, you may feel most comfortable working with OpenSCAD, which is a code-based 3D modeling platform. But you can also build your own parametric modeling tool. Creative coding platforms, such as Processing and openFrameworks, offer many good libraries and resources for programming parametric forms. One benefit of building your own custom parametric modeling tool is that it gives you exceptional control over data integration, user interaction, and customization in your design. See the tutorial at `https://github.com/madelinegannon/BodyArchitectures` for a step-by-step walkthrough on how to make 3D-printed bracelets using Processing.

Summary

People are fairly particular about what they put on their bodies, so wearables have a demanding list of requirements they need to satisfy. To some degree, wearables need to be functional, beautiful, and comfortable. Adding to the complexity is that everyone's *body* is different: a wearable that is comfortable for your body may not be for mine; one that is functional for mine may not be for yours. These requirements—or *design constraints*—are particularly challenging when *digitally* crafting wearables.

This chapter discussed commercially available software for creating 2D and 3D digital designs. It also highlighted current limitations for designing for the body. To overcome these limitations, you saw two techniques for customizing existing digital design tools. You learned about ways to bring in physical bodies as digital references in a virtual modeling environment and about principles of parametric design for designing wearables. You also saw how parametric modeling uses the full potential of digital design for wearables by letting designers rapidly explore a design space, customize a design, and integrate personalized data into the design of a wearable.

The next chapter goes over how to translate digital designs into physical artifacts using a variety of fabrication machines.

CHAPTER 9

■ ■ ■

Digital Fabrication for Wearables

To integrate new materials, we sometimes have to develop new machines. For example, to use fiber optics in clothing, Harry Wainwright (who was introduced in Chapter 1) created a special machine to weave the fibers into fabric, and this enabled him to design more intricate light patterns in the fabrics. Fabrication techniques for manufacturing wearables have been mentioned in previous chapters, but this chapter takes a closer look at some of these processes, especially newer and more cutting-edge techniques.

Some of these processes are related to making reactive clothing, and others have been developed in search of more efficient and economical manufacturing processes. Regardless of the application, a fascinating variety of new styles and techniques have emerged from the integration of digital fabrication methods with traditional textiles. Fashion designers have been presented with a new toolset of software and machines that challenge their process. Some designers have embraced this toolset and are defining the future of textiles manufacturing, whereas others believe the new trends do not mesh with their style.

Lasering

I will start with the *laser cutter*, perhaps because it is my favorite digital fabrication tool. To give a quick overview of how it works, I will first define the key component, the *laser*. Although you are probably familiar with lasers, it may come as a surprise that the word *laser* is an acronym for Light Amplification by Stimulated Emission of Radiation. The acronym is useful because it also defines the term; a laser emits light through optical amplification based on the stimulated emission of electromagnetic radiation.

In a laser cutter, the high-power output of the laser is manipulated through an optical chamber, which directs the beam based on instructions from a computer. Using a focused laser beam, the machine is able to cut through several different materials with extreme precision. If you slightly unfocus the beam or lower the intensity, it can also engrave or etch patterns on the surface of materials, even those it cannot cut through. For example, most laser cutters can cut and engrave through fabrics, paper, thin wood, acrylic, and foam and can additionally engrave harder materials like stone and glass. The ability of the laser cutter to cut through different materials depends on the power of the laser and the ventilation system.

The laser cutter was invented in 1965 to drill holes in diamond dies. In the early 1970s, it was adapted to cut non-metal materials such as fabrics. In the 1990s, British fashion designers, including Janet Stoyle and Janet Emmanuel, began to experiment with using laser cutters for textiles and other unconventional techniques. In 1998, Integrated Laser Systems patented the first laser-cutting machine specifically for cutting fabric and textiles. The company continues to manufacture these machines today and also offers custom cutting services; it is one of many laser-cutting companies that has shifted its focus to textiles.

© Sibel Deren Guler, Madeline Gannon, and Kate Sicchio 2016
S. D. Guler et al., *Crafting Wearables*, DOI 10.1007/978-1-4842-1808-2_9

Laser Cutting

Laser-cutting fabrics offers a great advantage over traditional methods of cutting fabric. For one thing, it is much more precise than a human hand could ever be. It is also usually much faster and can cut through multiple layers of fabric at once, increasing the efficiency of the process.

Laser cutting works best on synthetic fabrics because the material in the fabric melts when the laser slices through it, creating a clean, sealed edge that won't fray. Although laser-cutting natural fabrics also creates a heated seal, the fibers are likely to be singed by the laser beam, resulting in a burned look that is not always ideal. The discoloration can sometimes be washed off, but the crisp, burned texture remains, which may not be preferred when using softer, thinner fabrics.

Although the laser cutter is a great tool for cutting templates and different shapes from textiles, it can also be used to create new patterns within the fabric. Traditional methods like weaving and crocheting can be used to design intricate patterns with gaps and holes. The most popular of these is lace, which can come in many different forms and patterns. Laser cutting offers an alternative method for creating these textures because the laser can simply cut the pattern out of the fabric. For example, a typical lace pattern could be cut from a piece of leather or polyester fabric. This new technique has inspired the use of unconventional materials to feature designs that are traditionally associated with a different material. Figure 9-1 shows samples of laser-cut leather with various designs.

Figure 9-1. *Dress made from laser-cut white leather from Louis Vuitton Spring/Summer 2012, pret-a porter*

The laser cutter can take any vector image and trace along the lines to create a new fabric pattern. This also opens the door to new types of patterns that can only be created using this process. Other cutting tools could be combined with pattern tracing, but this is an extremely tedious process that is not as accurate as using a laser cutter. Additionally, laser-cut patterns can be more freeform; you can take any image, hand drawn or digital, and cut it out of any fabric. You can also engrave the pattern into the fabric, as explained in the next section.

Laser Textures

Laser-cutting patterns is not the only way a laser cutter can be used to create new fabric patterns. *Laser etching* is another unique and exciting process in textile manufacturing. Instead of cutting through the fabric at high power, the laser is programmed to etch a pattern at lower power by moving across the surface of the fabric and melting it away. The depth of the pattern—in other words, the amount that is removed from the surface layer—is determined by the laser's power, speed, and resolution settings. Etching is usually optimal at lower power settings, high resolution, and slow speeds, depending on the composition of the fabric.

Laser etching presents a lot of possibilities for experimentation. First, depending on the composition of the fabric, the surface layers will melt in a specific way, creating a smooth or rough surface texture. Designers have found that laser-etching woven textiles that are composed of various fibers works well, because the laser can be set to remove one element of the textile, revealing a different color or texture underneath. Some designers weave fabrics specifically for laser etching. By constructing the fabric with certain fibers, they can be sure that melting away the fabric will give the result they intend.

Another interesting feature is that the etching pattern can vary in depth. The laser can be programmed to etch certain parts of the pattern at one setting and other parts at a different setting, resulting in a depth gradient across the surface of the textile. This variation can also be achieved by attaching a thin stencil to the surface of the fabric, with certain parts of the fabric exposed according to the pattern on the stencil. The laser etches at uneven depths as it goes over the surface of the stencil and fabric.

Laser Welding

Laser technology is not limited to creating patterns and textures; it can also be used to fuse fabrics together, eliminating the need for stitches. This process, known as *laser welding*, has been a primary area of research for The Welding Institute (TWI), an engineering research facility in Cambridge, UK. In laser welding, the thermoplastic properties of synthetic fibers are used to melt layers of fabric together, resulting in a smooth, strong bond that offers an alternative to stitching. Not only must the textile be highly thermoplastic in content to enable melting, but the composition must also allow the energy from the laser to transmit through the fabric, which is not a property that most designers are interested in. This property is not usually measured or known by the manufacturer and has led to some new scientific methods for evaluating fabric.

Kate Goldsworthy, a researcher and textile designer who has made tremendous contributions to this field, collaborated with TWI during her doctoral research to find environmentally friendly techniques for textile finishing. Goldsworthy's thesis, titled "Laser-Finishing: A New Process for Designing Recyclability in Synthetic Textiles," explores techniques for manufacturing and re-manufacturing textiles with an emphasis on the sustainability of this process as it relates to the life cycle of the material. Figure 9-2 shows Goldsworthy's Mono Finishing project, which consists of a series of fully finished textile samples, each demonstrating a different technique she developed at TWI.

Figure 9-2. Swatches from Dr. Goldsworthy's Mono Finishing project (photos courtesy of Kate Goldsworthy)

During her research, Goldsworthy realized that this process produced superior results compared to traditional methods. She found that welding bonds the layers of fabric together without disrupting the surface, although denser materials sometimes display melting and destruction. The welding technique can also be used for stitch-free surface embellishments including beading, sequins, foiling, and embroidery.

Goldsworthy's more recent works include a project called Zero Waste, which uses a single-step digital manufacturing process to cut, etch, and weld garments using laser technology. This research is particularly promising because it allows designers to create small runs of custom pieces without having to cut and sew by hand. Whereas a small run of a custom garment normally would lead to an abundance of waste and high energy consumption, Goldsworthy has developed a way to eliminate several steps, resulting in a *zero waste* (zero compared to normal, that is) process. Additionally, the synthetic fibers used are suitable for full chemical recycling if the garment is disassembled.

3D Printing

3D printing, also known as *additive manufacturing*, has become immensely popular in the last decade. It is the process of synthesizing a three-dimensional object with a computerized numeric control (CNC) machine. I remember the day I walked into Staples and saw a 3D printer on display: I was filled with excitement that the store had been so quick to adopt this new trend.

3D printing was invented in the 1980s, but it wasn't until 20 years later that an open source version of this project was conceived, known as the RepRap. In 2009, about 10 years after this initiative began, an affordable printer was released in kit form called the BFB Rapman. Since then, other affordable kits and prebuilt printers have been flooding the market.

There are several types of 3D printers, which vary based on printing process, printable platform size, and printable materials. Some are to be used only with metal, whereas others can print several different kinds of materials. The most common 3D printers work by melting thin 2D layers of thermoplastic such as polylactic acid (PLA) on top of each other to create a 3D object. These objects can be printed hollow, partially filled, or completely solid, depending on the desired outcome. Some printers use a temporary material called *support* to fill in any gaps during the printing process. The printer software calculates where the support fill may be needed during the printing process. For example, if the object is wide on the top and bottom and thin in the middle, it may use some support fill between the two ends so that the object does not collapse during the print. This support fill can be chipped away or dissolved by putting it in a chemical bath.

Although 3D printers have become more affordable, they may not seem like a worthwhile investment for a designer who just wants to try a few pieces or a hobbyists who would like to do a one-off print from time to time. Several 3D printing platforms have emerged that can print a file for you. All that is required is the design file and material specification, and your custom-printed object is sent right to your door. Companies like Shapeways offer several kinds of printing services with a wide range of materials and resolution.

3D printers have been used to make just about anything wearable, from jewelry to shoes to hats. Companies like Nike and New Balance are using 3D printing technologies to create custom-fit shoes for athletes, and jewelers and artists are using the technology to make molds and casts from digital models. 3D printing has been disruptive to many different industries, and wearables are no exception. There are entire books about the 3D printing process and applications, but this books focus of course, are those that pertain to wearables. The following sections introduce printing techniques and materials that are particularly interesting or disruptive for fashion and apparel. Chapter 10 introduces some technologies that can be combined with 3D printing to bring the fabrication of wearables to a new level.

Flexible Filaments

Objects printed with flexible filaments have rubber-like elasticity after they have been printed. Depending on the form and composition of the filaments, these objects can be stretchy, bouncy, or bendable. Wearable applications of flexible filaments include the following:

- *Eyeglass frames:* As discussed in Chapter 7, eyeglass frames are generally made from a shape-memory alloy or polymer.

- *Bathing suits:* Flexible filaments have been used to 3D-print bathing suits, which are normally constructed out of ultra-flexible materials. 3D printing allows the designer to experiment with different 3D textures and shapes to create unique forms.

- *Jewelry:* Flexible filament is ideal for making custom bracelets and watchbands, because it offers a more form-fitting solution. Depending on the design, the wristband can stretch to fit over the wearer's wrist or bend to more comfortably wrap around the wrist.

- *Athletic accessories and shoes:* The customization potential of 3D printing, combined with flexible material that can conform to the movements and changes of the body, present ground-breaking opportunities to increase an athlete's performance.

Danit Peleg, an Israeli fashion designer, recently launched a line of 3D-printed garments. Peleg uses FilaFlex (a brand of flexible 3D filament) to create plastic textiles with various patterns and textures. The textiles are flexible, allowing them to comfortably fit the wearer's body. The garments bounce up and down when lifted or shaken. Figure 9-3 shows Peleg's 3D-printed skirt, which responds to the model's movement by bouncing back and forth. The model is also wearing red 3D-printed shoes.

Figure 9-3. *3D-printed skirt and shoes from Danit Peleg's first collection (courtesy of Danit Peleg; photo by Daria Ratiner)*

The DREAMS Lab from Virginia Tech and members from the TransLab have collaborated to develop 3D-printed flexible textile structures. They were inspired by the additive 3D-printing process because it is more eco-friendly than conventional subtractive methods. The goal of this work was to create fabric that is both flexible and rigid, meaning the shape remains fixed when the fabric is manipulated. The resulting textile uses interlocking Mobius motifs that can conform to the skin.

4D Printing

3D printing is fairly straightforward to imagine, because it literally refers to printing a three-dimensional object. By this logic, *4D printing* refers to printing in the fourth dimension, and this opens up a discussion about what that means. 4D printing refers to a 3D-printed object that remains dynamic—in other words, it is able to change over time after it has been printed.

There are several different approaches to this concept, some involving self-folding and others responding to physical changes. The self-folding techniques employ some of the smart materials introduced Chapter 7. Using a tool called a *filament extruder*, researchers have experimented with creating their own filament that is a mixture of materials like Nitinol and PLA. The result is a 3D-printed object that reacts to a change in temperature or light or the presence of electric current. Depending on how the structure is designed and the smart material in the filament, the object can change shape and embody several different states.

The Self-Assembly Lab at MIT is experimenting with many different processes of 4D printing and has joined forces with Stratasys and Autodesk, two leading firms in the 3D-printing industry. Using Stratasys's Connex multimaterial printer technology, they have developed a way to embed functionality directly into the material, including actuation, sensing, and material logic. With a single print, a product or mechanism can transform from a 1D strand to a 2D surface and into a 3D shape. The Connex technology allows researchers to program the material while printing it out. The geometry of the materials gives them water-absorbing properties that activate a self-assembly process. Depending on the material composition and design of the object, carefully placed joints and hinges allow it to morph in response to water, heat, or light. This is a fairly new technology, and there are several potential applications for this process, including the creation of garments that respond to the wearer or a fluctuating environment.

Nervous System, a Boston-based jewelry and accessory company, has a slightly different approach to 4D printing. Its Kinematics project is a system for 4D printing using foldable forms. Large objects are compressed into smaller 3D shapes for production, resulting in a more efficient and practical way to print these textures. The designs are composed of several interlocking components that behave as continuous 3D-printed textiles. Figure 9-4 shows an example of a 3D dress that was printed using Kinematics; the size of the dress is reduced by 85%, making it printable as single object. This process is particularly useful for creating intricate wearables that conform to the body.

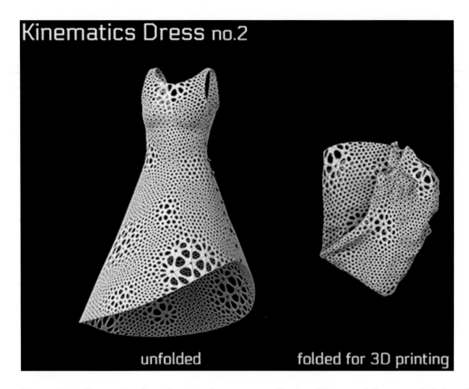

Figure 9-4. Kinematics dress showing the compressed printed form and the expanded dress (rendering by Nervous System: Jessica Rosenkrantz and Jesse Louis-Rosenberg)

Printed Casting

Lost-wax casting is a method that jewelers use to cast metal sculptures from an original nonmetal model. The way the process normally works is as follows:

1. A *positive* model is made from a castable substance like clay or wax.

2. A *negative* is made by making a mold of the model from a flexible material like silicone or rubber.

3. The model is removed from the mold, and the mold can be reused to make replicas.

4. A second ceramic mold is made, and the molds are sprued, burned, and treated in preparation for the metal (I will not go into these steps, but there are many instructions available on the internet if you search for "lost-wax molding"). Finally, hot metal is poured into the cast, creating a metal positive when it cools.

The first step of this process, making a model, is one of the most time-consuming phases. If the design is very intricate, it can be difficult to sculpt a small item such as a ring from wax. 3D-modeling the item using CAD software is much less frustrating, because one mistake does not ruin hours of work and material. Unlike a mistake made while sculpting which can ruin hours of a work, a mistake made by modelling can be reversed with one click. Figure 9-5 shoes two rings side by side: the 3D-printed wax ring made for casting, and the final silver ring made from the cast mold.

Figure 9-5. A 3D-printed wax ring printed on a Formlabs printer, and the cast silver ring (courtesy of Formlabs)

Many 3D printers can print using metal filament. In this case, there is no need to make a wax model and go through the casting process, because the ring can be printed directly from the computer model. However, depending on the type of metal you want to use and the number of replicas you would like to make, finding a 3D printer that can print out a metal version may not be the best route. In this case, it is easier to combine new and old techniques, making a digital model of the piece and then continuing with traditional casting methods. (Plus, the cost of a 3D printer that prints metal can be 10 to 50 times higher than a 3D printer that can make a wax model suitable for casting.)

Digitized Machines

Unlike laser cutters and 3D printers, which were not originally designed with textile or jewelry manufacturing in mind and have been hacked by designers, several machines were design to digitise textile manufacturing. This section looks at two of these machines, which are particularly disruptive to the manufacturing processes they replace.

Digital Knitting

Knitting machines are use to create knitted fabrics and are partially or fully automated. Industrial knitting machines have become a crucial part of the mass customization of apparel. They are able to knit large quantities of a specific product very quickly and efficiently. Some machines, similar to 3D printing, can knit a 3D garment, meaning an entire sweater can be knit in one piece without any seams. But these machines also have drawbacks, especially for small designers who are not interested in mass production. They are difficult to program and are usually operated by skilled technicians. Additionally, they are not economical for one-off designs because of their high operational costs.

Recent developments in knitting machines have led to a new alternative to fully automatic sewing machines. Shima Seiki, a leading company in knitting-machine manufacturing, has a line called WHOLEGARMENT that can knit a 3D garment using four needle beds; this allows it to produce 3D garments with different patterns and textures, including ribs. The machines are equipped with a computer control system that provides controllable sections, allowing the designer to manipulate the tension and shaping of the garment during the knitting process.

KNYTTAN is an early-stage company with great potential. It is developing a digital platform for sharing and purchasing knit designs. Similar to the 3D-printing services mentioned earlier, like Shapeways, KNYTTAN lets users order customized knitwear. The company is developing an easy-to-use interface where users can select ready-made designs or customize their own garments from fully tested templates. This simplifies the designer's interaction with the manufacturing process, making it possible for you to design a garment without learning the intricacies of an industrial knitting machine.

With these new advances in knitting-machine technology, the $200 billion knitwear market has the potential to become democratized, causing a tremendous disruption to current manufacturing systems.

Digital Embroidery

The first mechanical sewing device was invented in 1755. More than 200 year later, the first computerized sewing machine was designed. Before computers became affordable, embroidery patterns could be "programmed" by punching patterns on paper tape and feeding the tape through the machine. In 1980, Wilcom created the first computer graphics system for designing embroidery, which ran on a mini computer. Over the next decade, several other companies developed technologies for this process, including Melco (later acquired by Saurer) and Brother. At first the computer interface still printed out the pattern on paper tape, but eventually the tape was replaced by floppy disks, which have since become obsolete. Modern machines can stitch patterns directly from a computer or SD card and have a built-in digital touchscreen interface.

These embroidery machines use a hoop or frame that holds the fabric taut like a canvas. The hoop is moved around under the needle so that the needle stitches across the fabric to create the programmed pattern.

The ability of the machine depends on the needle. Some machines have up to 20 needles, each threaded with different color yarn and capable of making different kinds of stiches. These include the following:

- *Satin stitch embroidery:* Also known as a zigzag stitch for its zigzag pattern.

- *Chain stitch embroidery:* A series of looped stitches that form a chain like pattern. These chain patterns come in many different varieties.

- *Applique:* One layer of fabric applied to the surface of another.

- *Cutwork:* A technique in which a hole is cut out of a portion of cloth and reinforced with embroidery to keep the raw edges from fraying.

SoftWear Automation

SoftWear Automation is an Atlanta-based company that is revolutionizing the cut-and-sew process and taking the sewing machine from digital to robotic. Its innovations improve the accuracy, efficiency, and ability of textile-manufacturing processes using methods like preprogrammed sewing paths. The company's automatic sewing machine uses ThreadVision, a machine-vision technology that monitors the stitches on the surface of a piece of fabric to ensure that they are even and notifies the machine when it comes close to the edge. Another product, called LOWRY, is a lightweight, four-axis robot used in fabric handling, pick-and-place operations, and direct sewing. LOWRY is able to track the sewing path and manipulate the fabric to prevent distortion. It can also feed fabric into and out of the machine. Figure 9-6 shows LOWRY in action.

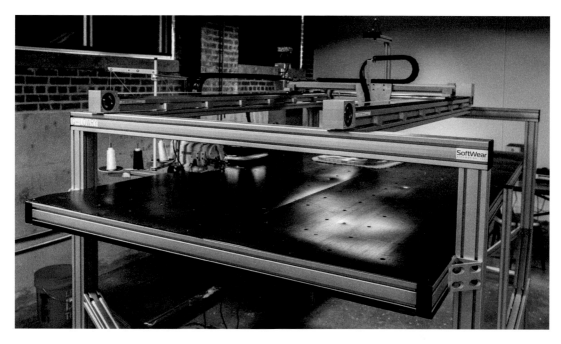

Figure 9-6. *SoftWear Automation's LOWRY, monitoring fabric during an assembly (courtesy of SoftWear Automation)*

Maker and Machine

These fabrication technologies have revolutionised practices that have developed over centuries. Additionally, the use of software to design clothing and accessories is a remarkable change to the design process. Similar to architecture and other fields that have relied on pen-and-paper models or laborious handcrafted 3D models, fashion is a field where instructing a machine rather than a human completely changes the process. The most obvious difference may be efficiency, because the time gained from having a machine do the work allows the designer to focus on other steps and potentially complete the process much more quickly than before. Additionally, a machine may be much better at handling certain materials, leading to smoother cuts and builds than are possible in a handcrafted piece. This has given rise to a debate about how these processes may distance the maker's relationship with their craft: the maker suddenly becomes isolated from the materials.

Three main barriers arise: the physical distance between the maker and the machine, the separation between maker and material, and the space between the maker and the software controlling the machine. In the case of laser cutting, researchers feel that this relationship is not lost, but rather if redefined. The laser-cutting process can be paused and resumed, allowing the designer to redesign during the manufacturing process. By pausing the laser, the designer can open the sealed chamber and touch the fabric to see if the desired result is being obtained. The fabric can be rotated, flipped, or repositioned before resuming the programmed process.

With a process like 3D printing, you must wait for the print to finish and cannot manipulate it during the printing process without sacrificing the resolution and stability of the print. Digital fabrication does make some of these material interactions impossible, but it also presents many new forms of interaction.

Summary

Digital fabrication is extremely interesting and useful when applied to wearables. Not only do these machines allow for precision that is nearly impossible to achieve by hand, but they also offer low-cost solutions to prototyping concepts and tools for wearables. For example, a friend of mine who was designing a pair of shoes for a doll was able to 3D-print a mold and laser-cut the leather for the shoes in an evening. Without these tools, he might have cast the molds for the shoes, wait for them to set, and cut the leather by hand, extending the process by days.

Researchers are exploring ways of developing custom software and hacking different kinds of sensors and tools to create new and exciting techniques to design for the body. The next chapter explains this process through the eyes of one of these researchers. Madeline Gannon is an architect and interaction designer exploring the boundaries between human and machine interactions. Her work has led to the development of several exciting systems that can be employed for wearable design.

CHAPTER 10

■ ■ ■

Designing for the Body, on the Body

Guest Chapter by Madeline Gannon

Designing for the body can be challenging with today's digital tools. 3D-modeling environments tend to be empty virtual spaces that give no reference to the human body. Chapter 8 showed how 3D scanning and parametric modeling can help tailor your digital tools for crafting wearables. But even with customizing, they still have limitations. At the end of the day, you are 3D-modeling in a tool that was built to design cars or buildings, not wearables. So, what would a digital tool native to wearables design look like? How would it help overcome the design challenges that are inherent to wearables?

This chapter looks at *Tactum*, an experimental interface that uses the human body as an interactive canvas for digital design and fabrication. Tactum, shown in Figure 10-1, is an augmented 3D-modeling tool for designing ready-to-print wearables *directly on your body*. This design system was created by Madeline Gannon's Madlab.cc. Instead of using a screen, mouse, and keyboard to 3D-model a design, it uses depth sensing and projection mapping to detect touch gestures and display digital designs directly on the user's skin. Using Tactum, a person can touch, poke, rub, or pinch the geometry projected onto their arm to design a wearable. Once a design is finalized, a simple gesture exports the digital geometry for 3D printing. Because wearables designed with Tactum are created and scaled to the user's body, they are ready to be worn immediately after printing.

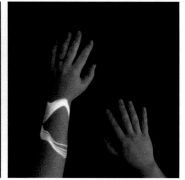

Figure 10-1. *Tactum is a gesture-based interface that lets you customize wearables directly on your body*

This chapter takes a deep dive into the technical details that made Tactum possible. It also gives you some background on computer interfaces that use the skin and discusses the future potential of augmented modeling tools.

© Sibel Deren Guler, Madeline Gannon, and Kate Sicchio 2016
S. D. Guler et al., *Crafting Wearables*, DOI 10.1007/978-1-4842-1808-2_10

Skin-Centric Interfaces

In the past ten years, a rich body of work has been developing for using your skin, instead of a screen, as the primary interface for mobile computing. Researchers have been working on various methods for sensing and displaying interactions with the skin. Figure 10-2 shows three recent research projects that explore the practicalities of using hands and arms for navigating menus, dialing phone numbers, and remembering input. The consensus among these researchers is that skin offers a surprising number of possibilities that smartphones lack:

- Skin interactions can be detected through devices worn on the body, in the body, or in the environment.

- Skin can be both an input and output surface by combining sensors and projectors.

- The human body has *proprioceptive* qualities--a spatial awareness of itself--which makes visual feedback not entirely necessary for effective interaction.

- Unlike your cell phone, your skin is always available and with you.

- Your skin innately provides tactile feedback.

- Because skin is stretchy, you can get multidimensional input.

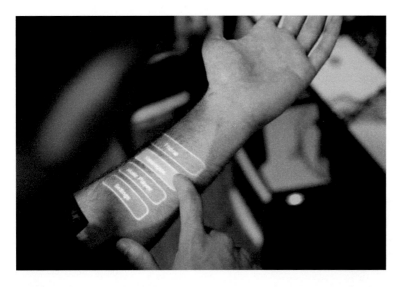

Figure 10-2. *Researchers in human-computer interaction have been exploring skin as an interface for mobile computing. This image shows Skinput, by Chris Harrison, et al. (2010), in which buttons projected onto the skin work just like buttons on a screen. (Images courtesy of Chris Harrison, Scott Saponas, Desney Tan, and Dan Morris, Microsoft Research; licensed under CC BY 3.0.)*

Tactum builds on this existing work by creating a way to 3D-model directly on the skin. Notice in the previous list that a few of the possibilities are particularly useful for 3D modeling: projecting onto the skin lets you map and simulate 3D models on the body; sensing diverse input lets you use a number of natural gestures for modeling; and multidimensional input has potential to use the skin as a digitally deformable surface. With these opportunities in mind, Tactum focuses specifically on designing for the forearm: not only is it easily accessible, but many wearables—including watches, gadgets, jewelry, and medical devices—can be made for the arm.

Sensing the Body

Tactum uses a single depth sensor to detect tactile interactions with the body. The system detects touch gestures by first tracking the medial axis of the forearm as is moves around the workstation. It can then isolate the small volume of space directly above forearm. When a finger enters this small volume of space, the system knows that a user is touching the skin. Tactum then starts tracking the behaviors of the touch—such as duration, position, velocity, and acceleration—to classify a specific touch gesture. Using this method, Tactum can detect up to nine different skin-centric gestures for 3D modeling. Figure 10-4 shows the range of natural gestures that are sent to Tactum's 3D-modeling back end.

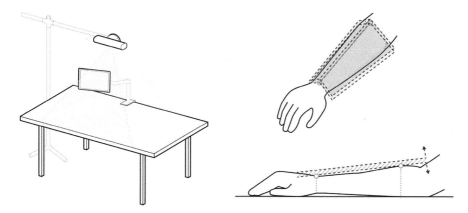

Figure 10-3. *(left) The initial workstation setup for Tactum. (right) The segmented, red touch zones on the forearm are tracked by Tactum's depth sensor as the user moves in the workstation*

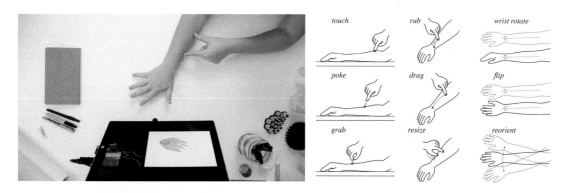

Figure 10-4. *Using a single depth sensor, Tactum can detect up to nine different gestures for 3D modeling*

Although the sensors may have changed, the principles for tracking and detecting the body have remained the same. Tactum uses depth data from the sensor as in the following example:

1. Find and segment the forearm.

2. Find the index finger and thumb of the opposite hand.

3. When the index or thumb enters the touch zone of the forearm, begin recording the gesture.

4. Identify the gesture, and send it to the 3D-modeling back end.

113

3D Modeling Back End

The gestures detected by Tactum's depth sensor are fed directly to a 3D-modeling back end. This is where digital geometry is processed without the designer having to know the details. In the example in Figure 10-5, a live 3D model is being wrapped and piped around an existing 3D scan of the forearm. As the designer touches and pinches the skin, their tactile interactions are sent to the modeling back end. From here, the wearable design's animated 3D-printable geometry is dynamically updated by a particular gesture. The updated geometry is simultaneously projected back onto the designer's body. Although Figure 10-5 shows a 3D scan of the body, it's not entirely necessary when designing in Tactum; however, working from a 3D scan helps ensure that the wearable has an exact fit once the printed form is placed back on the body.

Figure 10-5. *The 3D-modeling back end dynamically updates the wearable design based on tactile interactions with the skin*

Fabrication-Aware Design

Fabrication-aware design embeds the technical expertise of an experienced fabricator into the workflow of a digital design environment. With Tactum, the internal digital geometry is built with an awareness of how it will be physically produced: it only allows for 3D-printable geometry to be generated. Therefore, no matter how much or little the geometry is manipulated by the designer, the digital geometry is always exported as a valid, 3D-printable mesh. Figure 10-6 shows the projected geometry that the designer sees. Once they achieve a satisfactory design, they can close their fist to export the geometry for fabrication.

Figure 10-6. *Dynamic 3D model being projected back onto the body. Once a desired geometry is found, the design can be exported for 3D printing*

Tactum keeps the animated digital geometry scaled and attached to the designer's body. This gives the printed form a level of ergonomic intelligence: wearable designs inherently fit the designer. Moreover, with the constraints for 3D printing embedded into the geometry, every design is immediately ready to be 3D-printed and worn on the body.

Intuitive Gestures, Precise Geometry

Gestures within Tactum are designed to be as natural as possible: as you touch, poke, or pinch your skin, the projected geometry responds as dynamic feedback. Although these gestures are intuitive and expressive, they are also fairly imprecise: they are only as precise as your hands. This means the minimum tolerance during design is around 20 mm—the approximate size of a fingertip. This 20 mm limit is adequate for many design scenarios, as in Figure 10-7, which shows the creation of a new design. However, to design a wearable around an existing object, such as a smartwatch, you need more precise control over the digital geometry.

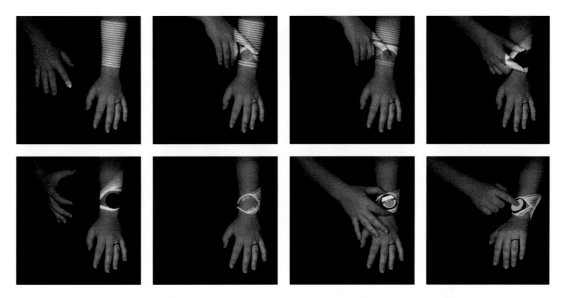

Figure 10-7. *This sequence of images shows the process of designing a smart watch band directly on the body with Tactum. The actual watch face can be used as a physical reference for the digital design*

Figure 10-7 shows how Tactum can be used to create a new watch band for a Moto 360 Smartwatch. As in the previous example, you can use skin gestures to effect the overall design: touching and pinching the skin lets a designer set the position and orientation of the watch face and the distribution of the bands. However, the watch-band design also requires mechanical components to function: it needs clips that hold the watch to the watch band and a clasp that holds the watch band to the body. Moreover, for the watch to fit and the watch band to function, these mechanical components require precise measurements and tolerances that go beyond what you can detect from skin gestures.

To overcome this limitation, Tactum can connect premade geometry that was precisely 3D modeled in a traditional CAD program to specific parts of a wearable design. In this example, the clips are first 3D-modeled using conventional modeling techniques. They are then imported and parametrically attached to the abstract design definition of the watch band: the two clips sit precisely 41 mm apart, but their position and orientation are entirely dependent on where the designer places the watch face on their skin. This parametric association between the overall watch-band design and any premade, imported geometry prevents a designer from directly modifying any high-precision geometry and preserves the wearable's functional constraints.

Tactum uses intelligent geometry to strike a balance between intuitive gestures and precise constraints. Here, the exact geometries for the clips and clasp of the smartwatch are topologically defined within the band's parametric model. In this example, the user-manipulated geometry defines the overall form and aesthetic of the watch band. The clips and clasp, although dependent on the overall watch-band geometry, cannot be directly modified by any gestures. The CAD back end places and generates those precise geometries, once the user has finalized a design. Figure 10-8 shows how the existing smartwatch fits directly into the watch band designed through Tactum.

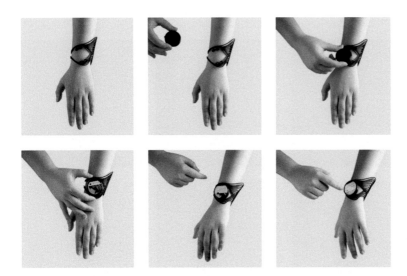

Figure 10-8. *Tactum can design wearables around preexisting objects, such as this watch band for a Motorola 360 smartwatch. Skin-centric gestures are used to set the overall design of the watch band. The high-precision mechanical components of the watch band can be imported from conventional CAD programs and parametrically attached to the overall design*

Pre-scanning the body is not entirely necessary when designing a wearable in Tactum. However, it ensures an exact fit once the printed form is placed back on the body. Between the 3D scan, the intelligent geometry, and intuitive interactions, Tactum is able to coordinate *imprecise* skin-based gestures to create very precise designs around very precise forms.

Physical Artifacts

Tactum has been used to create a series of physical artifacts around the forearm. These artifacts test a range of different interactive geometries, materials, modeling modes, and fabrication machines. Figure 10-9 shows a PLA print made from a standard desktop 3D printer, a nylon and rubber print made from a selective-laser sintering (SLS) 3D printer, and a rubbery print made from a stereolithography (SLA) 3D printer.

Figure 10-9. *Tactum has been used to fabricate a number of wearables using different 3D printing processes. (left) An armlet printed from PLA on a desktop FDM printer. (center) A splint prototype printed from nylon and rubber on an SLS printer. (right) A cuff printed from a rubber on an SLA printer*

Future Applications

Although Tactum is an experimental interface, there are real-world implications for skin-centric design tools. Many wearables today are still made using high-skill analog techniques: for example, a special-effects artist sculpting a mask onto an actor; a tailor fitting garments to a client; a prosthetist molding a socket on a residual limb; or a doctor wrapping a cast around a patient. These professions may benefit from integrating digital technologies into their workflows, but they should not have to abandon the dexterous abilities of their own two hands. Skin-centric design tools show a potential for balancing the best of digital and analog techniques for on-body design.

Summary

This chapter profiled *Tactum*, an experimental interface that uses the designer's body as an interactive canvas for digital design and fabrication. You learned about related work in skin-based interfaces and saw how Tactum uses depth sensors to detect tactile gestures on the skin. This chapter also showed how gestures—although relatively imprecise—can be used to 3D-model precise, functional objects directly on the body. Finally, the chapter concluded with a series of 3D-printed artifacts fabricated using a range of printing processes. In the next chapter, we look at how wearables can integrate into our everyday lives for health and wellness.

PART III

■ ■ ■

Fashion and Product

CHAPTER 11

■ ■ ■

Wearable Wellness

Can wearables improve our quality of life? This is perhaps the most important question we need to answer. How can we convince people all over the world that wearable electronics are a necessary evolution of our wares? Thus far, you have been presented with different methodologies and toolsets for exploring and inventing wearables. 3D printers and laser cutters are opening doors for democratizing the design and manufacturing process. Digitized sewing and knitting machines are translating computer code into embroidery and stitch patterns. However, for the most part, these tools are used in short-run boutique or independent projects; they have not been adopted for mass production. Perhaps you are not yet convinced of how wearable technologies could become a part of your wardrobe.

The next part of this book tries to convince you otherwise. It explains how and where wearable technologies are disrupting and revolutionizing various fields of research and industry. This chapter focuses on wearables for wellness. Health-related gadgets are designed to encourage people to be healthier. From tracking the number of steps you take to helping improve your diet, these metrics are meant to give you a perspective of how you can take better care of yourself. There are several different ways in which these gadgets can be worn; some are embedded in accessories, and other are incorporated directly into the fabric of clothing. The design and form of these gadgets will continue to evolve in the future. The next few sections highlight some technologies that have become increasingly popular over the past few years.

Fitness Trackers

Fitness trackers have created a huge buzz in the last couple of years and have been quickly adopted by those who are looking to add personal style to tracking their health. Data that was once only measurable by a doctor or specialist can now be sent to your phone and then analyzed and explained to you in a custom daily report. The power to improve your health and track your progress on a daily or even hourly scale has never been easier. An estimated 25 million people purchased fitness trackers in 2015; however, the number of people who use their new gadget for more than 6 months is up for debate.

Several focus studies have shown that fitness trackers are the ultimate motivational tools, rather than the ultimate health-monitoring tools. They very successfully encourage users to rethink their daily habits, like taking a longer route when walking, eating less, and generally paying more attention to their sleep cycles. This is most likely because of the user interaction they foster. Every time you look at your phone, check your email, or glance at the touchscreen on your device, you are reminded of your daily progress. Not only that, but many of them have the ability to network to other fitness trackers so you can compare your activity to that of your friends and family.

© Sibel Deren Guler, Madeline Gannon, and Kate Sicchio 2016
S. D. Guler et al., *Crafting Wearables*, DOI 10.1007/978-1-4842-1808-2_11

An important question that many people have about fitness trackers is, what happens to all the collected data? Currently, the information is private and only accessible to the devices you connect to your tracker. However, several other industries would love to have access to this information. Some obvious groups include doctors, who would be able to analyze what may be the largest data pool ever, and advertisement agencies that could target you when you are most alert. This issue is discussed in greater detail in the last chapter. This may not be a huge concern right now, though, because studies show that none of these fitness trackers are particularly accurate. When tested simultaneously, each one overcompensated in some areas and undercompensated activity in other areas. Figure 11-1 shows three different fitness trackers that were tested simultaneously by one user, who found that the results varies tremendously from device to device.

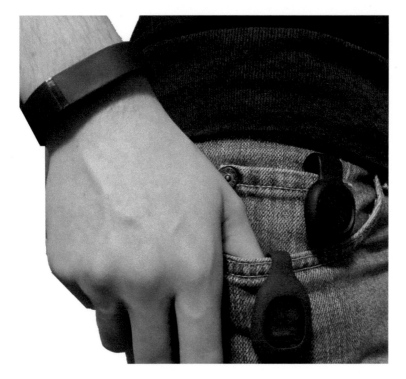

Figure 11-1. *A reviewer testing three fitness trackers simultaneously: from top-left to bottom, Fitbit Flex, Jawbone UP MOVE, Fitbit Zip*

Today, the three most highly reviewed fitness trackers are the Fitbit, Jawbone, and Garmin Vivosmart. There are hundreds of others on the market, not to mention smartwatches like the Apple Watch that have integrated fitness trackers. Following are some distinguishing aspects of the top three:

- *Fitbit HR*: A thin wristband with a small digital display that can show your statistics as well as caller ID for a paired smartphone. Its strongest feature is the heart-rate-monitoring sensor, which appears to be more accurate than other brands.

- *Garmin Vivosmart*: Has been praised for offering measurements that are equally accurate to those of the Fitbit and Jawbone, but features a larger screen and has a more user-friendly integrated notification system. It is waterproof, whereas most are only splash proof, and performs better when tested by runners. It is also said to have a very comfortable band.

- *Jawbone UP MOVE:* Designed a bit differently and does not feature a display on the device, encouraging the use of other devices with the wristband. It has a very strong sleep-monitoring system.

Smart Clothing

Smart clothing refers to e-textiles or clothing embedded with electronics. Smart clothing is being researched and developed in several different areas, primarily focusing on fitness, fashion, and health.

Techstyles

Fashion designers are working with high-tech textile manufacturers to redesign classic articles of clothing. Ralph Lauren, for example, has developed the PoloTech Shirt: a smart shirt that is able to track your biometrics and pair with a Bluetooth-enabled device. The shirt was created in collaboration with Canadian smart textile company OMsignal.

Smart textiles companies each emerge with a specific focus or specialization. Most are working to integrate wireless sensors that transmit data to a smart device, but some are developing ways to embed real-time displays on the clothing. Gymi, for example, is embedded with an LED display of your heart rate, a reps counter to show how close you are to a set goal, and an extra display to show the readout of another person for partner-training purposes. Following are three big names in the smart textile industry that have different applications:

- *Hexoskin*: *Hexoskin's* biometric shirt can provide more biometric data than any other wearable on the market. It can monitor heart rate, breathing rate, ventilation, recovery, cadence, and oxygen levels. It is designed to be an equally effective sleep-tracking device. Hexoskin is used by space agencies, military organizations, and sports teams around the world. The shirt pairs with an app that tracks the wearer's performance across different activities and can be used to monitor health, fitness, and more. It is machine washable and comes in several different models for men and women.

- *Clothing+*: Clothing+ is a leading e-textile consultancy firm that helps brands create with e-textiles. It offers expertise and experience with e-textiles systems and works with brands to infuse new technology into their clothing. Clothing+ was the first company to create a wearable heart sensor that could be washed. The company continues to innovate new solutions for embedding electronics in fabrics with new tools and materials. It works with clients throughout the process of selecting the right sensors, fabrics, and software tools for each project. Clothing+'s services also include configuring a mass-manufacturing and supply chain, allowing brands to produce smart clothing on a large scale. Clothing+ specializes in smart clothing for fitness and healthcare and has shipped more than 50 million sensory clothing units.

- *iTBra*: The iTBra is a more localized article of smart clothing; it is a bra that can detect signs of breast cancer. The bra contains intelligent breast patches that detect temperature changes within breast cells. This information is sent to a smart device and processed through a predictive analytic software algorithm. The software is able to categorize abnormal temperature and cellular signaling patterns in otherwise healthy tissue. Clinical trials show that the data from the iTBra is just as accurate as mammography. It is targeted at women who are looking for a more discrete and accessible way to monitor their health that does not involve radiation and scheduled doctors visits.

Several other e-textiles companies are working on the cutting edge of integrating this technology into everyday clothing. For example, AIQ is innovating new techniques for major brands. It often works together with Kings Metal Fiber, a company that specializes in thermally resistant conductive threads and fabrics.

Fit Like a Glove

LikeAGlove is a new wearable service that ensures you find the right size jeans, shirts, dresses, and more. The company has made smart elastic leggings that automatically take your size measurements and send them to an Internet shopping profile; an app then presents you with several pairs of jeans that are guaranteed to fit you perfectly. You're probably wondering how it works. Here is an overview. The smart leggings appear to be a normal pair of leggings with a large button on the front below the waist. They are embedded with conductive fibers and sensors that provide precise measurements of the length of your leg, waist, thigh, inseam, and hips. Once you put them on, you push the button, and it automatically collects data from these sensors and transmits it via Bluetooth to an app. The app loads the measurements in 5 seconds and filters through a database of jeans to present you with models and brands of jeans that are guaranteed to fit you.

If you have ever struggled through several ill-fitting pants and dresses to find ones that fit just right, your next question is probably, where can I get this? The leggings are currently available for preorder from `www.likeaglove.me` for $69; this price is expected to double when the product is fully launched. The product video also features a smart shirt that will measure your torso to help you find the perfect dress.

Wearable Baby Monitors

Wearables are not just for adults; they are revolutionizing babywear. Several companies are developing wearable sensors to help parents and doctors keep track of an infant's vital signs:

- *Mimo Baby*: Mimo Baby has developed a small turtle-shaped monitor that attaches to a custom "kimono" onesie. The turtle monitors the baby's sleep position, body temperature, activity level, and breathing and sends this information wirelessly to an app that reports the baby's status. Mimo recently partnered with the home automation system Nest so that you can adjust the temperature in the baby's room based on the information from Mimo. You can even use a Nest Cam to watch and listen to your baby, ensuring that you have peace of mind when you are away. The system retails at about $200 depending on how many kimonos you choose to invest in.

- *MonBaby*: MonBaby is a similar to Mimo, but instead of clipping onto a custom onesie, it is a small button that can be attached to any article of clothing. The button is embedded with sensors for measuring properties similar to those monitored by Mimo; it sends this data to the MonBaby app. The company has also launched the SafeSleep project: an online platform for sharing resources and tips to help track and improve your baby's sleeping patterns.

- *Owlet*: The Owlet Smart Sock, shown in Figure 11-2, monitors a baby's heart rate and oxygen level while they sleep. The sock comes with an Owlet monitor base that can be placed in the parent's bedroom and acts as an alarm that is designed to trigger based on incoming information from the sock. The sensor can be removed to wash the sock, which comes in several different sizes for growing babies.

Figure 11-2. *Owlet and a smartphone showing the app (photo by Westin Dangerfield © Owlet)*

Bracing Yourself

DIY braces and casts are popular projects among hackers and medical experts. By taking advantage of the lower cost of digital-fabrication machines, they can make custom-fit prosthetics, splints, and more at much lower costs than ever before. One example is the e-Nable Community, an incredible global organization of doctors, makers, and hobbyists who have come together to create prosthetic 3D-printed hands for children in need. The community began as a husband and wife maker team who posted a video on the Internet of a metal puppet hand they had designed for a steampunk convention in 2011. The video went viral, and they discovered they had a much larger fan base outside of the steampunk community. Their project gave hope of restoring limbs with affordable DIY methods to thousands of people around the world with upper limb differences. Today, this online platform provides resources for designing mechanical hands, getting started with 3D printers, support for families, and more. Other prosthetic initiatives are discussed in Chapter 13.

Quell is a knee brace that uses *wearable intensive nerve stimulation* (WINS) to treat chronic pain. The brace stimulates sensory nerve fibers in the upper calf, which activates descending pain-inhibition systems in the brainstem. Then, high-frequency nerve stimulation triggers a cascade of processes that block pain signal transmission and result in widespread pain relief. The brace is embedded with sensors such as accelerometers to transition between therapy levels based on the wearer's activity. User studies show that 81% of people who use Quell reported an improvement in their chronic pain, and 67% reported a reduction in their use of pain medication. The product is FDA approved, and the starter kit can be purchased for $250.

Kinetic is another company that is rethinking medical braces. Its smart back brace can detect when you are lifting an object and which muscles you are using during the act. It pairs with a wristband that receives information from the brace. The brace uses this data to determine whether you have put your back at risk and are lifting the object safely. If it seems you are performing an unsafe action, the brace signals the wristband to vibrate. The device was invented to help reduce the number of work-related injuries that result from unsafe lifting and bending, and help employers save on workers compensation claims. The brace also sends collective data to an app that a manager can use to see how their team is performing at any given moment and provide suggestions for redesigning the workspace to optimize workflow.

For Better Posture

"Stop hunching"—words my mother and grandmother have said to me more times than I can count. Although the reminder helps, it's often not enough to keep me standing straight for the whole day. So, what is? A range of products that aim to help correct posture have come to market in the past few years. They typically involve a sensor that detects when you are slouching and sends you a friendly reminder to straighten up via a buzz from a small pager motor in the device. Following are some wearable posture sensors that take different approaches to form and style. The one thing they all have in common is that they pair with an app:

- *Lumo Lift*: A small plastic sensor that is worn like a pin just below your collarbone. It is held in place using a magnetic clasp, as shown in Figure 11-3. Once you have attached the sensor to your shirt, you double-tap to calibrate the patented angle-displacement sensor and set a training program through the app. Depending on the coaching settings you have selected, the sensor vibrates to remind you to correct your posture. The app also keeps track of your progress over the long term to show how you have improved. Lumo can measure additional metrics like the number of steps you take and the calories you have burned. I tried a Lumo Lift for several months and found that it was indeed quite helpful, but it did not work with looser tops. The company is working on ways to attach the sensor to wearables that give more reliable feedback, such as bra straps, but it largely depends on how the clothing fits on the user.

Figure 11-3. *Lumo Lift worn on a blouse, with a diagram of the entire system (© Lumo Body Tech)*

- *UPRIGHT Posture Trainer*: A small, curved device that attaches to your lower back and vibrates when you slouch. It is not the most discrete tool, but it is easily hidden by a shirt or jacket. It uses built-in sensors that automatically calibrate to your body and then detect changes to your posture and send an activity log to the app.

- *JINS MEME*: A product that stands out for taking a different approach to measuring posture than you may expect. It is a pair of glasses that measure your eye movements and ear and nose position to determine whether you are tired and have poor posture. The smart glasses frames have embedded *electrooculography* sensors near the bridge of the nose to monitor changes in your eye movements, gyroscopes to detect changes in your body, and two six-axis acceleration sensors in the earpieces to check for posture and general body state. This data is sent to an app, which analyzes your state and can help you optimize your form and function. For example, if the glasses detect that you are drowsy while driving, they send you an alert. The glasses come in a few different styles including a Darth Vader model.

- *Prana*: A bit different from the others on this list in that it is not specifically for improving your posture; it is designed to improve your breathing. However, good posture facilitates good breathing, so the Prana can also be used to keep track of your posture. It is a circular disc, about one inch in diameter, that clips to your waist. Prana measures your breath with its patented sensors and sends this data to an app that passively notifies you of your status. It is popular among meditation and yoga communities.

The last part of this chapter provides a recipe for creating your own DIY pair of posture-sensing suspenders!

Concept Products

Here's a futuristic wearable that takes things to another level: smart contact lenses. The project was originally announced in 2014 as a collaboration between American tech company Google and Swiss pharmaceutical company Novartis and is expected to be on the market by 2018. The lenses are embedded with a tiny circuit that measures the blood glucose levels of diabetics and wirelessly sends this data to a device.

The team has filed for a patent on the technology, which suggests that they are already planning to use it in other areas. The lenses could be adapted to improve vision loss due to age by autofocusing on distant objects like a camera lens or to detect and report your blood alcohol content. It could even be used to sense environmental conditions like allergens and dust and to verify the wearer's identity.

Posture Suspenders Project

This project was developed by Tobias Sonne during his research at Carnegie Mellon University and can be seen at http://tobiassonne.com/?p=272. Although the sensors are quite low tech compared to the technology in the products mentioned earlier in this chapter, you will gain an understanding of how posture sensing works.

■ **Note** You need prior microcontroller experience before attempting this project, although it is fairly simple and would make a great early project for a beginner. You also need to be comfortable with sewing electronics, because this tutorial does not go into detail about sewing circuits.

Begin by collecting the following materials:

- 1 pair of suspenders

- 2 DIY bend sensors (tutorial in Chapter 7)

- 1 microcontroller (preferably sewable like the LilyPad or Flora)

- Conductive thread

- LiPo battery (rated for the microcontroller you are using)

- Desired output: sewable vibration motor or LED

- Alligator clips (for prototyping)

- 2 10k ohm resistors

Follow these steps:

1. Prototype your circuit as shown in the diagram in Figure 11-4 (colored lines represent alligator clips).

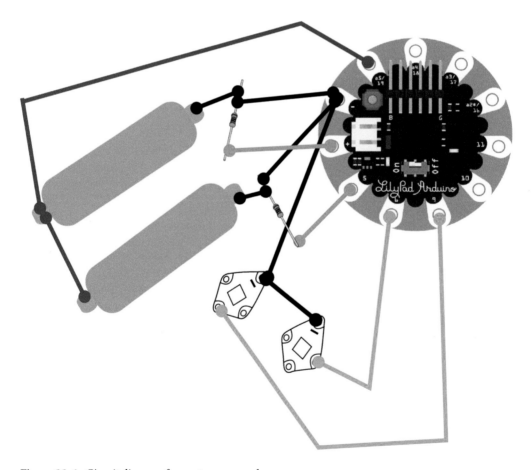

Figure 11-4. *Circuit diagram for posture suspenders*

2. Loosely attach the bend sensors to the suspenders with safety pins or double-sided tape. Make sure to place them on your upper back in an area that changes shape dramatically if you start to slouch.

3. Connect your microcontroller to the computer, and upload the following program to measure the values coming in from the sensor:

```
int sensorleft = A0;      // left bend sensor
int sensorRight = A1;     // right bend sensor
int Right = 0;            // variable to store the value coming from the right bend sensor
int Left = 0;             // variable to store the value coming from the left bend sensor

void setup() {
Serial.begin(9600);
}

void loop() {
  Right= analogRead(sensorRight);
  Left= analogRead(sensorLeft);
  Serial.println("right:" + Right);
  Serial.println("left:" + Left);
  delay(200);
}
```

4. Analyze the data to find the threshold value: that is, the point at which the value changes dramatically when you begin to slouch. Values on one end of this threshold value mean you are standing upright, whereas values on the other end signify that you have started to slouch.

5. Connect the output to your circuit—either an LED or a vibration motor—and upload the following code to your microcontroller. Now, when the bend sensor detects that you have started slouching, it should trigger the output to turn on:

```
int sensorleft = A0;      // left bend sensor
int sensorRight = A1;     // right bend sensor
int Right = 0;            // variable to store the value coming from the right bend sensor
int Left = 0;             // variable to store the value coming from the left bend sensor

int threshold= 500;       // change to your observed threshold value
int vibe = 9;

void setup() {
Serial.begin(9600);
pinMode(vibe, OUTPUT);
}
```

```
void loop() {
Right= analogRead(sensorRight);
Left= analogRead(sensorLeft);
digitalWrite(vibe, HIGH);
if (Right >=threshold){
digitalWrite(vibe, LOW);
delay(2000);
}
else if(Left >=threshold){
vibe= HIGH;
delay(2000);
}

}
```

6. If you are happy with your circuit, you can replace the alligator clips with conductive thread! Before you start, you may want to refer to Chapter 5 for a refresher on how to sew with electronics. Here are some tips:

   • Curl the legs of the resistors with pliers to make loops to sew through, as shown in Figure 11-5.

Figure 11-5. *Resistor with curled legs for sewing through*

   • When sewing to a pad on the microcontroller, be sure to loop through the pad a few times, until the connection feels secure.

   • If there is not enough room to attach the microcontroller to the suspenders, you can sew on a patch of fabric to create a larger surface.

   • You may want **to sew** a pocket for the battery to sit in on the back of the suspenders so that it stays in place.

   • Be careful when placing the components. Make sure all the negative rails go along the same side of the suspenders, and the positives on the other side— remember not to cross the paths.

7. Try out your suspenders! Do they help you improve your posture? Try different outputs and output patterns on the suspenders to see what works the best, as shown in Figure 11-6. You could make a light fade in and out or a buzzer increase in intensity depending on the angle of slouch—be creative!

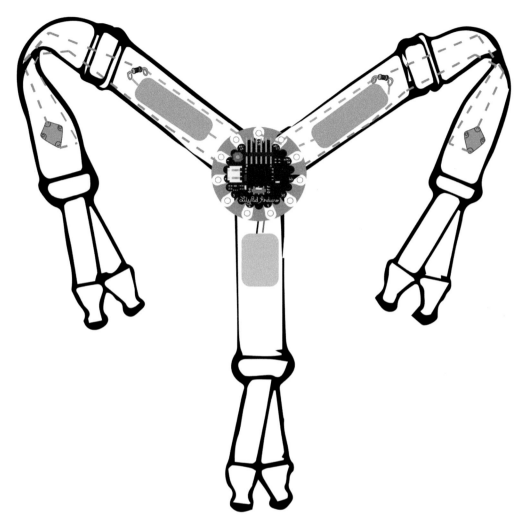

Figure 11-6. *Completed posture suspenders*

Summary

The technologies and products describes in this chapter are just a small percentage of the amazing wearables being developed for medical and wellness applications. Ultimately, these technologies can only become as successful as we allow them to be, so the design and interface of these gadgets is extremely important and, arguably, has much room for improvement. As more people adopt these gadgets for help with monitoring their infants' conditions, tracking their daily calorie intake, or checking their posture, manufacturers will get more feedback about which features work best. Calibrating sensors to adapt to the physically and environmentally dynamic conditions of our bodies is another challenge that requires much research and development. These technologies show great promise and will likely improve exponentially in the next few decades. The next chapter examines techniques and projects that offer less visible alternatives for wearables.

CHAPTER 12

■ ■ ■

Beauty Tech

Beauty and *technology* are two words that are not often used together. Technology might be described as being beautiful, in the sense that it is simple and well designed, but can beauty be technological? The term *beauty technology*, coined by computer scientist Katia Vega, is an emerging field of wearables that refers to electronic devices that are attached to the surface of the body and enable the wearer to interact with the digital world. These interactions are not disruptive to the wearer's everyday routine; on the contrary, they are designed to integrate into natural tendencies and actions such as blinking or waving.

Beauty technology has been applied to different fields such as fashion, makeup, and medicine. Chapter 2 mentioned X-ray technology as a method of getting under a person's skin; beauty tech is a method for sticking to the skin. Both medical and design researchers are developing sensors that can be applied directly to a person's skin. This can be extremely beneficial for taking accurate measurements of body parameters or tracking movement. This chapter discusses various projects that use beauty technology to create more advanced or intimate wearable experiences.

The Beauty Technologist

Katia Vega is a beauty technologist working at the intersection of invisible computing and fashion. Vega's work is inspired by magic and empowering human capabilities with technology. During her doctoral studies, she worked as a research assistant in the Wearables Lab at Hong Kong Baptist University, where she noticed that a lot of women wore fake eyelashes, nail stickers, and makeup on a daily basis. She thought, "Why not add a little technology to these elements?" This question led to her invention of beauty technology. Vega works to create beauty enhancements that can give the wearer robotic powers but are completely imperceptible from the outside. Furthermore, they do not fit any traditional robot aesthetic. She wants her "magical" electronic devices to be hidden on the body, emphasizing the feeling that they are giving the wearer secret powers. She is currently a postdoctoral associate at the MIT Media Lab, where she researches beauty technology, wearable computers, and human-computer interaction (HCI). The following sections highlight some of her inventions; you can follow her work online at `http://katiavega.com`.

Hairware

Vega's latest project, called Hairware, uses metalized hair extensions as a capacitive touch interface. Hairware explores the conscious use of unconscious auto-contact behaviors. Touching or twirling a strand of hair is a common comfort behavior that women unconsciously perform. Hairware takes this behavior to a new level by triggering actions when the wearer touches the metalized capacitive touch-sensing hair extensions.

© Sibel Deren Guler, Madeline Gannon, and Kate Sicchio 2016
S. D. Guler et al., *Crafting Wearables*, DOI 10.1007/978-1-4842-1808-2_12

Artificial hair is chemically metalized, which makes it conductive while keeping its natural color. Layers of nonconductive hair are attached around the conductive hair to protect it from the wearer's skin. Depending on which part of the extension the wearer touches (top, middle, or bottom), the sensor sends out different output values, which are input into a microcontroller to control digital devices. For example, when the wearer touches certain points on her hair, a signal is sent to her phone to send out her geolocation.

Hairware allows the wearer to use her auto-contact behaviors as a secret interface. This raises an interesting debate about the advantages and disadvantage of disguising technology on our bodies. Is it fair to hide these interactions in social situations, or will it become so common that it is expected? These questions are discussed further in Chapter 16.

More than Makeup

Conductive ink was introduced in Chapter 6 as a recommended material for your wearable toolbox. Conductive ink allows you to draw circuits on fabric, paper, and even skin! Katia Vega and her collaborators began experimenting with conductive makeup in 2010 by creating eyeliner from conductive ink. This technique proved to be problematic because although the ink is not hazardous to the body, it is not approved for use on skin. Additionally, the ink is water-soluble, and the humidity from the wearer's eyes and skin can cause issues. The group decided to take another approach to applying conductive makeup to the skin: stickers. They created makeup stickers by covering thin conductive tape with makeup ink. For example, a thin, black, conductive makeup sticker can be applied as eyeliner. The stickers do not cause irritation and are easily removable.

Another makeup product the team electrified is fake eyelashes. Instead of applying liquid conductive mascara, fake eyelashes are chemically metalized, which allows them to keep their black color. The metalizing process involves two parts: first the eyelashes are activated with hydrogen and tin chloride, and silver nitrate is added to prepare the eyelashes to catalyze the electron transfer. Second is an electrolysis phase, during which a layer of nickel is deposited on the eyelashes to plate them. The plating contains copper, which makes the eyelashes electrically conductive; and black nickel, which gives the natural black color of the eyelashes (see Figure 12-1).

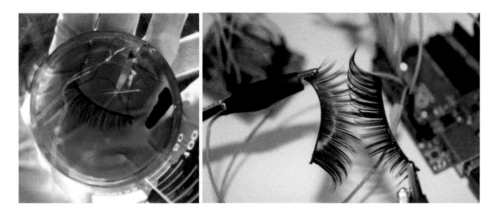

Figure 12-1. *Fake eyelashes being metalized at EQA lab (left) and tested (right) (photos courtesy of Katia Vega)*

Following is a list of Vega's projects that use conductive makeup technology:

- *Blinkifier*: A wearable computer that amplifies the action of blinking without using intrusive devices on the face. As the muscles around the eye contract, a series of LED lights, embedded in a wearable headpiece, display different patterns depending on the blinking gesture. The project uses conductive eyelashes to capture the blinking motion. Every time the wearer blinks, the metalized lashes come into contact and close the circuit, thus acting as a switch input. The eyelashes on the top eyelid act as one side of the switch, and the bottom lashes are the other side. This input signal is transmitted through conductive eyeliner stickers to an Arduino in the headpiece that sends an output signal to trigger the LEDs.

- *Kinisi*: An FX e-makeup application that was designed to turn skin into an interface that is controlled by a smile, a wink, or the raising of an eyebrow. It is similar to Blinkifier in that conductive makeup is used to control light patterns of LEDs. Instead of a wearable headpiece, the LEDs are applied directly to the skin and hair of the model and covered with FX materials, as shown in Figure 12-2. In addition to the metallic lashes and conductive eye makeup, conductive lipstick was developed. Vega and her team collaborated with Larca Meicap, a special effects makeup artist, who added her FX materials to the Beauty Technology sensors to precisely apply the sensors on specific muscles.

- *Superhero:* An e-makeup circuit that triggers output or levitates an object when the user blinks. The circuit is made from conductive makeup, black metalized fake eyelashes, and a radio transmitter. Like Blinkifier, the metalized eyelashes are used as a switch input to the transmitter. Each time the user blinks, a signal is sent to the radio receiver, hidden in a handbag nearby. The receiver is programmed to output animated images—"POW," "BAM," and "ZAP"—that are displayed on a screen each time it receives a signal. In another version of this circuit, blinking is used as an input to trigger infrared commands that are then decoded for the remote controller of a toy helicopter. By blinking her eyes, Vega is able to launch the helicopter into flight!

Figure 12-2. *Kinisi model with LEDs lit up around her eyes and in her hair (courtesy of Katia Vega)*

Beauty Tech Nails

Another technology developed by Vega is her Beauty Tech Nails. These are fake fingernails that are embedded with RFID tags, small magnets, or conductive nail polish. These elements enable the wearer to interact with other electronic wearable devices or objects in their environment. The RFID glass capsules embedded in the nails are used with an RFID reader that can identify each individual tag and trigger an application based on the input of one nail or the combination of a sequence of nails in a specific pattern. The magnets can amplify the wearers' sensing abilities by allowing them to sense magnetic fields and objects with magnetic switches, such as smartphones and tablets. The conductive nail polish can be used to complete a circuit when it comes in contact with other conductive materials.

136

Following is a list of projects that use Beauty Tech Nails:

- *Gimmickiano:* In a live performance, DJ Maribel Tafur wore RFID nails to "play" the piano. The nails are shown in Figure 12-3. As she moved around the auditorium and waved her fingers over a wearable belt embedded with an RFID reader, the belt sent the notes to a computer through a radio module. Depending on the input pattern received, different notes were played by a computer interface.

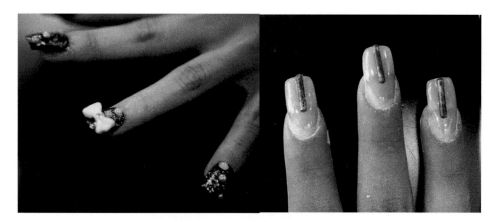

Figure 12-3. *Decorated RFID nails from Gimmickiano (left); exposed RFID tags on nails (right) (courtesy of Katia Vega)*

- *Abrete Sesamo:* This project was inspired by the ancient Ali Baba tale, in which a cave that holds a treasure can be opened with the words "iftah ya simsim" ("open sesame" in English). Vega and her team created a version of this lock, using a combination of finger movements instead of a secret phrase to open the door. RFID glass capsule tags are inserted into gel nails and hidden with nail polish and decorative crystals. An RFID reader receives the input combination from the nails and transmits it to a microprocessor that opens the door when the correct code is entered.

Living Makeup

Makeup and electronics are not only being applied to the face with new conductive materials; they are also being projected onto faces as dynamic masks. Omote is a project led by Japanese producer Nobumichi Asai, who is known for his work in projection mapping, to create what is being referred to as *living makeup. Omote* translates as *face* or *mask* in Japanese. Using advanced face tracking and projection mapping, the team has invented a system to project images onto a user's face in real time that can simulate anything from makeup to cascading water. Asai states that he was inspired by the medium of the human face, which he considers to be the most "powerful but delicate medium for art."

Face tracking is widely used in security and marketing applications, but Asai wanted to use this technology in a different way: to express beauty and the art of makeup, specifically Japanese beauty. He was inspired by Japanese aesthetics and *Japanimation*, a term referring to the Japanese anime subculture. Updating the image with every slight movement of the user's face required a much more precise algorithm than other face-tracking systems. Coordinating the timing of the computer graphic renderings to match the face is impressive. He hopes to continue to develop new technologies that express beauty with new media. A model with an Omote mask that seamlessly changes from one projected image to another is shown in Figure 12-4.

Figure 12-4. *A model wearing an Omote mask that changes from one projected image to another (©nobumichiasai.com)*

Dermatology and Technology

Wearable technologies are being researched and developed for more than makeup and masks; researchers have also been exploring the potential of wearable technologies for dermatology. The applications of these technologies range from anti-aging to dermo-therapy. Studies have shown that although medical tracking devices like the Fitbit (discussed in Chapter 11) are very promising, the majority of users do not use them for more than 6 months. Therefore, researchers are trying to redesign these devices to be smaller and less invasive. Doctors and medical experts are looking forward to these advancements and believe that with the help of these sensors, they can lower the rate of ER visits and keep patients healthier. The following two companies innovating in this field, sometimes referred to as the *Internet of healthy things*:

- *MC10:* The MC10 BioStamp is a temporary tattoo, the size of two postage stamps and thinner than a Band-Aid, that acts as electronic skin. A picture of the stamp on human skin is shown in Figure 12-5. Using common sensors like accelerometers and gyroscopes, the BioStamp can monitor temperature, movement, heart rate, brain waves, and more. It then transmit wirelessly to a computer program that analyzes the data. The stamp is waterproof and powered by a thin film battery that can last more than 24 hours and is charged wirelessly. One concern is that because it is a skin patch, wearing it for too long could cause dermatitis.

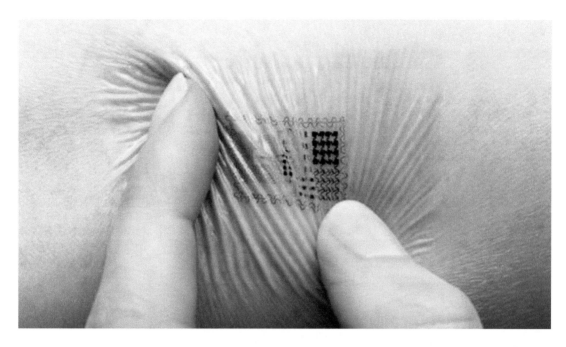

Figure 12-5. *The BioStamp, which has five built-in sensors, wireless communication, and more (© MC10 Inc.)*

- *Feeligreen:* Feeligreen is a French company that has developed a line of makeup and skin patches that address aging and other skin-related conditions. The dermoPatch is an under-eye adhesive sticker that applies a microcurrent technology across the skin. The microcurrent technology increases the pharmoco-kinetics of ionized drugs and transdermic diffusion of active molecules, thus improving their efficiency in the treatment of certain types of local pathologies. Feeligreen says this could be applied to a large range of drugs that treat neuropathic chronic pain, skin cancer, bedsores, arthritic pain, and diabetes; provide needleless vaccines; and can be used for cosmetic applications such as anti-aging, depigmentation, and cellulitis.

Another interesting technology that plays into this field is *transient electronics*. These are tiny, biocompatible electronics that dissolve after a set amount of time. They are encased in layers of silk protein extracted from silkworm cocoons and are fully biodegradable. Researchers have discovered how to adjust the properties of the silk such that it dissolves at a specific time. They believe that this technology will be widely used in medical implants, consumer electronics, and environmental monitors. Although this technology is still being tested and developed, it is extremely promising for wearable applications.

Conductive Tattoos

Along with medical and beauty products, conductive tattoos are popular among artists, designers, and hackers. Some of these tattoos use conductive inks, such as Bare Conductive. Although these inks are safe to use on the skin for short periods, they are not recommended for long periods, as Vega discovered in her research. Amrita Kulkarni, an Indian designer, has been experimenting with conductive ink in her henna designs. Using small LED lights and coin-cell batteries, she draws intricate patterns on her skin and embeds simple light circuits throughout. Chaotic Moon, an Austin-based design firm, is using this ink to prototype more complex skin circuits for DIY health monitoring and embedding banking information onto the skin to replace credit cards. The company refers to this concept as a *tech tat*.

The Design Probes team at Phillips released a speculative concept video called "SKIN: Electronic Tattoo" in 2007. In the video, two lovers touch each other's bare skin, activating an electronic tattoo that spreads across the body. The video "explores the body as a platform for electronics and interactive skin technology." The electronic ink that forms the tattoo is touch sensitive and is therefor visible only when contact has been made. Similar interfaces are being researched in academic labs around the world as well as in industry. For example, Google recently filed a patent for an electronic skin tattoo that couples to a mobile device. The application describes a neck tattoo that would pick up sound from the wearer's vocal cords ("fluctuations of muscle or tissue in the throat," to be exact) and wirelessly send it to a device.

DIY LED Tattoo Project

This section guides you through how to make a simple tattoo circuit with LED lights. The project uses off-the-shelf components that can be ordered online through sites like Amazon and also found in local hobby electronics stores. Some of these are shown in Figure 12-6.

You need the following materials:

- Conductive Ink

- Small coin-cell battery (CR1220)

- Chibitronics circuit stickers (LEDs and sensors)

- SMD LEDs

- Tweezers

- Glue dots

- Conductive tape

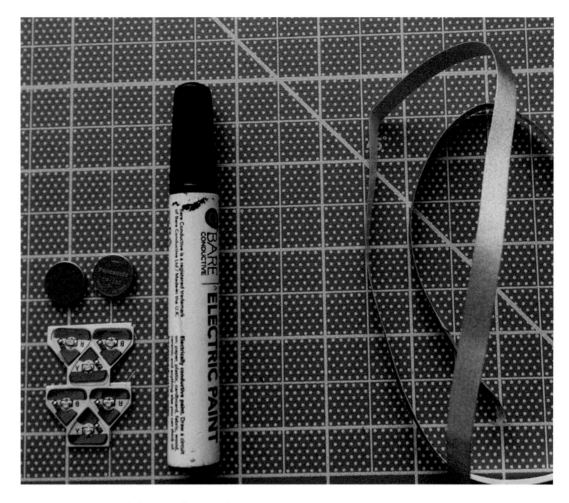

Figure 12-6. *Materials for a conductive ink tattoo*

Design and Sketch

Following is a series of question to consider while making this and other beauty tech projects:

- What is it? Decide what aspect of beauty you'd like to focus on.

- Attachment: how is it attached to the body? Does this cause any problems? If you are focusing on something that attaches to the skin, research the properties of skin. Could humidity cause problems for your device? If it is something that attaches to your nails, could it cause complications with your daily habits? For example, if it involves magnets, could it trigger unexpected interactions with your devices?

- What does it do? This is the most important part of your concept. What superpower will your device give you? How will it change your interaction with the world? Will it be a secret, hidden device, or will it pop out and help you express yourself further?

Steps to Make a Temporary Light Tattoo

Follow these steps:

1. Once you have your circuit design, sketch it out on your body using a pen or thin marker. Remember, the positive and negative traces of the circuit cannot overlap. Additionally, there should be small gaps where you plan to place the LEDs and battery. The forearm is a good place to start, because it gives you a lot of surface area.

2. Outline the circuit traces with conductive ink, and wait for it to dry (15 to 20 minutes), as shown in Figure 12-7.

Figure 12.7. Conductive ink drying on skin

3. Carefully place the LED circuit stickers on your arm. You may want to use tweezers for this part.

4. Now to attach the power. Place a small glue dot on the bottom (negative side) of your battery, such that half of the surface is exposed. Place the negative side of the battery over the end of the negative trace outlined with conductive ink, such that the glue dot does not cover the ink and the surface of the battery is making contact.

5. To connect the positive side of the battery, you can either draw with conductive ink from the end of the positive trace on your tattoo to the top surface of the battery, or use another material like conductive tape to close the final gap. Once the ink is dry, the LED should light up, as shown in Figure 12-8.

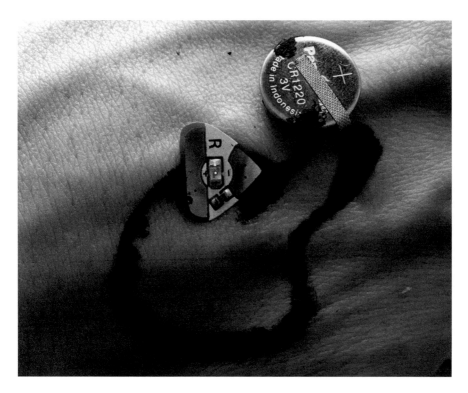

Figure 12-8. *Test circuit drying on a hand*

6. If the battery is loose, you may want to experiments with various tapes and more glue dots to hold it down, or a small Band-Aid may do the trick. If you want to cover the tattoo traces and/or circuit sticker, you can use foundation or other makeup.

Summary

Beauty technology extends into many areas of research, from medical and wellness to performance and art. I find these applications to be particularly exciting because of the way electronics and digital devices can be disguised and embedded on the body. These projects are intentionally crafted to be applied to the body through invisible means—in other words, they feel like a natural growth or extension of the wearer's skin and hair. This is a powerful step forward for wearables, showing that these devices can shrink and evolve so much that we might not even notice them or, more important, feel them. The next chapter will look at some examples of how to take wearables from on the body and embed them in the body!

CHAPTER 13

■ ■ ■

Superhumans and Cyborgs

When you hear the word *cyborg*, your mind probably jumps to superhero comics and sci-fi TV shows or movies featuring creatures with one eye in the middle of their forehead, robotic limbs, and green skin. Although these are, indeed the cyborgs we are familiar with from the media, there are many other cyborgs living among us, some with less obviously unusual features, and some who could be spotted a mile a way. You may be surprised to find out how little it takes to be known as a cyborg. Several cyborg enhancements are used frequently to restore a person's natural abilities and may not seem like a superhuman feature. The term *superhuman*, however, is more specific and refers only to qualities that exceed human capability. These are for the most part fictional qualities like superhuman strength or sixth and seventh senses. Superhumans are a subset of cyborgs; a superhuman ability may have resulted from a cybernetic implant or enhancement.

Another term pertinent to this topic is *cybernetics*, which is defined the science of communication and control theory as it applies to the comparative study of automatic control systems. However, the term is broadly used to refer to any controlled system that uses technology. Thus cyborgs are a derivative of cybernetics. As you may expect, many cyborgs are people interested in or involved with the field of cybernetics.

Chapter 2 touched on the history of cyborgs and bionics and how they have been used in media and popularized by certain iconic characters. This chapter elaborates on forms of cyborgs and artificial enhancements. These include wearable enhancements such as hearing aids and special eyeglasses, as well as implants and prosthetic wearables. You also learn about organizations and societies that have formed around the culture of cyborgs and bionics.

Cyborgs and Bionics

Before delving into the world of cyborgs, let's evaluate what makes a person a cyborg, or bionic.

■ **Note**   *Cyborg* and *bionic* basically have the same meaning and are used to describe the same devices throughout this chapter. *Cyborg* is a noun and more often refers to a person, whereas *bionic* is an adjective.

By definition, a *cyborg* is a person who is aided by or dependent on a mechanical or electronic device. This means anyone who is wearing a fitness tracker to help monitor their health is in fact a cyborg. Alternatively, cyborgs are people with medical or experimental implants that restore or modify their behavior and function, such as a cochlear implant, which is used to restore hearing. Researchers believe a wave of cyborgism has already started on a small scale and may become widespread in the near future. On the far end of the spectrum, they speculate that there will come a time when humans and machines have become one, which is referred to as *singularity*. There is some opposition to singularity from those who believe the world will collapse before this occurs. In other words, they think the technology we create will impose the end of humanity before it can effectively merge with humans. This, of course, is a longer and more philosophical discussion, as found in books such as *Future Shock* by Alvin Toffler and *The Singularity Is Near* by Ray Kurzwell.

© Sibel Deren Guler, Madeline Gannon, and Kate Sicchio 2016
S. D. Guler et al., *Crafting Wearables*, DOI 10.1007/978-1-4842-1808-2_13

Cyborgs for Art

Artists have used cyborgs in their work in many different ways, from creating work about cyborgs, to altering their own bodies to become cyborgs. The latter, known as *cyborg artists*, are often trying to add a cybernetic extension to their body that they can share with their audience. In these cases, the device is the heart of the piece. The following sections introduce a few artists who have paved the way for cyborgism as an art form.

Stelarc

Stelarc is an Australia-based performance artist who is famous for pushing the limits of becoming superhuman with his body modifications. His performances involve displays of his extended abilities, such as being hung from hooks that have been implanted in his back. He regularly collaborates with robotics engineers, experimenting in the space between virtual and reality. During one performance, his body was controlled by electronic muscle stimulators that were connected to the Internet.

In his *Ear on Arm* project, he had a third ear implanted onto his forearm and connected to his auditory system by a team of surgeons and stem-cell experts. Initially, Stelarc wanted to implant the ear on his head, but the doctors were not able to perform this procedure. As Stelarc explains, "I have always been intrigued about engineering a soft prosthesis using my own skin, as a permanent modification of the body architecture. The assumption being that if the body was altered it may mean adjusting its awareness." To carry out this quest, he experiments with prosthetics in unconventional ways to see if he can rearchitect his body's senses and systems.

Neil Harbisson

Neil Harbisson is a British artist and activist raised in Barcelona who was born completely color-blind. He studied music and art and pursued a degree in music composition in the UK. In 2004, Harbisson had an antennae implanted in his skull, allowing him to use audible vibrations in his skull to communicate information such as measurements of electromagnetic radiation, phone calls, music, as well as video and images. Figure 13-1 shows Harbisson in front of one of his prints. He is most famous for being the first cyborg recognized by a government: his UK passport features a photo of him with his antennae.

Figure 13-1. *Neil Harbisson and his eyeborg (photo by Dan Wilton, licensed under CC-BY-2.0)*

The antennae's main function is to treat his color-blindness. It translates light frequencies of the visible color spectrum as well infrared and ultraviolet light to sound. Harbisson has memorized these frequencies and claims he is able to "hear color" through this process. The antennae consists of two antenna implants, one vibration/sound implant, and a Bluetooth implant that allows him to connect to the Internet. The Internet connection makes it possible for him to receive color information from satellites and other people's cameras, as well as receive phone calls directly into his skull. Currently five people, each on a different continent, are allowed to directly send him images, sounds, and videos.

Harbisson regularly gives lectures to raise awareness about cyborgism at universities, museums, conferences, and other venues. He also continues to produce work as an artist, most commonly in the form of music and color prints, and has performed and exhibited globally. For example, his series *Color Scores* consists of a series of painting in which he paints what he hears. As Harbisson explains, his ability to hear color means common sounds such as voices and music are all associated with a color. Thus he is able to paint speeches and music that correlate to the colors in which he hears them. Similarly, a walk through a park or a supermarket fills his ears with the sounds of all the brightly colored objects he passes.

Moon Ribas

Moon Ribas is a cyborg activist, choreographer, and dancer known for her *Seismic Sense* project. In March 2013, Ribas permanently attached a sensor to her elbow that vibrates whenever an earthquake occurs in the world; she has been wearing the sensor since then. The frequency of the vibration relates to the strength of the earthquake and is wirelessly connected to seismograph data on the Internet. With her sensor, Ribas created the solo dance performance *Waiting for Earthquakes*. In this performance, the dancer stands still until an earthquake is felt, and the intensity of her movements reflects the magnitude of the earthquake.

Her other projects include *Speedborg,* which began as a speedometer glove that translates the speed of objects around her into vibrations that can be felt by her hand. After months of wearing the glove, she found she could sense different speeds depending on the interval of the vibrations. Another version of the project used earrings instead of gloves that similarly vibrated when there was a nearby presence. She wore the earrings while travelling around Europe, and in each city she collected data to find the average walking speed of the citizens. She used this data to create *The Speeds of Europe*, a video dance that demonstrates the walking speeds of the citizens in the cities she visited.

By 2009, Ribas found she was very familiar with her own speed. With this information, she created *Green Lights,* which is choreographed in relation to a set of eight traffic lights on Barcelona's Rambla de Catalunya. She first studied the traffic-light timings and measured the distance between traffic lights; she then calculated the speed at which she had to walk to such that she was not interrupted by a red light and was able to get from one end of the avenue to the other end without stopping.

Wafaa Bilal

Wafaa Bilal is an Iraqi-American artist and assistant professor at the Tisch School of the Arts at New York University. His art focuses on provoking a dialogue about international politics and dynamics; Bilal has lectured internationally about the critical situation in Iraq and Sadam Hussein's regime. He uses technology and media in his work to connect to his audience and invite them to participate in his performances.

In his piece *3rdI*, he became a cyborg artist by surgically implanting a camera on the back of his head. The camera had a USB connection to a lightweight laptop that Bilal carried with him, which had a 3G wireless Internet connection. With this system, the camera automatically captured one image per minute from his daily life and transmitted them to a web site (www.3rdi.me) where they are visible to the public. As he explains, the piece is a platform for telling and retelling a story, and the artist is the storyteller.

The piece was exhibited at the Arab Museum of Modern Art in Doha Qatar. NYU asked Bilal to cover the camera while on campus due to security concerns; he had the camera removed in February 2011 due to constant pain.

147

Cyborg Foundation

Neil Harbisson and Moon Ribas founded the Cyborg Foundation in 2010 with the mission of helping humans become cyborgs, promoting the use of cybernetics as body parts, and defending cyborg rights. They believe that cybernetic extensions should be treated as parts of the body, not artificial extensions. The foundation does not focus on helping repair senses and does not discriminate between people with disabilities and those without. They believe if we extend our senses, our perception of the planet will change, as will our behavior, and this will lead to a connected world that is more respectful to the environment and one another. They launched the initiative Cyborg Nest in 2015 in collaboration with Younivis, an "incubator for social superheroes," in order to architect new senses for the cyborg generation. You can visit the Cyborg Foundation online at `www.cyborgfoundation.com`.

Cyborg Research

Artists have made tremendous contributions t the advancement of cyborgism, but many of these would not be possible without the help of scientists and engineers. Steve Mann and Kevin Warwick are two scientists who are instrumental in this field.

Steve Mann

Steve Mann was mentioned in Chapter 1 for his work on wearable headsets and is revisited here for his contribution to cyborg research. It is believed that Mann was the first cyborg, because he has been wearing his computer-aided vision system since the 1980s to enhance and record what he naturally sees. In addition to several inventions in the field of computational photography, Mann is extremely active in issues of cyborg rights and cyborg law. He keeps an online blog at `http://eyetap.blogspot.ca` detailing his own experiences as a cyborg. In July 2012, Mann was physically assaulted by a McDonalds employee who tried to pull his headset off and proceeded to push him out the door of a McDonalds in Paris. Following the incident, Mann teamed up with several international organizations and leading industries to propose the Mann-Wassel law for presentation to the New York legislature. The goal of this effort is to create a legal policy and social climate to counteract such incidents by companies that could negatively interfere with the research and use of *augmediated reality* technologies.

Mann has coined the term *sousveillance*, which refers to the recording of an activity by a participant in the activity, typically by way of small wearable or portable personal technologies. His *Anonequity* project is an ongoing collaboration with several other researchers and focuses on the ethics, law, and technology of anonymity, authentication, surveillance, and sousveillance as they relate to cyborg law. He is a tenured professor in the Department of Electrical and Computer Engineering, with cross-appointments to the Faculty of Arts and Sciences and Faculty of Forestry, at the University of Toronto, and is a professional engineer licensed through Professional Engineers Ontario. He is also general chair of the Institute of Electrical and Electronics Engineers (IEEE) International Symposium on Technology and Society and Associate Editor of *IEEE Technology and Society*.

Kevin Warwick

Kevin Warwick is an engineer, professor, and deputy vice chancellor at Coventry University in the UK. His research centers on artificial intelligence, biomedical engineering, control systems, bioethics, and robotics. He is best known for his project *Project, Cyborg*, an ongoing project in which Warwick has implanted an array in his arm with the goal of becoming a cyborg or, as his nickname says, "Captain Cyborg." The project began in 1998 when an RFID tag was implanted under his skin, allowing him to control doors, lights, heaters, and other computer-controlled devices based on his proximity. This served as a test to see how the body would react to the implant.

The next stage was to implant a neural interface that consisted of a BrainGate (a brain-implant system built by the company Cyberkinetics) and an electrode array connected to an external gauntlet that contained other necessary electronics. The array contained 100 electrodes, 25 of which could be accessed at once. The median nerve, which the system monitors, carries many times that number of signals. The interface was designed by Warwick's former PhD student Dr. Mark Gasson and his team. It was successfully implanted into his arm in March 2002 and directly interfaced into his nervous system. The implant also connected Warwick's nervous system to the Internet at Columbia University in New York. This allowed him to send a signal to control a robot arm at the University of Reading that was built by one of his colleagues and obtained feedback from the sensors in the fingertips. The signal from the array was complex enough that the robot arm was able to mimic the actions of Warwick's arm. He was also able to connect ultrasonic sensors to a baseball cap and experience extrasensory input from them. The side effects of the implant on Warwick's hand function were measured using the University of Southhampton Hand Assessment Procedure, a clinically validated hand-function test, and no measurable effect or rejection was found. The nerve tissue grew around the electrode array, enclosing the sensor.

Warwick is not the only person who went through this operation. A similar array was implanted into his wife with the goal of inventing a form of telepathy or empathy, using the Internet to communicate signals across long distances. The operation was successful and proved to be the first direct and purely electronic communication between the nervous systems of two humans.

Warwick believes that *Project Cyborg* could pave the way for new medical tools that treat patients with damage to the nervous system. Additionally, it is speculated that a similar technology could be used for technology-facilitated telepathy. He has written or edited 27 books, 3 of which are about *Project Cyborg*. He holds honorary degrees from several universities around the world and several visiting professorships. He has also been awarded many honors including earning the title of one of the "only 7 eminent scientists" from the Institute of Physics, the others being Galileo, Einstein, Curie, Nobel, Oppenheimer, and Rotblat. His implants are on display at science museums in London and Naples.

Bodyhacking

■ **Note**   This section explains some unconventional body modifications. If you do not enjoy reading about these types of things, please proceed with caution.

Most of the cyborg implants and enhancements presented so far have a specific purpose. The cyborg has chosen to have a procedure performed as part of an art project or proof of concept. Neil Harbisson initially wanted to find a different way to perceive color because he was naturally color-blind. He then began to experiment with his implant and has used the device to serve other purposes. This curiosity alone can be a reason for an implant.

Bodyhackers, also referred to as *grinders*, are people who modify their body with technology and thus fall into the arena of cyborgs. Bodyhackers experiment with different ways to extend human capabilities, or become superhuman, by implanting electronics and other small objects under their skin. The procedures are usually carried out by a body-implantation specialist or doctor and are performed at the risk of the recipient. Different people have different reactions to their implants; some are able to live with no complications, whereas others face infections and disease after the operation. The following sections review four of the more common body hacks.

Near-Field Communication Chips

Near-field communication (NFC) microchips are in many of the electronic devices we own. NFC chips enable a communication protocol between two electronic devices when they are in a certain range (about 10 cm) of one another. They are used in contact-free payment systems, where simply holding your card in front of a device like a smartphone with a payment application is enough to process a transaction. They are also used in car keys, to unlock the doors automatically when the key is a certain distance from the car. They are much less expensive than similar technologies such as Bluetooth.

Once the chip is synched with a device, it basically acts as a key to enable communication. A grinder who has this key embedded in their finger can automatically unlock keypads and phones using the technology. It is believed that this implant will be more useful in the future when it is compatible with more devices. One risk is that the chip could be hacked to carry spyware and spread viruses to all devices it comes into contact with.

Magnetic Implants

Other grinders have had a small neodymium (rare-earth) magnet implanted in their fingertip in order to gain an extra sense. The procedure involves slicing the tip of the finger, inserting a magnet, and gluing the incision together. Once the incision heals, the magnet is ready for adventure. For starters, people with this implant can pick up small metal objects like paperclips and bottle caps with the tip of their finger, as shown in Figure 13-2. Depending on the strength of the magnet, they may even be able to demagnetize credit cards and hotel key cards.

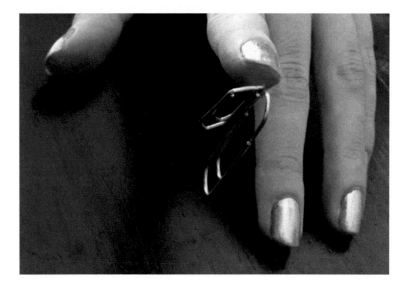

Figure 13-2. *Woman with a magnetic implant lifting paperclips*

A more interesting effect is the new sense of magnetic awareness. A person with a magnet in their finger can literally sense the presence and strength of a magnetic field. Dann Berg, a writer who had a magnet implanted in his pinky finger in 2009, tells his story of how his everyday experiences changed. He says that suddenly things like power transformers and microwaves became interactive; he could feel this new invisible layer as a tingle in his finger. He explains, "Each object has its own unique field, with different strength and 'texture.'" Berg recalls the first time he went into a retail store and felt the strong magnetic waves emitted by the device used to remove tags from clothing. He could feel the magnetics embedded in electronic devices like speakers. Some of these magnets were so strong that they could flip the magnet in his finger!

Berg notes that he is generally happy with his magnet and cannot think of many negative consequences. He does not believe the magnet has given him a sixth sense, but rather it has extended his sense of touch and allows him to interact with objects more intimately, letting him perceive them without physically touching them. The magnet has not been a problem in airport security and does not damage his electronics. In fact, the magnet is not as strong as it first was. One major issue he is aware of is that he would have to have the magnet removed if he needed to have an MRI—and if he forgot, the machine would probably rip the magnet out for him.

Another, less common, version of magnetic implants involves embedding magnets in the ears. In 2013, Rich Lee had sound-transmitting magnets implanted in his ears that, when paired with an amplifier and coil necklace, allow him to play music without headphones. In order to use the magnets, an amplifier is plugged into a media player and sends signals to a coil worn around the neck. The coil creates a magnetic field that sends signals to the magnets and is perceived as sounds that only the wearer can hear.

LED Compass

Pittsburgh-based bio-hacking collective Grindhouse Wetware recently tested the first version of its latest creation: a small circuit board, a bit larger than a coin, embedded with five LEDs that are activated by a magnet. The board is covered in a special silicone casing, which took months to develop. The most important part of the design is to ensure that the board does not make contact with the body. Three members of Grindhouse had the board, known as the NorthStar v1, implanted into their hands by a Swedish tattoo and body-modification artist in November 2015. The NorthStar can serve as a backlight for a tattoo or mimic the natural phenomenon of bioluminescence, where living organisms are able to glow and emit light.

When a magnet is placed on the board, the LEDs blink for 10 seconds. The team predicts that the battery on the board will be able to light it up about 10,000 times. At that point, the device will have to be surgically removed. When asked why they created this device, the team stated that the community wanted a way to light up their tattoos. They plan to sell about 100 of these devices to tattoo parlors in the next year. Their research is mostly self funded, with some outside investment; it does not comply with bioethics standards, so they usually are not able to work with doctors or medical experts.

The NorthStar is the next iteration of the Circadia 1.0, a health tracker around the size of a pack of cigarettes that cofounder Tim Cannon previously had implanted. He removed it after three months due to discomfort. The NorthStar is considerably smaller, but the group wants to shrink it even more and expand its capabilities. For example, a future version could wirelessly deliver biometric data such as blood pressure. Another version will be able to track the motion of the person's hand, enabling the hand to become a wireless controller. The implant will recognize movements and transmit them via Bluetooth to a gesture controlled device that can be controlled with gestures. They like to think of this as the next level of Siri, who you don't need to talk to. As Cannon explained in an interview with Vice, "We want to transform science fiction into reality.... This is about passion and citizen science."

Cyborg-Themed Products

This section presents some products that are working to give a new outlook or perception for how people experience the world. Some of these are similar to the superhero products presented in Chapter 2.

To Better See You With

Devices that improve or correct vision are one of the earliest forms of wearables, as you saw in Chapter 1. The ability to magnify or extend vision makes people curious, from wondering what it would be like to have "eyes in the back of your head" to being able to see through walls. This section highlights some newer wearable concepts that are trying to extend vision.

Night Vision

There is a reason I prefer not to drive at night: I cannot see as well. This is because humans in general are not able to form images in the dark; we need light to reflect off an object in order to form the image in our eyes. Luckily, the invention of night-vision goggles works to combat this inability. Night-vision goggles are commonly used by the military to aid soldiers who need to find their way in the dark, but they can also be purchased at sporting good stores to help you see your way through the woods when camping. They range in price from $10 to $600, depending on how high-tech you want to get.

On the lower end, you may only be able to find glasses with a reflective coating, similar to the material used to illuminate roads at night. On the higher end, you can get a more complex optical system. Night-vision devices work by amplifying what little light is present in an environment. They can do this in two ways. The first, called *light amplification*, involves collecting a small amount of light, even from the lower infrared spectrum that is imperceptible to human eyes, and then amplifying it to the point that you can see the image. The second method, *thermal imaging* or *heat vision*, uses the higher end of the infrared light spectrum, which objects emit as heat. If an object is giving off heat, the thermal-imaging device can capture this and translate it into a loosely defined image in the visible spectrum.

Eidos Eyewear

A team of designers from the Royal College or Art prototyped a set of wearable headpieces called Eidos that augment perception; see Figure 13-3. The first device resembles an oversized mask that is embedded with a camera and a display and enables the wearer to see motion. The incoming images from the camera are sent to a computer and processed by an application that creates an output with a ghosted trail, similar to that of long-exposure photography. The output is then sent to the display in the headset, altering the wearer's perception of the outside world. The team believes these nuance patterns and traces of movement will be useful in many different applications. For example, if used in sports, the technology would allow players to visualize and improve their techniques in real time. Alternatively, if worn by an audience at a dance performance, viewers would have personalized experiences of the event, whereas these types of projections are usually applied to the stage.

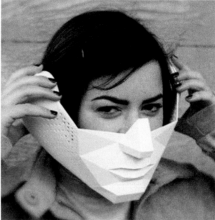

Figure 13-3. *Woman wearing the Eidos eyemask (left) with ghosted trail highlighted to show how she would perceive the image, and earmask (right) (photos by Tim Bouckley)*

To Better Hear You With

This section describes wearable technologies that augment or enhance auditory senses—in other words, the way we perceive sound.

Eidos Earwear

The second mask of the Eidos project allows the wearer to selectively hear speech. A directional microphone embedded in the device captures audio and processes it through an application that reduces background noise. The sound is then transmitted to the listener through headphones in the mask and a central mouthpiece. The mouthpiece passes the isolated sound directly to the inner ear through vibrations, which are processed by bone conductance. As the team explains, this creates a unique feeling, as though someone is talking directly inside your head.

Headphones, Reimagined

Doppler Labs is a San Francisco-based startup working on a new type of earbud. The wireless earpieces pair with a smartphone app that allows you to adjust the volume, EQ settings, and other effects. The earbuds, called Here, let you personalize your listening experience. For example, you can add an echo or cancel out specific background noise, like the sound of a crying baby. The app transmits the settings to Here via Bluetooth, which unfortunately does not deliver the best sound quality. The earbuds work best at short distances, which could pose a problem when your smartphone is turned off on an airplane. They retail at about $200 and are not intended to be marketed to a wide audience, but rather to music-savvy audiophiles who may be looking for a new listening experience.

Nuheara is another company working on a similar product, but its earphones are not just intended for listening to music. They will also be used for telephone calls or conversations with Siri, similar to the earpiece in the movie *Her*. Nuheara expects to release its product in late 2016 at a retail price of about $300. Several smartphone manufacturers, such as Motorola and Samsung, have developed Bluetooth earpieces that pair with the phone and transmit sound, but augmenting that sound is a new development.

VibeAttire

Whenever you walk into a loud concert or movie theater, you may perceive the loudness in your ears as well as other parts of your body. Or you may have experienced discomfort from a car passing by, blasting the bass of a song that is otherwise inaudible. This is because sound waves cause vibrations: to your ear, these vibrations are perceived as sound, but they can cause other parts of your body to vibrate as well, such as your chest. This generally is not dangerous unless the sound is extremely loud or you suffer from a lung or heart condition that could be affected by the vibrations.

Aubrey Schick, a designer and engineer at Intel, founded a company based on her project *VibeAttire* while working as a researcher at the Quality of Life Technology Center at Carnegie Mellon University. VibeAttire essentially works to benefit from the vibrations of sound and give the wearer a different type of sensory sound experience. It is a vest embedded with several vibration motors that pulse in response to an audio signal. Schick wrote a program that determines how different parts of an audio signal (treble, bass, volume, and so on) cause vibrations in the body and mapped the frequencies from the sound to a matrix of vibration motors embedded in the vest.

The vest was initially developed to allow deaf people to compose their own auditory experiences and later marketed as audio-enhancing tool to the general public. The targeted user applications are as follows:

- Music, gaming, and multimedia enthusiasts

- People with hearing impairments

- Therapy

I tried an early prototype of the vest and was amazed to find that I really felt as though I could hear music through the vest. I first used the vest with headphones so that I could both hear and feel the music at the same time; I then turned off the headphones and found I could still hear the song in my head through the feedback from the vibration. However, when I turned the vest on without hearing any of the music, my predictions about the music were way off. For example, from the vibrations, I interpreted a song to be in the genre of hip-hop or R&B—but when I turned up the headphones, it was a country song!

Medical Bionics

In medicine, bionics are divided into two categories: restorative and enhanced. *Restorative* technologies restore a lost function, organ, or limb. The defining factor is that something is being replaced or repaired. A common medical bionic is a cochlear implant, which is an electronic device that provides a sense of sound to a person who is deaf or hard of hearing.

Enhanced bionics, on the other hand, aim to extend past natural function or capability and provide a new, superhuman power. An example would be implanting a pair of legs that are able to run faster than any human.

Brain-Computer Interface

A *brain-computer interface* (BCI) is a direct communication pathway between an enhanced or wired brain and an external device. They are most commonly used to research, map, assist, augment, or repair human cognitive or sensory motor functions. The BCI field primarily focuses on neuroprosthetics that restore hearing, sight, and movement. The brain has amazing *plasticity*, meaning it can quickly readapt. This means the brain can interpret signals from prosthetics as it would natural sensor and effector channels. These can fall under the categories of both restorative and enhanced bionics, depending on the functionality of the device and how it is interpreted and adapted by the brain.

Invasive BCIs are implanted directly into the grey matter of the brain) during neurosurgery. These devices provide higher-quality signals but are prone to scar tissue build-up, which eventually weakens or totally blocks the signal from reaching the brain.

Retinal Implants

Retinal implants are a common invasive BCI that can partially restore vision to patients who have lost their sight due to degenerative eye conditions. In this procedure, a low-resolution image is created by electrically stimulating surviving retinal cells. Researchers have found that in these cases the photoreceptors of the eye have been damaged, but the nerve cells that relay the signal to the brain are still intact. This means it is possible to directly stimulate these retinal nerve cells and produce signals that are perceived by the brain as vision. Scientists have researched different methods to stimulate retinal nerve cells, including neurotransmitter release, magnetic, mechanical, and electrical stimulation. Currently, three types of retinal implants are being developed by private companies and research institutions around the world.

Noninvasive BCIs

The alternative, noninvasive BCIs, do not require surgery; they involve placing electrodes on the head but have poor spatial resolution because the skull dampens the signals. The most studied form is *electroencephalography (EEG)*. In an EEG, electrodes are placed along the scalp and measure spontaneous electrical activity, usually over a period of 20–30 minutes. By placing several electrodes around the scalp, more precise data analysis can be performed to deduce where signals are being fired and to filter out noise. EEGs are most commonly used to diagnose coma, sleep disorders, epilepsy, and brain death.

Recently, smaller, low-cost EEG headsets have been developed for the consumer market. NeuroSky Inc. is a Silicon Valley–based company that specializes in creating EEG headsets for consumer applications. Its products include Mindflex, a game released by Mattel that involves wearing an EEG headset to measure your brain waves and steer a ball through an obstacle course. The headset in the game is widely used by hackers and hobbyists who want to implement a low-cost BCI device into their projects. A few years later, NeuroSky launched MindSet, a research and developer multimedia headset with free software developer tools. The company also partnered with the Japanese organization Neurowear to create Necomimi, a headband with a brain-wave sensor that controls motorized cat ears that turn up or down based on the EEG readings. Figure 13-4 shows several members of the press trying Necomimi at a launch event.

Figure 13-4. *Necomimi launch event featuring attendees trying on the headsets (photo by Doug Kline, licensed under CC-BY-2.0)*

Technically, this device is not able to read your mind; but depending on where the sensor is located on the head and how noisy this area is, it can read your brain state quite accurately. There are currently many research initiatives to create smaller, more portable wearable EEGs. They have promising potential not just for games and smart accessories, but also for helping to monitor and diagnose chronic health conditions.

Prosthetics

A *prosthetic* is defined as an artificial device that replaces a missing body part. The reason a prosthesis is needed can vary from trauma to disease and is treated accordingly. The earliest known prosthetic was created by the early Egyptians and was discovered on a mummy, who is thought to have been buried in 950–710 B.C.E., in the form of a big toe made from wood and leather. Other early developments included an iron hand and a peg leg developed in the 1500s. The first electronically enabled prosthetic was developed in the 1990s. Known as the *intelligent prosthesis,* it was a microprocessor-controlled knee.

Many new materials and technologies in recent years have been used in the development of artificial limbs. Carbon fiber, for example, allows limbs to be stronger and more lightweight, thus making them easier to design and operate. Additionally, the use of electronics has become more common.

Myoelectric limbs can be controlled by converting muscle movements into electrical signals that are picked up by electrodes. The muscle movements are read from the surface of residual skin, such as flexing an elbow or ankle. This system uses the neuromuscular system of the body to control an electrically powered limb, as shown in Figure 13-5.

Figure 13-5. *The myoelectric arm of a U.S. Marine*

The alternative approach, *cable-operated* limbs, offers a more immediate response—the myoelectric system often has a slight lag time. The cable-control system harnesses the energy of a healthy shoulder or wrist and is referred to as *body-powered prosthesis*. Another advantage of this system is that the wearer can feel what is being held, thanks to the inherent biofeedback system.

A third approach involves *robotic prostheses*. These devices have several components, including biosensors, such as surface electrodes that detect electrical activity on the skin, needle electrodes implanted in the muscle, or solid-state electrode arrays with nerves growing through them. These sensors collect feedback from the wearer's body and communicate with a central controller system that triggers *actuators* in the device. Actuators are electronics that mimic the actions of a muscle to produce movement. The controller is connected to the wearer's nerve and muscular system and monitors and controls the movements of the device.

Robotic prosthetics offer much more fine-tuned control of the device. The *i-limb* hand launched in 2007, invented by a team at Princess Margaret Rose Hospital in Edinburgh and manufactured by Touch Bionics, was the first commercially available hand prosthesis with five individually powered digits. Other features of the hand include precision power, key grip modes, and a manually rotatable thumb that is passively operated by the wearer. Another example of robotic prosthetics is ReWalk Robotics' prosthetic legs, which are bionic exoskeleton attachments that enable paraplegics to stand upright, walk, and climb stairs.

Customized Prosthetics

Some patients see a prosthesis as a chance to alter their body in a new and unique way. For example, Chef Eduardo Garcia, who lost his arm in a hiking accident, has experimented with several different prosthetic substitutes that allow him to continue his passion of cooking. As a bionic chef, he has to be careful when selecting what type of prosthetic to wear, because he is constantly exposing it to water, heat from a stove, and cold from a freezer. However, he is also interested in exploring potential benefits of an artificial limb that could replace his built-in senses. He dreams of a limb that could detect pH and bacteria levels in the food he comes into contact with and display the results on an LED screen. His dream device would also be able to provide sensory feedback about temperature and texture. His current mechanical hand attachments include a hook that can expand to act as tongs to lift the lid on a pot. This may bring to mind Edward Scissorhands, a fictional character whose hands were literally scissors that he could use to trim bushes and cut through many different materials. He also has a myoelectric arm that can control 25 different functions via Bluetooth from a smartphone.

Another chance to customize prosthetics is the design of the outer shell. Because it can be made from synthetic materials, there is no need to make it blend in with the rest of the body; some designers are taking prosthetic design in a new direction. Alleles Design Studio is a Canadian company specializing in high-fashion prosthetic covers. The inspiration came from a research project by cofounder McCauley Wanner during her thesis project for her industrial design degree. Wanner found a gap in the prosthetics market for fashionable options. Most companies focused on function rather than aesthetics, leaving the consumer with few, if any, customizable options. Wanner interviewed many amputees and doctors and knew that she wasn't the only one who wanted to spice up these artificial limbs. Many amputees want to draw attention to their artificial limbs and are constantly trying to find unique ways to do so. For example, some want to customize them by imprinting a nostalgic image, a bit like getting a tattoo for an artificial limb.

Alleles Design Studio is working to fill this gap by creating affordable, customizable prosthetic covers. It currently only designs leg covers and has a few different collections people can choose from; the company also offers custom designs for those who are looking for something different. Alleles plans to release about two collections per year and keep the cost of the product in the $200–$400 range. Figure 13-6 shows a leg cover from the Racer collection.

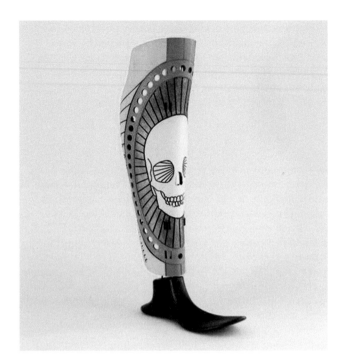

Figure 13-6. *Racer prosthetic cover by Alleles Design Studio (courtesy of Alleles Design Studio)*

Open Bionics

The Enable Foundation, an organization dedicated to helping people design and 3D-print bionic hands, was mentioned in Chapter 11. Another company working in this realm is Open Bionics. It has developed a prosthetic hand model composed of four lightweight 3D-printed parts that can be produced in about 40 hours. The current wait time for artificial limbs can range from weeks to months. Additionally, prostheses can cost thousands of dollars, whereas this one costs less than $100. The Open Bionics hand, which also plans to go fully open source, uses EMG sensors attached to the amputee's skin to provide individual finger movement such as opening and closing the fingers.

Similar to Alleles, Open Bionics is concerned with the wearer's aesthetic preferences. In order to increase the company's reach, it has released a line of superhero-themed bionics to appeal to children. The line includes a Jedi lightsaber hand that lights up and a hand with blue sparkles modeled after Elsa, the main character in Disney's hit movie *Frozen*.

Superhuman Bionics

So far, you have seen bionics and prosthetics that fit in the restorative category, but not prosthetics that are designed to enhance human capabilities. One approach to enhancing prosthetics is to embed them with small gadgets and devices. For example, instead of wearing a smartwatch, you could have it built into a prosthetic arm. Computer programmer Jerry Jalava has a prosthetic finger after losing his in a motorcycle accident. He decided to add a new function to his prosthetic and has a 2.0 GB USB port installed in the finger. The drive does not upload information to his body, but it certainly must come in handy when Jalava needs to store information.

However, not all bionics are designed for people who have lost a bodily function; others are designed to enhance the average person's functionality. Some of these were presented in Chapter 2, including superhero exoskeleton technologies. A collaborative project between researchers at Carnegie Mellon University and North Carolina State University released last year offered a different kind of exoskeleton that is not electrically powered but, rather, is purely mechanical. It is an ankle attachment that helps people walk using less energy. Studies show that people spend more energy walking than in any other daily activity. This energy, of course, becomes more precious as people become older or develop mobility issues. This system is said to reduce the metabolic cost of walking by about 7%. This difference equates to taking off a 10-pound backpack while walking around. The device is composed of a mechanical clutch that engages when the foot makes contact with the ground, and disengages when the foot is lifted into the air. The clutch replaces the function of the calf muscle in this motion, providing the force needed to launch the body forward without consuming any energy. This in turn decreases the overall metabolic rate of the activity.

Summary

This is perhaps the most graphic chapter of this book thus far, focusing more on fringe wearable projects in the medical, art, and cyborg enthusiast realms. Naturally, there will be curious researchers who try unconventional techniques and push things to the limit to see what is possible. Some of these efforts have led to breakthroughs in medical technologies, while others are perhaps a bit ahead of their time and have not shown any life-changing applications for the average person. Nonetheless, these experiments are crucial to understanding how these wearable technologies could alter people's interactions with the world. A magnetic finger implant may not seems like much more than a strange party trick, but the way the brain processes the information from the magnet shows that humans can quickly expand their existing senses and potentially form new ones. The last chapter 16 elaborates on the potential risks and challenges of a wearables-driven world.

CHAPTER 14

■ ■ ■

Activated Garments

This is perhaps the chapter you have been waiting for: what are fashion designers doing with technology? How can technology actually be integrated into clothes and accessories? What do these clothes look like, and how do they fit? These are important details when imagining the future for wearables. You have seen several wearable devices that match different styles and trends, but mostly from a functionality perspective of the wearable, rather than an aesthetic perspective.

Often, the "fashion" aspect of wearables feels like an afterthought. A tech company finds a fashion label or brand to make the device wearer-friendly, but the focus is really the accuracy of the engineering design, not the fashion design. Not all wearables are created this way, of course; many adventurous fashion designers want to work with technology and initiate a collaboration or partnership with technologists and engineers. Some of these designers research and develop their own techniques and methods for fitting electronics into their envisioned garments. A few of these projects have resulted in toolsets that are commercially available, as discussed in Chapter 6.

This chapter presents the latter approach: what happens when designers treat electronics as ingredients for their collections. How does fashion design change when the toolset is expanded from the thread, fabrics, and buttons discussed in Chapter 4 to a collection of electronic components? The designer is not limited to one set of colors, textures, and materials; these are all factors that can be changed from an app or in response to sensors embedded in the garment. For example, using a programmable LED to set the color of the fabric on a shirt means the shirt can shine green one day and blue the next. A fashion designer must decide how the garment responds and adapts to the wearer. Fashion designers are using electronics to add not only another wave of style, but another layer of interaction. They are literally *activating clothing*.

Fashion for Safety

In 2005, Anna Haupt and Terese Alstin were studying industrial design at the University of Lund in Sweden, when a law was passed that made helmets mandatory for all cyclists under the age of 15. As debates brewed about whether this law should be extended to adults, the team saw this as an opportunity to redesign the helmet. The problem they foresaw was that most adults do not prefer to wear helmets. Some think they are too cumbersome to carry around, and others may not want to wear them because they don't match an outfit. Whatever the reason, these hesitations result in a huge safety risk. Haupt and Alstin designed an inflatable helmet that sits as a collar around the wearer's neck until triggered, at which point it inflates to encapsulate the wearer's head, protecting the wearer from potential harm. Figure 14-1 shows the helmet before and after it has been triggered. The device, much like an airbag in a car, has several built-in sensors that trigger inflation when they sense impact or a sudden change in speed and orientation. The design has won several awards and led to the development of their company Hövding, which manufactures and sells the helmets worldwide.

© Sibel Deren Guler, Madeline Gannon, and Kate Sicchio 2016
S. D. Guler et al., *Crafting Wearables*, DOI 10.1007/978-1-4842-1808-2_14

Figure 14-1. *Hövding deflated collar/helmet (left); inflated (right) (courtesy of Hövding)*

Once inflated, the helmet covers a larger area than a tradition bicycle helmet. Additionally, it provides soft and gentle shock absorption on impact. The air pressure in the helmet stays constant for several seconds after impact, ensuring that it can remain effective from multiple impacts that may result from a single accident. The gas inflator uses helium and is responsible for the bulk of the weight; it rests on the rider's back. It is ergonomically designed with even weight distribution across the shoulders.

The helmet collar is made from ultra-strong nylon fabric that doesn't rip when scraped against the ground. It is waterproof and provides great protection for the built-in airbag system. The collar itself is not washable but is encased in a shell that can be washed. This shell protects the collar from sweat and dirt. The shells come in several different colors, allowing the user to personalize the item and choose their preferred shell.

A similar product is the In&motion ski vest. The vest contains an inflatable airbag that inflates before the skier makes contact with the ground during an accident. The In&motion system also analyzes data collected at the time of the fall and sends this to the user to help them better understand the causes of the accident.

To Safely Reach Your Destination

An interesting concept that has appeared in science fiction stories as well as design theory is the idea of self-navigating shoes. These are shoes that have little vibration motors around the heels, one on the left shoe and one on the right shoe. The shoes are synced with mapping software that tells the shoes which direction you need to turn while walking to a destination. If the wearer has to turn left, the motor on the left shoe vibrates; similarly, turning right is indicated by a vibration from the right shoe. Indian company Ducere Technologies has taken this concept to market under the brand name Lechal and is manufacturing stylish navigating shoes for both men and women. The company also sell insoles to convert normal shoes into *haptic* shoes. A portion of each sale of a pair of shoes goes into the Lechal Initiative, an organization that subsidizes the cost of the shoes for visually impaired people who cannot afford them at full price.

No Contact Jacket

Every woman has had the experience of walking alone at night and feeling uneasy about her safety. (Although men may also experience this feeling of vulnerability, it is unfortunately more common for women to be in danger.) The No Contact Jacket was created in 2003 by industrial designer Adam Whiton and apparel designer Yolita Nugent in attempt to provide an extra layer of comfort and protection. It is a stylish, sporty woman's outerwear garment with a secret power: it can repel an assailant with 80,000-volt shock! The shock is not lethal, but it is certainly enough to make a person take a few steps back, not to mention the side effects of disorientation, discomfort, and loss of balance. The wearer of the jacket is protected from the electrical charge by insulation, enabling her to escape.

The jacket is composed of several layers; the innermost layer is made from a conductive fiber and powered by a 9-volt battery. The battery is connected to a circuit that allows it to build up a high-voltage, low-amp charge, similar to the technology used in commercial stun guns. To activate the jacket, or charge it up, a small lock on the outer sleeve is opened using a key. Next, the wearer must press a button, which is attached by a cord to the inside of the sleeve so that she can easily hold it in her palm. This charging process may take a few minutes, so the ideal use case involves preactivating the jacket in situations where a woman may feel at risk. This way, she can feel confident and secured against any surprise attacks. However, it was found that even when the jacket is not activated, audible crackle sounds and visible electric arcs serve as a sufficient warning that the jacket is dangerous.

The jacket was prototyped in petite sizes so that men would have a hard time trying to use it against women in the event that the jacket was stolen. The team chose to embed the technology in a jacket over other articles of clothing to ensure that the woman can always have it with her, if not on her—in other words, they wanted an item that the women would use on a daily basis. The cost of the jacket on a small manufacturing scale was estimated to be about $1,000.

The team continues to work in the realm of creating new wearable technology for defense and protection. Nugent also founded R4R and manufactures conductive ribbon (invented for this project), which was discussed in Chapter 7.

Fashion for Privacy

Smartwatches and phones are not the only way to carry information on your body. Data chips can be embedded in almost anything. As you saw in Chapter 13, they are even placed in prosthetics! One issue that arises with all of this data storage is security. If your phone or smartwatch is stolen, the device is not the only thing you lose; the new owner also has access to your passwords, message logs, and more. Fortunately, there are many systems in place to lock a device as soon as it goes missing, making it impossible to break into—but sometimes it may already be too late.

One way to protect your digital information is to make it less detectable. This is the approach Susan McGregor took when designing *Hiding in Plain Sight*. The project incorporates USB keys into wearable accessories like jewelry, where they are invisible from the outside. This gives the wearer an increased sense of privacy and security. McGregor also wanted the project to be accessible to those who may not consider themselves technically savvy. The use of jewelry and other common accessories invites the user to explore other places and tools for storing information, taking the high-tech process of protecting data and making it simpler and more personal. A necklace with a USB drive hidden in the gems is shown in Figure 14-2.

Figure 14-2. *A USB necklace from the Hiding in Plain Sight project (courtesy of Susan McGregor)*

Emotional Style

Chapter 11 presented wearable biotechnology that measures the wearer's health or emotional state. The emotional state of the wearer is very important in fashion design. For one thing, clothing can develop a strong emotional and nostalgic purpose for the wearer. A brightly colored shirt worn on a memorable day may carry feelings of warmth and happiness. Several fashion houses across the world are exploring this potential of digitally enhanced wearables that connect more deeply to the wearer's emotions.

Social Body Lab

The Social Body Lab, led by wearables expert Kate Hartman at the Ontario University of Art and Design, researches meaningful and provocative interactions between humans and technology. The lab develops prototypes and projects that combine playful speculations about the power of technology with wearable garments that manifest human values and desires.

In the project *Prosthetic Technologies of Being*, the team collaborated with Jamie Sherman from Intel Research to explore ways in which technology can be manipulated to feel like an extension of the body. The prototypes in the series extend the wearer's ability to sense their surrounding while providing a new output to express their emotional reactions. The first prototype, Monarch, is a muscle-activated wearable form that attaches to the shoulders. The form expands and contracts in response to the movement of the wearer's arm muscles, as shown in Figure 14-3. The physical extension provided by Monarch heightens the wearer's personal expression.

Figure 14-3. *Monarch, activated by the wearer flexing her muscle (courtesy of Social Body Lab, photograph by Marc De Pape)*

The second prototype, called Nautilus, follows a similar theme of extending muscle movements and using them to trigger a change of shape in wearables. Nautilus takes the form of a wearable hood that covers the wearer's head when triggered to create a sense of personal space and division from the outside world. This time, the sensors are placed along the neck to sense when the wearer is shrugging. The shrug activates servomotors embedded in the hood to raise the fabric around the head or bring it back down.

Cardinal is the third prototype created in collaboration with former lab artists in residence Erin Lewis and is in the form of a cape. Cardinal investigates how wearables can enhance the wearer's sense of directional awareness and connectedness. The surface of the cape has designs made from thermochromatic ink (introduced in chapter 7) and is embedded with heating wire that changes the color of the designs. The heating wire is activated by a change of orientation of the wearer. When the wearer is facing the direction of their home, the colors change. The heating wire also provides a sensation of warmth to the wearer.

Other projects from the Social Body Lab are mentioned later in this chapter. You can also see documentation of their work online at `http://research.ocadu.ca/socialbody`, including videos of the prototypes from *Prosthetic Technologies of Being*.

HugShirt

CuteCircuit is a London-based fashion house that has been at the cutting edge of wearable technology since its launch in 2004. Its clients include celebrities like Nicole Scherzinger and Katy Perry. Prior to founding CuteCircuit, founders Francesca Rosella and Ryan Genz collaborated on several projects including the HugShirt, a shirt that helps people send long-distance hugs. The HugShirt is a long-sleeved t-shirt embedded with sensors that measure the strength, duration, location, heartbeat, and skin temperature from a hug. This information is recorded and then transmitted via Bluetooth to the HugShirt app. Each HugShirt has a partner shirt, and the recorded hug from one shirt is sent the to partner shirt through the synced app. Thus sending a hug is no different from sending an email or text message from your smartphone.

The goal of the shirt is to provide a more intimate human connection to the wearer when they are away from their friends and loved ones. It has been tested for various applications including medical studies with the elderly and children. Studies show that people are happier when they receive physical contact from each other. The shirt has been remade several times with improvements to the technology. It is rechargeable and washable.

No(where)Now(here)

Montreal-based fashion designer and professor Ying Gao works at the intersection between fashion and technology. In her project *(No)where(Now)here*, she created two interactive dresses that are made with photoluminescent thread (described in Chapter 6) that glows in the dark, and super-lightweight organza. The dresses are embedded with eye-tracking technology that triggers the dresses to move when someone is looking at them. The inspiration for the dress came from Paul Virilio's essay entitled "Esthétique de la disparition" ("The aesthetic of disappearance"), which questions the concepts of appearance and disappearance. As Gao explains, "A photograph is said to be 'spoiled' by blinking eyes—here … the experience of chiaroscuro (clarity/obscurity) is achieved through an unfixed gaze." The photoluminescent thread illuminates the dresses when they are in the dark. One of the dresses is shown in Figure 14-4, but I recommend watching the video to understand the movement and interaction of the dresses. The video can be accessed online at http://yinggao.ca/eng/interactifs/nowhere-nowhere.

Figure 14-4. *Ying Gao's (No)where(Now)here dress (courtesy of Ying Gao, photo by Dominique Lafond)*

Studio XO

Another fashion house that is making a big splash in wearable technologies is London-based Studio XO. Studio XO is led by fashion designer Nancy Tilbury and creative technologist Benjamin Males, who are interested in taking science-fiction fantasies to a new level with fashion and technology. Their process involves a speculative approach in which they envision a concept and build a narrative around it, helping them bring their visions to life in a believable form. In 2006, Tilbury was part of a team at Phillips Electronics, led by body architect Lucy McRae, who created the iconic Bubelle Dress. The dress responds to the wearer's emotional state by blushing. An inner layer is embedded with biometric sensors. These readings are then projected onto a second layer of fabric, mapping the wearer's mood to color and light patterns that result in a change of appearance and style of the actual dress.

Tilbury was contacted by artist Lady Gaga and her technical department, TechHaus, who were enamored with the Bubelle Dress. They commissioned the team to make several dresses for Gaga's ARTPOP campaign. Although all of these dresses share a wildly new and interesting aesthetic, one stands out among the others: Volantis is a dress that can literally fly! Using six drones attached to a taller middle stem structure, the team was able to create a wearable costume that Lady Gaga can step into and be propelled from the ground; the dress is steered by the pilots of the drones.

In addition to Lady Gaga, Studio XO works with several artists and performers including the Black Eyed Peas and Wayne McGregor. They have expanded into a collective of fashion designers, engineers, material scientists, and product designers. Their work centers on the theme of connected bodies, using technology to expand the emotional intimacy of fashion. The team believes that authentic fashion shares the desire to create a spectacle.

Their current endeavor, called XOB, works to use their network of high-fashion celebrities as icons for the general public to become interested in and engaged with the future of fashion. XOB is a ready-to-wear fashion label that uses biotechnology in the form of digitized skin. As Tilbury explains, their goal is to take these clothes from the stage and offer them to the people. While watching fans take photos of the clothing they had designed for a Black Eyed Peas performance, Tilbury and Males realized they could harness this enthusiasm to create connected clothing for everyone, not just celebrities. The line uses Studio XO's own emotional sensor technology, called XOX, which is said to be able to read the wearer's psychic state. XOB is intended to serve as a platform for other brands and designers to use in their collections. The team ultimately wants to teach and spread the concept of *digital skin* throughout the world. Digital skin goes beyond dresses and shoes embedded with LEDs to a more connected level, where the lights have function and can download and display information.

McRae has also continued to make incredible works combing science fiction, fashion, and speculative design, which you can see on her web site at `www.lucymcrae.net`.

Chromat

Chromat, a fashion house led by designer Becca McCharen, was mentioned in Chapter 3. This section revisits it to take a closer look at some of the interactive apparel it has created. Many of Chromat's garments combine 3D-printed forms with electronics to create interactive garments. Chromat's current work centers around creating a fierce, bold image for women with an obvious underlying theme of "girl power." In addition to its consumer brand, Chromat has worked with many artists to create custom outfits, including Nicki Minaj and Beyonce.

Following are examples of Chromat's work:

- *Adrenaline Dress*: Composed of 3D-printed panels and a carbon-fiber framework that can expand and contract. The back view of the frame and dress in a resting pose is shown in Figure 14-5. If the structure becomes activated, this lattice can morph into other, more provocative, forms. The garment is embedded with sensors that can sense adrenaline, triggering the carbon fibers to form an imposing shape. The project was inspired by biomimicry and fight-or-flight mode behavior, which describes an animal's physiological reaction that occurs in response to a perceived harmful event, attack, or threat to survival. During this reaction, hormones such as adrenaline increase at a measurable rate.

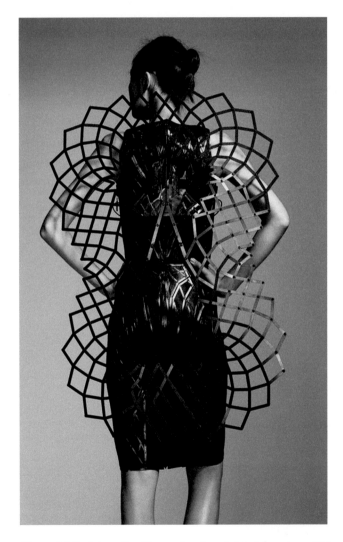

Figure 14-5. *Adrenaline Dress: view from behind (courtesy of Chromat, photo by Christelle de Castro)*

- *Laser Chakra Dress*: Another 3D-printed dress. This piece is embedded with laser diodes that simulate synthetic neuron connections in the brain. Laser ports are positioned at the seven *chakra* points on the body, representing energy vortexes. Optical amplification from the lasers serves as a physical representation for these chakra points on the dress. The word *chakra* translates to "wheel" in Sanskrit and is believed to be a part of the body that represents the center of spiritual power. It is used in many forms of meditation, such as yoga, to help focus the practitioner's energy.

- *Bionic Bodies collection:* Embodies the story of a love affair between a human and a robot. As McCharen explains, the collection was inspired by people's obsession with screens and technology. The garments attempt to provide the experience of going into the screen, or digital realm, by covering clothes in LED lights and metal. The final pieces are covered with rings of LED lights that were inspired by global energy usage topographies and interactive maps of web sites like Tweetping and Reddit.

Other projects and products can be seen on Chromat's web site: `www.chromat.co`.

Environmentally Reactive

Activated clothing can really make a statement when compared to "in-activated" clothing. Covering an outfit with lights and motors obviously stands out in a crowd of plain cotton and denim. Activated clothing does not always imply garments covered in bright lights, however sometimes they are more subtle and only visible in certain conditions.

Sparkle Booties

CuteCircuit's Sparkle Booties may look like typical fashionable stiletto-heeled boots, but when hit with direct light, they reveal a special power. The leather of the shoe is coated with reflective micro-perforated fabric containing thousands of glass microspheres that illuminate the surface of the shoe. Figure 14-6 shows the shoes after they have been triggered by light. CuteCircuit recently teamed up with EasyJet to redesign the airline's cabin/crew outfits. The flight attendants' new uniform includes a pair of Sparkle Booties so that they can illuminate the plane's corridors! The shoes are available in several different sizes and retail for 600 £.

Figure 14-6. *Sparkle Booties after they become illuminated (courtesy of CuteCircuit)*

Dissolving Clothes

Hussein Chalayan, one of the leading innovators in fashion design, unveiled a new creation at the spring 2016 Paris fashion show at Palais des Beaux-Arts. At the finale of the show, two models stood on a stage wearing stiff-collared, thigh-length overcoats. A portion of the ceiling was punctured by holes above the models that began to shower the models with water. As the water made contact with the coats, they began to dissolve and melt away, revealing patterned dresses lined with Swarovski crystals! The jackets were made of a paper-based material that disintegrated when exposed to water.

The concept is obviously not very practical, although many potential user scenarios come to mind. For example, what if, when you jumped into a pool, your shorts and t-shirt disappeared, leaving you with only a bathing suit? You wouldn't get that pair of shorts or t-shirt back—they would have totally disintegrated. Chalayan's goal was to make a commentary on how disposable fashion has become. And what better venue to make this statement than at a show where everyone is on the edge of their seats waiting for a fresh new look to be unveiled?

Wearable Façade

Wearable Façade is a project by design research studio POPKALAB for the Connecting Cities network. Connecting Cities was initiated by Public Art Lab in Berlin to create a connected infrastructure of media facades, urban screens, and projection sites to circulate artistic and social content. It has now become a worldwide network.

The project was inspired by the increasingly number of *media facades* that are being installed in cities around the world. Giant LED screens cover buildings and line walls that surround roads and parks. Almost every big city has a Times Square full of these media displays. In cities like Hong Kong, most of the building are lit up. *Wearable Façade* builds on this idea of using buildings to display information and reapplies it to fashion. In a sense, wearables media facades are even more influential because they are always updating based on their surroundings. They are smaller, mobile, and more accessible when displayed on a person rather than a building.

Wearable Façade is a garment embedded with a micro-camera and LED display that captures the colors and shapes of the wearer's environment and translates them into computer-generated patterns displayed by the LEDs. As the wearer walks through a city, *Wearable Façade* provides a reflection of the architecture and patterns recorded by the camera. The display offers a new perspective on the wearer's surrounding that is not static like a printed imaged on a billboard, but rather dynamic and animated with lights.

Garments as Interfaces

The concept of using a garment as an interface was mentioned in previous chapters. Although *Wearable Façade* is environmentally reactive, it could be seen as a wearable interface for advertising. Chapter 3 discussed Google's Project Jacquard, where researchers are working to create a new type of fabric interface that can be connected to existing hardware and electronics. Some designers are already putting this concept into practice, effectively creating garments that serve as an interface.

Digitizing Shoes

In the early 1990s, light-up sneakers were a must have for children everywhere. Popularized by the brand LA Lights, a product of American shoe company LA Gear, about 5 million pairs of these shoes were sold each year in the 1990s. LA Gear was not even the only brand selling such shoes, although it had the highest distribution channels. Light-up shoes have been one of the most successful products in the history of the athletic shoe industry, with more than 100 million pairs sold. Lights are still a popular feature of shoes, especially for children, but other outputs are also possible. Designers are experimenting with new ways to add interactivity to shoes.

POPKALAB just released *Sound Steps*: a pair of multitech shoes that produce sounds and music through the wearer's movements. The project was created in collaboration with Phonotonic and Stephane Gontard. The music is broadcast through a built-in speaker in the shoe that synchronizes with each step. The sound is customizable and can be changed by the user. The goal of *Sound Steps* was to create a product that democratizes the creation of music through a more ubiquitous outlet: shoes.

Nudgeables Accessory Kit

The Social Body Lab's (mentioned earlier) director Kate Hartman has designed several interactive wearable projects that she has expanded on with her research group. One of these projects, called the *Nudgeables Accessory Kit*, provides a customizable, secret communication tool. Hartman's motivation for the project was to find a way for clothing to communicate secret messages. Her solution is a modular hardware kit with an XBee radio transceiver called the Nudger and a receiver called the Notifier that enable a pair of people to nudge each other from across a room. The communication distance is limited by the bandwidth of the XBee.

The *Nudgeables Accessory Kit* can be embedded into a variety of different wearables such as headbands, scarves, and ties. The web site offers some ideas and tutorials on how to best attach the hardware to different materials. To trigger the Nudger, the wearer must push a button or other type of switch. The kit comes with a small push button that could be embedded into clothing, although the guide explains how to make your own switches out of conductive fabrics, much like the projects in Chapter 5. This is perhaps the most interesting part of the kit, because it encourages the user to design a personalized switch for their clothes. For example, someone who plays with their hair may want to embed the switch in a headband or barrette, whereas a person who adjusts their necktie may prefer to hide the switch in the tie. It is important to find a gesture or interaction that comes naturally, so as not to draw attention to yourself when you are nudging or being nudged.

The notifier delivers an output signal that can be connected to a small vibration motor or LED light. Depending on the application of the nudgeable, the wearer must decide if they prefer a visible notifier or more discreet nudge from the pulse of the motor. Additionally, the pair can develop a communication system around the nudges. A series of short nudges could be code for "Let's go home," and a single nudge could simply translate into "Hello."

TshirtOS

Imagine a t-shirt that had the ability to transform into hundreds of other shirts. How could this be possible? One way to achieve this is to create a shirt with a dynamic display that can be programmed on a daily, hourly, or even minute-by-minute basis. The outer border fabric of the shirt stays the same, but it's like owning hundred of graphic t-shirts in one!

TshirtOS is a t-shirt embedded with a flexible, washable, 1,024-color LED matrix arranged in a 32×32 grid (see Figure 14-7). But that's not all: the LED matrix is Bluetooth enabled, meaning you can set the pattern for the shirt from your phone; it also has built-in Twitter integration. You can program the shirt to display an animation, tweets from a Twitter feed, a simple message, or any other image you choose to input. It's a wearable platform for self expression. Features of the LED screen include brightness adjustment and flexibility. It also includes a built-in micro-camera, a microphone, an accelerometer, and speakers for other potential applications. For example, the shirt may react to the wearer's movements or a sound in the environment. The battery powering the LED panel lasts a few days once charged. TshirtOS was invented and developed by CuteCircuit, and the first units of the product were used for an advertising campaign by Scottish whisky label Ballantine's. It has now been brought to market by CuteCircuit and renamed InfiniTshirt.

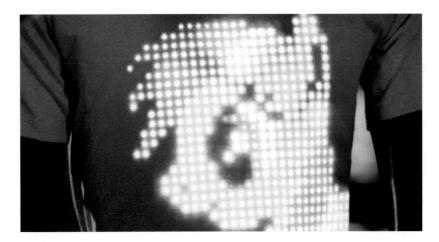

Figure 14-7. InfiniTshirt displaying a graphic (courtesy of CuteCircuit)

M-Dress

The *M-Dress*, or mobile dress, is another project by CuteCircuit that transforms clothing into an interface. The dress was conceived from the realization that most women's clothing does not have a place to hold a phone, like a pocket or pouch. This leads to many missed calls, extra accessories like a purse to hold a phone, and other inconveniences. CuteCircuit has designed a solution to this problem by embedding the phone in the dress itself!

The wearer inserts a SIM card in a slot under the label, and the dress can then receive calls to the wearer's mobile phone number. When the phone rings, the dress actually rings. It can even be programmed to produce different ring tones for different numbers. Custom gesture recognition software, developed by CuteCircuit, controls the hardware embedded in the dress. The simple gesture of bringing your palm to your ear activates a sensor that answers the call; bringing the palm away from the ear functions to hang up the call. As for making calls, the phone book can only store a few numbers. The dress is made from an elegant silk jersey material, and all the electronics are concealed.

Mirror Handbag

Another eye-catching accessory by CuteCircuit is the *Mirror Handbag*. It is made out of solid brass coated in a noble metal finish of ruthenium, palladium, or gold. The surfaces of the bag are made from a layer of laser-etched acrylic mirror that cover a matrix of white LEDS that shine through the mirror to create a dynamic light display. The LEDs can be programmed to display messages, tweets, and animations via Bluetooth though CuteCircuit's Q app. The bag is rechargeable via USB and retails for 1,600 £.

Illuminated Garments

Many other top fashion designers have debuted illuminated clothing over the last few decades. Unfortunately, a single chapter cannot present them all. If you are interested, there are books dedicated to cataloging these impressive creations. Following is a list of designers and brands with particularly interesting or beautiful pieces that are worth investigating:

- Pankaj &Nidhi's Geometrica collection

- The Crated

- Wearable Experiments

- Tamar Areshidze's illuminated crystal shoes

- Pauline van Dongen

- The Unseen Emporium

- Vega Wang's bioluminescent dresses

- Anouk Wipprecht

Summary

The inspirational pieces presented in this chapter may make you want to get straight to the studio and the drawing board. The concept of adding emotional and environmentally reactive functions to clothing is very exciting. If you look at clothing as a second layer of skin, it is natural to want to activate this skin in the same way as the first layer (that is, the skin on your body). Skin reacts to temperature and light, and it may tense up when you are afraid and smooth out when you are relaxed. What if your clothes could also behave this way—would they feel more natural? This chapter reviewed several examples of how clothing can enhance the wearer's body and experiences in meaningful ways, but in the end these are unique personal experiences. Every user, or wearer, has a different idea of what they'd like their clothes to be able to do and how their clothes could come to life. With initiatives like Studio XO's XOB, you may be able to share and collaborate on these ideas in the future, leading to an enormous collection, or closet, of dynamic and active clothing.

The next chapter, by guest author Dr. Kate Sicchio, expands on the use of wearables for aesthetic and design purposes to show how they are used in performance and costume. Dr. Sicchio is an award-winning media artist, choreographer, and performer whose work explores the interface between choreography and technology. She presents the history of the use of new technologies in performance and provides an outlook on how to design and develop new interactions and relationships in this realm.

CHAPTER 15

Wearable Costumes

Guest Chapter by Kate Sicchio

Since the 1960s, performing artists and creative engineers have embedded various wearable technologies into costumes for performance. From dance to music and theatre, the idea of digital interfaces that use the body spans many disciplines and works. In these performances there is usually a performer who is somehow either triggering or responding to a wearable device on their body. For example, a musician may wear gloves with bend sensors in them. When they bend their fingers, they can trigger a sound from a synth or a sample in a music software package. Instead of playing a traditional instrument, they are playing music through their own gestures. Figure 15-1 shows a costume housing biosensors for a performance at a music festival. Often this is thought of as interactive performance because it is allowing the performer a new way of creating the performance through interactive technologies.

Figure 15-1. *Biosensing Garment for controlling video by Camille Baker, worn by Kate Sicchio*

A range of performing artists have explored wearables, including Troika Ranch, Johannes Birringer and Michele Danjoux, Julie Bokoweic and Mark Bokowiec, Palindrome Intermedia Group, Amanda Parkes, Imogen Heap, Stelarc, Georg Hobmeier, Camille Baker, and others. This chapter aims to explore what kind of wearable technology is found in performance and costumes, which artists have used these types of devices in their work, and ways to incorporate wearables into interactive performances.

What Kinds of Wearables Are Found in Performance?

When exploring wearables in performance, there are a few general categories that most costumes and interactive designs fall into. These includes sensing systems, actuating systems, and energy-harvesting systems. All have different approaches and purposes for use in performance and artistic considerations.

First are *sensing systems*, which sense or measure some aspect of the body as an input to an interactive system. This encompasses a lot of the work with wearables and performance. This could be in the form of biological sensors (heart rate, breath rate, temperature, galvanization, brainwaves), motion sensing (accelerometers, gyroscopes, flexion), touch (pressure, location), or combinations of these sensing techniques. Often the sensor is somehow controlling another aspect of the performance, such as the music, video projections, or even the stage lighting. These systems are often designed with the idea of the body somehow controlling aspects of the performance through the wearable.

There are also systems designed to *actuate and output to the body*. This means a device is somehow creating a physical sensation on the body of the performer. This may include haptic feedback systems (vibrations, small motors), audio systems (speakers embedded in costumes), lights (LEDs, El wire), or, in the case of some avant-garde performance art, electrical impulses (electric shocks that stimulate muscle movement). As outputs, LEDs have become a popular way of costuming performers because they make a theatrical statement with their bright colors and impressive patterns onstage. However, the area of haptic feedback in performance is growing as a way of working with dancers and other participants in different artworks.

Finally, there have been some performance works exploring the notion of *harvesting energy* from the body. In these works, different techniques are used to capture the energy produced by performers and convert this into a power source. In these performances, the energy that is being harvested is often used to charge batteries, which then power the sound or light of the performance piece itself.

These three categories start to describe the technology that is often used in costumes and performance. How they are used becomes individualized to artists and often even individual artworks. By exploring artists and artworks more, how wearables can be embedded into costumes may become clearer.

Sensing Performers

In 1989, Mark Coniglio and Dawn Stoppiello (also known as Troika Ranch) started working with their initial sensor system at CalArts University. They created the Midi Dancer system as a way for dancers to control media in real time in dance and theatre performance. Midi Dancer focused on flex sensors on the joints of the body, including the wrists, knees, and elbows. It translated the amount of bend in these joints and wirelessly transmitted these as a MIDI (music protocol) signal. The amount of bend could then be translated into the dancer controlling sound, video, or other aspects of the performance. This was demonstrated in the 1994 piece, *In Plane*, where the sound, video projections, and a robotic set piece were all controlled by the performer's movement of her joints.

Because Midi Dancer was designed to be used in various works (and the company dedicated ten years to working with various versions of this system), it was less of a costume and more of a collection of wearables that could be worn under costumes. There was a clear aesthetic decision to make the device subtle, rather than a unique costume itself. The flex sensors were embedded in skin-tone cuffs made of stretch fabrics that slide over the elbows, knees, and wrists. These were then hard-wired to a belt, which sent the sensor data wirelessly to a computer. Although there are now many options for wireless communication, this early sensor system was built before many of these protocols become available or became reliable for performance.

More recently, the musician Imogen Heap has developed a wearable sensor system based on gloves for her live performances. The gloves have several sophisticated ways of sensing and are constructed using a variety of electronics and soft-circuit techniques. These includes flexion sensors in the fingers, accelerometers and gyroscopes in the wrists, as well as conductive fabric between fingers that detect how far each finger is from the next. The gloves themselves have had clear iterations, with the most recent versions using softer circuitry and conductive materials such as threads and fabrics to give them a lighter and more sophisticated appearance. The color has been considered as well in the most recent version, which has much more sense of being a costume beyond the practical functions of playing music.

In performance, Heap sings, samples her voice, adds effects, and plays prerecorded tracks and samples, all by gesturing with her hands and fingers. Her use of this technology to play her music live has also influenced her song writing. Her latest song (written exclusively to be performed with the gloves) is entitled "Me and the Machine."

Biophysical sensing, or sensing the different signals of the body, is another category of sensors often found in performance. This may include such sensors such as heartbeat monitors or respiratory-rate sensors. Biosensors can be of varying grades and used in various other fields including medicine and sports. However, there are ways of making DIY biosensors as well, such as using infrared LEDs to detect the pulse or crocheted breath sensors to detect the expansion of the rib cage. An example of this in performance is the work of Kate Sicchio and her DIY breath sensor used in a solo dance piece in 2013, as shown in Figure 15-2.

Figure 15-2. *A DIY crocheted breath (stretch) sensor by Kate Sicchio*

A combination of pink cotton yarn and conductive yarn are crocheted together to form a band that is worn in performance around the dancer's rib cage. This specific sensor is attached to an Arduino LilyPad as a microcontroller and a Bluetooth module to allow for wireless communication. The sensor captures the increase and decrease in size of the rib cage when the dancer breathes. It is not by any means a medical measurement of breath, but the change is great enough that it is recognizable and can be used to trigger and change other aspects of the performance. In this piece, it is used to change sound in the dance and influence the accompanying electronic music composition live. As a costume, this is an interesting piece because it looks like a cross between something your grandmother would make and a hacker would program. It contains a mixture of electronics, circuit boards, and bright pink yarn. It is also small enough that it can be worn over dance clothing or even under another costume piece to hide it. However, the choice to display the piece was very deliberate, because it allowed the audience insight into how the dancer was affecting the music in the performance.

Actuation, Haptics, and Performance

Another way of working with wearables in costumes is using the technology as an output device. This may include lighting up performers with LEDs or providing haptic feedback through small motors. In some ways, actuation is the opposite of sensing technology, because it is providing something on the body or costume that is controlled or programmed externally from the performer yet complements or affects the performance.

LEDs and El wire have become a way to create a dramatic impact on the stage, particularly in dance performance. Figure 15-3 shows a pair of sneakers enhanced with strips of LEDs. Shows such as *Artist of Light* by iLuminate (as seen on *America's Got Talent*, 2011) focus on lighting up unique patterns made on costumes with highly precise timing to create illusions and visual effects that help convey narratives as well as highlight the movement of the dancers. This works for a large visual impact and a theatrical effect for the audience that is very different from performances that aim to give control to performers through sensors as described previously.

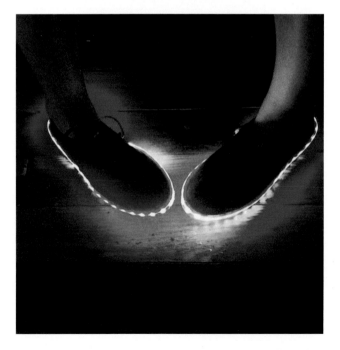

Figure 15-3. *LED sneakers for hip-hop dance performance (made by Kate Sicchio)*

Since 2013, Kate Sicchio and Camille Baker have been working with dancers and haptic feedback in costumes to convey choreographic instructions in their projects under the umbrella name of *Hacking the Body*. They have designed wearables using soft circuits and crafting techniques, as well as collaborated with interactive designers such as Becky Stewart and fashion designers such as Tara Boath Mooney. In performances, dancers respond to sensations on their bodies ranging from vibrations from vibe boards (similar to vibrations found in mobile phones) to custom-made devices. These actuators are sometimes triggered by Sicchio in live-coded performances. Other times, sensors on the dancers activate them.

The newest work to première in 2016 for *Hacking the Body* is titled "Flutter/Stutter" and includes custom-made fabric capacitance sensors and custom haptic actuations. A still from the research and development phase can be seen in Figure 15-4. These haptics are created using servomotors that tickle dancers with small strips of fabric on the back of each dancer's neck. They are sewn into a shoulder piece worn by the dancers. There are also small vibe board motors embedded in another costume piece that is worn around the dancer's waist. When wearing these brightly colored costumes, dancers respond to different sensations and feelings on their bodies that are created through the haptic feedback, and create an improvised dance. For example, the feeling of the tickle on their neck may cause the dancer to move their shoulders or use sudden or light quality in their movement. With a strong buzzing on their hip, they may move more dynamically and travel across the space, leading with that hip. The haptic devices in the costumes on the body become triggers for the movement in the performance.

Figure 15-4. *Dancer Phoebe Brown performing with the custom haptic system in Hacking the Body's "Flutter/Stutter"*

Energy Harvesting

In Prue Lang's ongoing collaboration with Amanda Parkes, titled *Un Réseau Translucide,* they explore how to make a completely energy-efficient dance piece and only use energy created during the performance to power the lights and music. Or, as they say, they are "developing a choreographic system in which the performers also generate the electricity." One of the systems in this work is the use of energy-harvesting shoes that collect energy through the use of piezoelectric materials. When performing with the shoes, one hour of dancing equals one minute of lights. Although energy harvesting is still not at a point where it is commercially viable, it is exciting to see this technology used in costumes and finding a purpose in a conceptual choreographic performance.

Technology vs. Performance

In many performance pieces that use wearables, a common question arises: are the performers still making art, or are they simply demonstrating a cool new technology? In many of these works, the technology as well as the piece are both experimental in nature, and this is a grey area. However, when thinking about the overall concept and how wearables can be uses as a tool (rather than the centerpiece of the show), the gimmick of the wearable tends to fade away, and the wearable provides a much richer artistic experience for the audience. Many of the examples discussed in this chapter use the technology to serve the performance, rather than make a performance around a new wearable. This is key in considering how to start using wearables in costumes and interactive performance.

How to Design Wearable Sensors for Performance

When working with sensors in performance, it is good to think about these guidelines: choosing a sensor, designing for the body, what the sensor will control, and devising and choreographing for the sensor. These may not necessarily happen in this order all the time. You may realize through devising the performance that the sensor needs to be located on a different part of the body. But by working through these concepts, you will find various ways to put sensors into performance works.

1. Choose a Sensor

Think about what are you sensing. Is it a biosensor that is tracking a biological signal of a performer, such as their heart rate? Or are you trying to capture movement and need an accelerometer or gyroscope? Many types of sensors are available, so work with one that is going to capture the information you want from your performers.

2. Design for the Body

Depending on what you are sensing, the location of the sensor on the performer's body or embedded in the costume may become critical. For example, most biological sensors have specific locations on the body where they work best, and some must be touching the skin of the person being sensed. Other sensors react differently and have different ranges of data depending where they are placed on the body. A flex sensor may only get a small range of changing numbers on the spine, but senses a wider amount of movement on the elbow because of the differences in the biomechanics of these body parts.

3. Decide What the Sensor Will Control

Once you know what sensor you are using and how it will be placed on the body, think about what this sensor is controlling in the performance. Is it manipulating sound? It is changing a video projection? Do the lights activate with the sensor? To connect your sensor to these other media, you may need to consider specialized software such as Isadora, MaxMSP, or Processing.

4. Devising and Choreographing the Sensor

Another important consideration is the actions of the performer. Do not take this for granted! If you are making a meaningful performance and not a demonstration of technology, the movement and intentions behind the work must be considered. Making a performer run aimlessly just to generate accelerometer data is not going to be a poetic or interesting performance for an audience. Consider this when working with sensor systems so that the performance is just as involved in the technical process as the making or sensors or the media it controls.

5. Repeating Is Necessary

Iteration in the process of using sensing systems in performance is a necessity. Be prepared to make changes and several prototypes before the overall performance is finalized. Do not bring a system to a performer and expect them to create magic with it without discussion and the possibility of making significant changes. You are not just making a costume—you are creating the opportunity for new performance systems to emerge.

Summary

This chapter explored how wearable technology may be used in costumes and performing arts. It gave an overview of sensing systems, actuating systems, and energy-harvesting systems and some of the different approaches and uses in performance for these technologies, as well as artistic considerations when using wearable devices. You saw various examples of artists and customs that use technology in new ways and tips to approaching this work yourself when designing wearable technology for stage performance.

CHAPTER 16

■ ■ ■

Speculations on Wearable Futures

From health trackers to digital makeup, this section of the book has explored many different practices that are embracing wearables in creative ways. There are certainly others that I have not touched on, but hopefully this has been a diverse and informative sampling of how different schools of thought are adapting to the rise of wearable technology. Reflecting on all this, you are now in a position to speculate about how these new devices will mesh with social structures and culture. What will it take for this technology to become as ubiquitous and seemingly necessary as the World Wide Web? Today it is hard to imagine a world without the Internet, even though the Internet did not really extend globally until recently, and there are still parts of the world where life goes on completely off the grid. Will the same attitudes one day apply to clothing? Will vintage clothes and accessories no long seem attractive and unique, but rather antiquated and inferior?

This last chapter features some truly futuristic fashion and speculates about how humans' relationship to wearables will change over time. These changes will not only occur in a personal level; the entire infrastructure around making, selling, and buying clothes will be affected. Let's look at some possible and probable trends in the near future and speculate about how this will trickle into other areas of the wearable world.

Fashion Pioneers

This section highlights two fashion designers who have been at the cutting-edge of new design and innovation for years. A look at their recent collections may help forecast the trends of the future.

Hussein Chalayan

The Turkish-Cypriot designer Hussein Chalayan has been at the forefront of reinventing fashion for decades. Chalayan's work borders between fashion, theater, and art, and his runway shows are always designed as theatrical performances involving these elements. The dissolving dresses mentioned in Chapter 14 are just one example of his incredible, astute perspective. Chalayan credits his perceptiveness to his general boredom with the world around him; he works to create objects that make the world more interesting. As he explains, "The way I see it, everything in fashion has been done over and over again ... the only way you can do something new is by using technology."

Chalayan uses technology and new materials in much of his work. His pieces and shows are planned and executed so carefully that the audience is able to perceive how Chalayan is creating an entire narrative with each piece; he is writing the story and creating the set and the characters.

In 2000, he presented his *Before Minus Now* collection, which featured the Remote Control dress: the first wireless device to be presented as a fully functioning fashion garment. The dress is composed of fiberglass and resin cast in a custom mold and is shown in Figure 16-1. The side and rear of the dress have mechanical flaps that open using a button on a remote control, revealing frothy pick tulle underneath.

© Sibel Deren Guler, Madeline Gannon, and Kate Sicchio 2016
S. D. Guler et al., *Crafting Wearables*, DOI 10.1007/978-1-4842-1808-2_16

During the debut show, a boy walked onto the catwalk with remote in hand and followed electronic instructions to operate the dress. Chalayan explained that he used the idea of controlling a person's clothes with a remote control to poke fun at the natural tendency to want to control life and people's unrealistic expectations of technology.

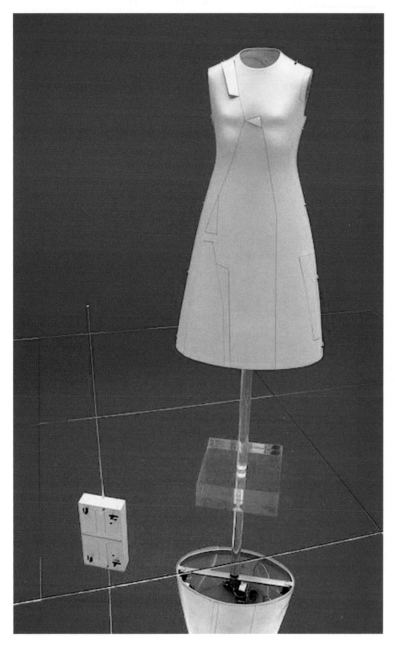

Figure 16-1. *Chalayan's Remote Control Dress (photo by Sascha Pohflepp, licensed under CC-BY-2.0)*

That same year, during his fall/winter show, Chalayan created a set of wearable wooden furniture. Four models wearing simple slips walked into a living room furnished with four chairs and a round coffee table and proceeded to remove the fabric covers from the chairs. The fabric covers transformed into four different dresses that the models put on over their slips. Then the chairs were folded into suitcases and placed next to each model, showing that she could carry her chair/dress with her. Finally, a fifth model walked onto the stage and approached the coffee table, removing a disc from the center and stepping inside the table. She then pulled the table up from the middle, transforming it into a tiered wooden skirt that she hooked onto her belt.

Other noteworthy collections by the designer include the following:

- *Transformer Dress*: In his spring/summer 2007 show, Chalayan revealed six different dresses that transformed automatically, including a skirt that suddenly flared out, a top that automatically unbuttoned, and a dress that disappeared into a hat. He was experimenting with the idea of clothes reacting to their environments

- *LED dresses*: That same year, for his fall/winter collection, Chalayan created a dress in collaboration with Swarovski that featured 15,600 LEDs layered behind crystals that acted as a display for a movie that played on the dress. Since then, he has produced several other illuminated garments.

Chalayan's work has been exhibited at museums around the world. He has been given the title British Designer of the Year in 1999 and 2000 along with numerous other awards throughout his career. He has worked with several high-profile brands during his career. He currently leads his own brand, *Chalayan* (since 1993), which recently opened its first retail store in London, and is the creative director at the German Sportswear label Puma. Chalayan has a powerful and exceptional ability to share and illustrate stories through couture.

Iris van Herpen

Iris van Herpen is a Dutch fashion designer who started her own label in 2007 after graduating with a degree in fashion design from ArtEZ Institute of the Arts, Arnhem. She regularly collaborates with famous artists, musicians, architects, and choreographers. From the beginning of her career, van Herpen has approached her pieces as sculptures, always experimenting with new forms and materials. She is credited for being the first designer to introduce 3D printing to fashion with her 2010 collection. Her collections are often inspired by patterns and processes in nature, such as crystallization or magnetic force. Her latest collection was themed around *terraforming*, which means modifying the biosphere of another planet to resemble Earth. The designer actually "terraformed" her materials, inventing new fabrication techniques in the process. For example, by combining stainless steel and silk into the same weave, she created a fluid new material.

Her 2013 collection *Voltage* opened with a model dressed in a metallic bodysuit swaying atop a Tesla coil as sparks of electricity spewed from her hands and head. The star garments of the show, however, were a skirt and cape 3D-printed on an Objet Connex, which can combine several materials in each print. The piece was created in collaboration with architect Neri Oxman, discussed later in this chapter, and 3D-printing company Stratasys. The garment is lined with thousands of tiny white anemone-like modules; some parts are soft and flexible, whereas other sections act as a kind of structural skeleton. As van Herpen explains, "The ability to vary softness and elasticity inspired us to design a 'second skin' for the body acting as armor-in-motion … we were able to design not only the garment's form but also its motion."

For her spring/summer 2016 (SS16) show, van Herpen created a dress that was woven live on actress Gwendoline Christie, of *Game of Thrones*! Christie lay motionless on a round concrete surface as three robot arms disguised as magnetically "grown" sculptures created by Dutch creative Jolan van der Wiel wove, 3D-printed, and laser-cut a dress onto her body. As the robots were working to complete the garment, models wearing van Herpen's SS16 collection entered the stage, donning futuristic garments composed of mesh, leather, and metallic pieces embedded with Swarovski crystals. If nothing else, the performance definitely felt other-worldly.

Figure 16-2. *3D-Printed Dress from van Herpen's 2012/13 "Hybrid Holism" collection*

Van Herpen says that her work is an expression of herself at the time of its creation. In a sense, she ia making the point that fashion is, in the end, an art; she uses her couture collections to create more experimental work. She employs her curiosities about nature, beauty, and regeneration in each piece, continuously pushing the boundaries of how clothing relates to function and movement of the human body. Her speculative and futuristic creations will definitely continue to keep us at the edge of our seats.

Future Fabric and Fabrication

This book has discussed new types of fabric that are embedded with conductive materials and electronics, but this is not the only focus of textile researchers. Chapter 9 presented digital fabrication machines that are being used in the production of textiles and apparel. Currently, designers and researchers experimenting with these techniques are limited to materials that are readily available. These materials, however, may not yield the best results; different material compositions may prove to be more efficient for these processes. This section examines some new forms of fabric for wearables.

Spray-On Clothes

A modern trend in fashion is skin-tight clothing. From skinny jeans to leggings, it seems as though clothing is getting tighter and tighter around the skin. London-based company Fabrican has invented a way to make clothing fit even closer to the skin: it patented an instant, non-woven, spray-on fabric. Yes, you read correctly: it is literally a can, similar to that used for whipped cream, silly string, or insulation, containing liquefied fibers that bond when sprayed (see Figure 16-3). As the spray dries, the solvent evaporates, and the result is a thin fabric layer that can be removed, washed, and reworn. These clothes are literally like a second skin for the wearer. The advantages of Fabrican over traditional fabrics include the following:

- It is a faster method for constructing garments.

- Garments can be easily repaired.

- Clothes can be sketch in 3D.

- Garments can be crafted without seams.

Figure 16-3. *Spray-on dress by Dr. Manel Torres, fabricanltd.com (photographer: Gene Kiegel)*

Fabrican has many applications other than fashion. The company has been adapting the material to be used for various purposes:

- *Medical applications:* Creating casts and bandages, and facilitating transdermal drug delivery

- *Hygienic tools:* Instant cloth and wipes

- *Spill management:* Maintaining spill positions, creating barriers, and containing spills

- *Automotive applications:* Car interior and electrical wire coverings, and so on

- *Design tools:* Prototyping and enabling consumers to easily customize objects at home

Catalytic Clothing

Catalytic Clothing is a collaboration between artist and designer Helen Storey and chemist Tony Ryan, to create clothing that filters the air around the wearer. The team has invented a way to attach *photocatalysts* to the surface of clothes by mixing them in as an additive to products like fabric conditioners. The active catalyst agent is held in a shell that binds to the surface of the clothing when it is released in the washing cycle.

A *catalyst* is a substance that increases the rate of a reaction without being consumed in the process. Photocatalysts can break down airborne pollutants by harnessing power from light. When light shines on the surface of the treated clothing, the electrons in the material are rearranged and become more reactive. They then react with the water in the air to break the molecules into two separate molecules called *radicals*. Radicals are extremely reactive molecules that cause pollutants to break down into harmless chemicals.

The main sources of air pollution are motor vehicles and factory waste. Many cities, like Beijing, suffer from extreme levels of air pollution, making it impossible for citizens to live in healthy conditions. The Catalytic Clothing technology is said to instantly break down pollutants that come in close proximity of the photocatalytic surface. The clothing cannot actively attract pollutants, and some may become attached to the surface without being broken down; in this case, they are cleaned off when the clothes are washed, as already occurs with normal clothing.

BioCouture

BioCouture is a London-based design consultancy led by fashion designer, TED fellow, and NASA/Nike material Innovator Suzanne Lee. Lee and her team are pioneering the use of biomaterials for creating new textiles for fashion, sportswear, and other industries. Instead of using weaving or other traditional textile-manufacturing processes, BioCouture fabrics are grown in a lab. The process is actually fairly simple: green tea, sugar, and microbes are combined to form a static culture. The microorganisms in the mixture eat the sugar from the tea as it ferments and spin tiny fibers made of pure cellulose in the process. After a week or so, these fibers stick together and form a mat on the surface that is about an inch thick. The sheet is then dried and can be cut or shaped and molded into clothes, shoes, and other wearables. The biomaterial and resulting wearables from this process are shown in Figure 16-4.

Figure 16-4. *BioCouture "grow your own leather" process and resulting jacket (©biocouture.co.uk)*

An obvious advantage of this process is that it is environmentally friendly and yields zero waste or toxins. Additionally, the materials are compostable! Not only are these materials biodegradable, but they can be mixed with vegetable peelings and other materials to compost back into the earth.

Lee predicts that in the future, clothing could be composed of living organisms that work symbiotically with the wearer to nourish the body or monitor for signs of disease. As she explains in an interview with *Dezeen*, "I can imagine that we will eventually move towards the material itself being living while it's on you, and having a direct relationship to your whole body in this happy micro-biome environment." In 2014, Lee launched the Biofabricate platform and annual conference to bring together scientists, designers, and researchers in effort to foster new collaboration and innovation for a sustainable future.

For more information about BioCouture and a recipe to grow your own fabric, visit `www.biocouture.co.uk`. And for more information about Biofabricate, visit `www.biofabricate.co`.

Mediated Matter

Neri Oxman, mentioned earlier for her collaboration with Iris van Herpen, is an architect, designer, and associate professor of media arts and sciences at the MIT Media Lab, where she founded and directs the Mediated Matter design research group. Mediated Matter works at the intersection of computational design, digital fabrication, materials science, and synthetic biology to enhance the relationship between built and natural environments. Although their work is applied to architecture, construction, and digital fabrication, several projects also fit within the realm of wearables.

To demonstrate the speculative and innovative quality of their work, let's look at their recent project entitled *Wanderers: An Astrobiological Exploration*. In this work, they created four 3D-printed wearables in collaboration with Stratasys that are designed to facilitate synthetic biological processes that could allow humans to survive on other planets. The garments are composed of capillaries infused with synthetically engineered microorganisms that help to create a habitable environment. The first piece is designed to interact with the atmosphere on Jupiter and is proposed to consume and digest biomass, absorb nutrients, generate energy from sucrose accumulating in the side pockets, and expel waste. The second, Zuhal, can adapt to the vortex storms on Saturn. Bacteria contained on the bodice's swirling textured surface would convert the planet's hydrocarbons into edible matter. The third, Otaared, is for survival on Mercury and provides a protective exoskeleton around the head that can be custom-fit to the wearer. The fourth, Al-Qamar, is a "wearable biodome" that is worn around the neck and over the shoulders. The exterior of the piece is composed of pods for algae-based air purification and biofuel collection that can produce and store oxygen.

Oxman and her group continue to develop new and exciting tools and environments that blend materials and technology. Although they are not always presented as alternatives to fabric, it is important to consider the integration of these new materials in manufacturing or fabrication processes for fashion and design.

Future Retail

This chapter has looked at the future of materials and fashion trends, but what will the retail experience be like for future fashion? If clothing indeed becomes more durable and long lived, as predicted, the desire for thousands of different styles each season may be significantly diminished. Consumers may only be interested in styles that are transformable between seasons. The color of the fabric may not matter if it can be programmed to change whenever the wearer wants. Fabric and fit as we know it may become a thing of the past. This is likely a future very far from now, because fashion and style are so embedded into our lives.

People have always preferred the convenience of having goods delivered rather than going out to fetch them. This has historically been a symbol of wealth and status, and it is the motivation for several app-based services that allow you to place orders through your phone or computer and have them delivered, sometimes the same day. This model is being launched and tested primarily in large cities like New York and San Francisco. Wearables have one advantage over other goods like food and office supplies: they offer a more intimate user experience. Although you may not think twice about ordering a bottle of shampoo online, you may not feel the same way about a new pair of shoes. You cannot be sure if you want them until you physically try them on, walk around a bit, and see how your feet react. Even if someone else leaves a rave review, when it comes down to it, no two feet are identical, and these experiences cannot be compared. Of course, you could always ship the shoes back if you don't like them and order another pair; but does this provide more convenience than going to a shoe store and having the ability to try on several different models in an hour?

Consumer preference, however, is not the only factor in this equation. There are also expense calculations to be analyzed. Eyewear brand Warby Parker offers the option of having five different styles of glasses sent to the customer's home at no charge, with the agreement that they will be returned after a week. This is, in a sense, a compromise; it blends the convenience of online ordering with options and time so customers feels as though they are getting an equal if not better experience than shopping in a physical store. This enables the brand to provide the same shopping experience to customers all over the world. Additionally, the company it saves on expenses because it no longer has to budget for rent, utilities, employee salaries, and other costs of operating a physical storefront.

Lifestyles and Experiences

Another solution to keeping up with the demands of future consumers is to reimagine the concept of a store. Retailers are experimenting with different approaches to the design and aesthetic of their spaces. Some are branching out to offer a lounge or coffee shop in the store, so that customers get a sense that they are not just buying a shirt or a watch, they are joining a culture. Brands have always promoted their own culture and lifestyle, but emphasizing this in physical stores is an increasingly popular experiment. The Samsung pop-up in New York City in the winter of 2014 contained an Illy coffee bar where customers could enjoy a free espresso, a photo booth, and a busy schedule of in-store events.

The pop-up store is one strategy to changing the retail experience. Instead of being tied to one location, stores can pop in and out of cities and provide the full experience to more potential customers, if only temporarily. Additionally, this idea that stores can migrate and adapt to new cultures may be more relatable to a generation of jetsetters who are constantly moving around for work. It may feel reassuring that their favorite brand is popping in and out of cities and countries too, sharing the global lifestyle experience.

A more extreme version of the pop-up store is the vending machine store, shown in Figure 16-5. Several brands have started to place vending machines full of their products in locations where they know customers are inclined to make impulse purchases. For example, flip-flop brand Havaianas placed vending machines filled with flip-slops at the beach, where people may decide to buy a new pair that they can use right way. Clothing brand Gap placed a vending machine full of collared shirts in an airport terminal for professionals who may have forgotten to pack a crisp, clean shirt for an important business meeting. This is another low-commitment experiment, in terms of the cost of maintaining the vending machine, that allows the brand to target customers in hyper-specific locations.

Figure 16-5. *T-shirt vending machine store (photo by Kojach, licensed under CC-BY-2.0)*

Analog to Digital

Another key aspect of new lifestyle trends is converting analog methods and objects to digital. Many everyday rituals now have a digital factor. For example, you can check the news or weather on your phone—you no longer have to flip through a physical newspaper. Checking to see whether a package has arrived can be done online by entering a tracking number—you don't have to wait until you go home and check the mailbox. How can digital elements be added to a store without doing away with physical stores completely in exchange for online storefronts?

FashionLike

Fashion retailer C&A has implemented a new marketing strategy in Brazil called FashionLike. The project involves a set of clothing hangers with a small screen embedded on the top of the hanger. The clothing collection is posted on Facebook when it is released in the store, for fans to vote on or "like" each article of clothing. The number of likes each item receives is displayed on the LED screen on the item's hanger. The idea is that shoppers can consider the popularity of each item as they browse the store's aisles. The result of this digitized hanger system showed that the store was able to engage 1,000 new fans per hour via Facebook, resulting in a collection being completely sold out in a day. The overall impact of the campaign was nearly 9 million people.

Virtual Dressing Rooms

The concept of a dressing room, or fitting room, has remained fairly consistent: a small room or closet where you can try on clothes in a store before deciding whether you want to purchase the items. Some dressing rooms are more comfortable than others, offering seating or refreshments, but beyond the furnishings there is not much variance. A virtual dressing room would introduce some real changes to the scene. Although there are different ideas for how a digital dressing room would be implemented, the basic system works like this: the customer enters a booth that is a mix between a photo booth and a dressing room and stands before a large screen. Cameras (usually Kinect depth sensors) in the room scan the customer's body and create a virtual model of the person that is displayed on the screen. The customer then selects the clothes they want to "try on" from a digital catalog on the side of the screen, or on a device such as an iPad. The clothes are then mapped onto the customer on the onscreen display, much like a virtual mirror.

Japanese fashion brand Urban Research began testing virtual dressing rooms in its stores in 2014. The image on the screen is said to respond to the user's movements in real time through "3D real-time fitting" technology. The company even says the system will be able to provide the virtual experience of feeling the texture of the clothes through "cloth simulation."

Interactive Retail Displays

Several stores and businesses are experimenting with digital in-store experiences. From window displays to interactive shelving and tables, various projection-mapping installations are providing entertainment and appeal. The experience of shopping online is very different than shopping in a store. For one thing, there is no tactile interaction with the object, so unless the consumer has previously seen the product, they are making the purchase based on an image. To make up for this loss, online stores provide more in-depth information about the product. Often the page includes a fit guide, customer reviews, and an anecdote about the product; this information works to provide confidence for the consumer. In a physical store, this information is sometimes written on the clothing tag, but shoppers are unlikely to carefully read the tags and labels in the store. However, researchers have found this information is present alongside the product on an iPad or other interactive device, it is more inviting and approachable.

Design studio Perch Interactive has created a customizable retail shelf and table that provide an interactive experience for shopping and projects information about the product on the surface that changes depending on user input. This makes the shopping experience feel more personal, halfway between browsing products at a store and being in a museum. The consumer gets the best of both worlds: the tactile experience of physically touching the garment, and the digital experience of consuming background information before making the decision to buy.

Culture and Society

These new trends and materials will ultimately lead to changes in the culture and societal norms around apparel. As you saw from the review of the history of wearables in Chapter 1, new technologies do not become widespread until they become affordable. Before this, they are viewed as rare luxury items for a select group of (often wealthy) people and do not have much influence power over society as a whole. Wearable technology is already following this pattern. Although it may be adopted in certain fields, such as medicine and sports, where the potential gains outweigh the expenses, it will not find its place in everyday fashion until it is less expensive.

The cost of bringing these goods to market, as you saw in previous chapters, is related to many factors such as materials, supply chain, and manufacturing processes. It will be difficult for all these factors to align without the support of large companies that can afford to experiment and take risks until the system is established. This is why the early adopters of this technology include big brands and companies like Intel, Google, and Levi's.

Costs and Benefits

The cost of a pair of Levi's jeans currently runs around $80; Levi's customer base therefore is composed of people who can afford and expect their pants to be in this price range. It is unlikely that the brand would release a pair of technologically enhanced jeans until it can price them in this range. Levi's is not looking to exclude its current consumers and shift toward a more exclusive market; doing so would hurt the brand and result in many unhappy people who would take their business elsewhere. Additionally, if Levi's were to release a short run of electronic jeans, it might face the same fate as other products that were released "at the wrong time," such as Google Glass. Similar to people with an NFC chip implant, users would quickly realize that although there were many things their pants were capable of doing, the infrastructure for this tool was not quite in place.

Brands that are likely to unlock the secret formula for weaving electronics into clothes are already investing funds and energy in ongoing research projects. This secret formula may take the form of a new weaving or sewing machine that can incorporate LEDs, conductive threads, and other materials into the fabric. Using high-tech camera vision like SoftWear automation's ThreadVision (discussed in Chapter 9), these machines could be repurposed to work with electronics. Machines like the MarkForged 3D printer that can print strong materials are also an exciting part of this solution. As apparel engineer Yolita Nugent (designer of the No Contact Jacket from Chapter 14) explains, "Imagine that they can print on textiles and then reinforce those textiles with Kevlar or space age materials such as polyimide aerogel. Then combine this technique with Voxel8's first 3-D printer for electronics. It's all very exciting."

Privacy Concerns

Susan McGregor's data jewelry from Chapter 14 demonstrated how wearables can be used to help facilitate data privacy, but other types of wearable technology pose a threat to privacy. Although wearable health trackers and monitors are constantly logging data about the wearer's biometrics, vitals, and possibly even location, this information is still kept confidential. What would happen if doctors and insurance companies had access to this information? One possibility is that insurance companies may subsidize these health trackers for patients who have chronic conditions. Or perhaps they would prefer that clothing be embedded with this technology. This may mean insurance companies would be dealing directly with fashion designers to negotiate prices and styles for these garments.

Another, more dystopian, possibility is that this information could be used to calculate the cost of human lives. Your health, bank, and social information could all be analyzed to predict your every move. Everyone with a social media profile is already voluntarily contributing part of this information. Most of the other channels are also online and could easily be uploaded to the same program that analyzes every digital representation of a person's life.

Social Robotics

You've seen the potential market and manufacturing impacts of wearable technology, but I haven't discussed the cultural and psychological impacts. As clothing and environments become smarter, how will people change? When you board a subway car in any big city, you'll probably notice that more than half of the commuters are glued to their smart devices, watching movies, playing games, and reading email. This results in a loss of connection with the physical environment; people are literally engulfed by a digital world, tuning out of much of the world around them. This image may make it seem as though digital technology is imposing an introverted nature on society, but this is hardly the case. On the contrary, people are more social and connected than ever before, at least in digital life, if not in real life.

As the work presented in Chapter 14 shows, technology can also be used to promote emotional expression and help users interact with their environments. One field that is particularly interested in this relationship is *social robotics*. Social robotics concentrates on the development and design of robots that are social: that is, robots that interact with humans, as other humans would. An example of how this fits in with wearables can be seen Adam Whiton's *Zipperbot*. The Zipperbot is a tiny robot that attaches to clothing and zips and unzips a zipper. It can be seen unzipping a skirt in Figure 16-6. The Zipperbot may fill the place of a friend who could help you with a zipper when your hands are full or, better yet, help you release a zipper that is stuck in place!

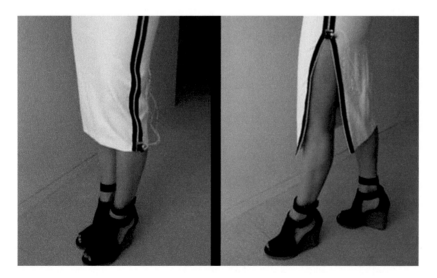

Figure 16-6. *Zipperbot adjusting slits in the side of a skirt (photo by Adam Whiton)*

On the other hand, people may have conflicts with their robotic clothing. It is already common to see people get frustrated with their smartphones and blame them for typos or mis-scheduling an appointment. Although the technology may not have functioned as it was supposed to and could be at fault, in the end the only one to blame for these mistakes is the user who trusted and relied on the technology. Introducing robotic clothing may release a whole new culture of technical difficulties. What if you programmed your shirt to glow red, and halfway through the day it turned green due to a software error and clashed with the rest of your outfit? Naturally, you would be upset with the shirt; but such disappointment is definitely a sign of intimacy and acceptance. To logically be upset with the shirt, you must admit that you put the shirt in the place of a social object that has the power to make you happy or upset. Hopefully the future does not lend itself to a time when people are walking around and complaining to their clothes—that would definitely be very strange.

Summary

This chapter has offered a sneak peek into the near future of the fashion and textiles world. What will come after these more predictable eventual changes is more difficult to imagine. As you have seen, these industries are linked and are becoming more connected and intertwined with each new technological development. A world where electronic textiles and clothes are as ordinary as cellphones is a world where fitness monitors are not an optional accessory but are woven into the fabric of wearables: a world where makeup not only shines, it lights up.

In the beginning of this book, I defined *wearables* as anything that is intended to be worn, although I made the distinction that the term has become widely adopted to mean "wearable technology." Perhaps at this point you also feel that *wearables* is not the best term for describing these creations. Some of these technologies are not intended to be worn on the body so much as applied or implanted. A more appropriate term for this field that is being adopted by designers and researchers is *body technology* or *body architecture*. *Body technology* is fairly self-explanatory and can refer to anything that combines technology with the body. Thus electronic shirts, cyborg enhancements, and new design tools for prototyping directly on the body all fit under this umbrella. *Body architecture* is in a sense a subset of body technology that refers more specifically to the manipulation of forms for the body.

You have almost reached the end—congratulations! I will leave you with one last tutorial in the appendix. Connected clothing with RFID tags visit `http://www.etologyglobal.com/`. This project was largely inspired by my research for this book, and I hope that you too will imagine new ideas and projects after reading the book.

As you travel further into the world of fashion and technology, discovering new innovations and techniques, remember to reflect on what you have seen. Fashion and technology are both interdisciplinary processes, spanning fields and toolsets. The most interesting and promising discoveries combine values and principles of fashion, design, and engineering, and work to create an exciting and accessible user experience. I encourage you to stray from the norms, try on things that you'd normally never wear, think dynamically, and design critically.

APPENDIX

■ ■ ■

Cyborg "Fingercaps" and Resources

While researching and writing this book, I came across several inspirational projects that led to many different project ideas of my own. One piece that I was especially drawn to was a set of 3D-printed fingernails developed by Studio XO (mentioned in Chapter 14) for Lexus. You can see the full video explaining the collaboration online at `https://vimeo.com/102814854`.

I had recently seen cyborg artist Neil Harbisson (mentioned in Chapter 13) give a talk about his experiences as a cyborg and the work he has done with the Cyborg Foundation. I found that I was curious about cyborg enhancements myself, but not enough to actually implant something in my body. I decided I wanted to create a way to try out different augmentations. The most common place to get this type of implant in the body seems to be the fingertip. Borrowing from the concepts of 3D-printed fingernails and Katia Vega's Beauty Tech nails (from Chapter 12), I decided to make a kit of *Cyborg Fingercaps:* a set of modular 3D-printed pieces that fit on the top of your finger and can be customized to include cyborg enhancements such as magnets, RFID tags, NFC chips, USB drives, and more. This project, shown in Figure A-1, ties together a lot of the themes and techniques explained in this book.

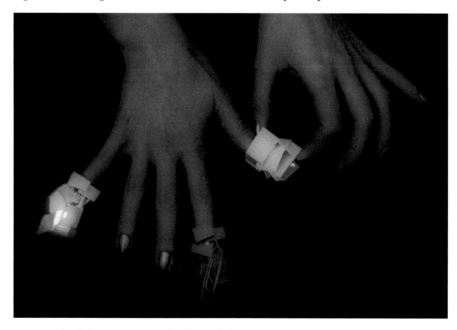

Figure A-1. *Cyborg Fingercaps by Deren Guler*

© Sibel Deren Guler, Madeline Gannon, and Kate Sicchio 2016
S. D. Guler et al., *Crafting Wearables*, DOI 10.1007/978-1-4842-1808-2

Harbisson made the important point during his talk that if we are able to turn the enhancements on and off, our brains won't accept them as an extension of our bodies. If you've ever removed a ring after wearing it for a long period of time, you've probably noticed that your finger feels a bit odd—some say their fingers feel "naked." With the fingercaps, my hope is that if worn continuously they may feel like an extension of the finger, a bit like a prosthetic.

Recipe for Cyborg Fingercaps

First I list the tools and materials I used when developing this kit. The fingercaps could be made with different methods—for example, they could be cast or carved. I chose 3D printing because it allowed for quick iterations of different designs.

You need the following materials:

- LED lights (3 mm or surface mount)
- Small coin batteries
- Rare earth magnet (14" disc or smaller)
- RFID tag
- NFC chip
- Thermochromatic paint
- Photoluminscent paint
- Tilt-ball switch
- Thin-gauge wire
- Nail polish
- Transparent filament
- Thin padding or cushion material
- Glue dots
- USB drive

You also need these tools:

- Soldering iron
- 3D printer
- Wire cutters and strippers
- 3D scanner (optional)
- Calipers
- Electrical tape

Follow these steps:

1. Measure your fingertips, around which the fingercaps will go. You can do this through traditional means by measuring them with calipers, or you can use 3D-scanning technology (described in Chapter 8).

198

2. Decide how you'd like the fingercaps to look, and model them. Figure A-2 shows three of the fingercaps I modeled. Several different modeling programs are available, many of which are detailed in Chapter 8.

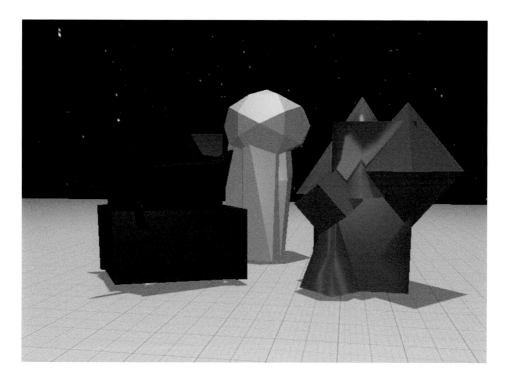

Figure A-2. *Three different fingercap models*

3. Print out the models on a 3D printer using transparent or white filament. If you do not have access to a 3D printer, you can most likely find one at your local makerspace, hackerspace, or fablab. 3D Hubs provides a database of venues with 3D printers around the world. There are also services online that let you mail-order 3D models to be printed, such as Ponoko and Shapeways. I used an Ultimaker Extended to print out my models at my local fablab; you can see a picture of the process in Figure A-3.

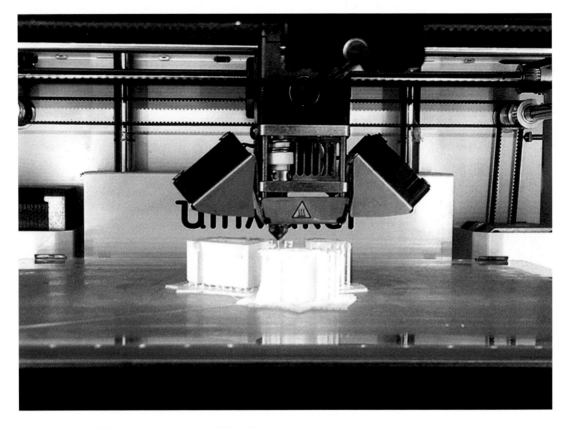

Figure A-3. *Models being printed on an Ultimaker 2*

4. Depending on the quality of your printer, there may be rough edges around the corners or your print. You can use sandpaper or a file to lightly brush off any unevenness along the surface. You want the surfaces to be smooth, especially if you are planning to paint them!

5. Build the circuits that you want to embed into the fingercaps. For the first version, I chose to build an *LED throwie*: a simple circuit composed of just an LED and a battery. To make these circuits resilient, I chose to solder them together.

6. Paint the fingercaps using your desired paints. I used a combination of nail polish, spray paint, thermochromatic (heat sensitive) and photochromatic (glow-in-the dark) paints. The thermochromatic paint serves as a temperature sensor, in that it changes color when it is over a certain threshold temperature as explained in Chapter 7. The photochromatic paint serves as a light sensor, in that it gives off a faint light or glow in the dark. You can see the parts and tools I used in Figures A-4 and A-5.

Figure A-4. *Parts and tools for building circuits and painting the fingercaps*

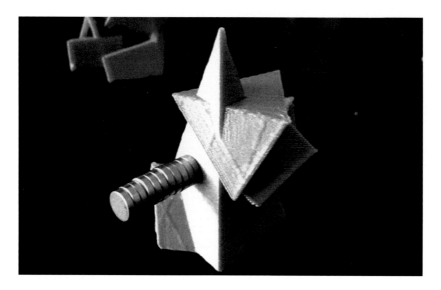

Figure A-5. *Closeup of fingercap embedded with a magnet*

7. Place the circuits into the fingercaps such that the LED lights shine through one of the sides. Other objects you wish to embed, like the magnet, you can attach with a non-permanent but strong adhesive such as glue dots. Test each fingercap to make sure the circuit or object is visible or effective from the outside.

8. Try them on! If they are uncomfortable or loose, you may want to add some thin padding or coat the inside with a thin layer of silicone. You may also choose to make some changes to the circuits based on how they feel and work when you are wearing them. For example, do you want the light to shine outward, away from your finger, or inward, toward your hand, like the thumb and index fingers in Figure A-6?

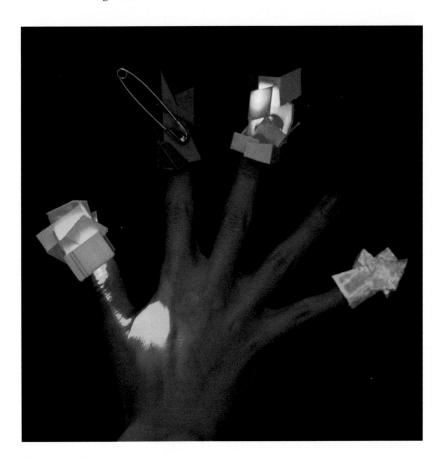

Figure A-6. *Trying on the fingercaps*

9. To notice the effects, you must wear the fingercaps continuously for a period of time—at least a few days. Depending on how comfortable they are, you will probably want to remove them at night. I chose a geometric design with a lot of sharp corners; I will try to make a version that is designed to be more comfortable in version 2.

Additional Resources

Following is a list of additional resources for topics discussed throughout the book:

Chapter 1: A Brief History of Wearables

- Steve Mann's blog: `http://eyetap.org/`

- Georgia Tech smart shirt: `www.gtwm.gatech.edu/`

- *Beat the Dealer: A Winning Strategy for the Game of Twenty-One* (Vintage Press), Edward O. Thorp's book about algorithms for card games

- History of wearable computing: `www.media.mit.edu/wearables/lizzy/timeline.html`

Chapter 2: Wearable Fictions

- Wikipedia on James Bonds gadgets: `https://en.wikipedia.org/wiki/List_of_James_Bond_gadgets`

- A list of sci-fi gadgets from books: `www.technovelgy.com/`

- Military TALOS suit: `https://en.wikipedia.org/wiki/TALOS_(uniform)`

- SixthSense Project: `https://code.google.com/p/sixthsense`

- A short essay on design fiction, by Julian Bleecker: `http://drbfw5wfjlxon.cloudfront.net/writing/DesignFiction_WebEdition.pdf`

Chapter 3: From Textiles to Wearables

- *Textile Messages: Dispatches From the World of E-Textiles and Education (New Literacies and Digital Epistemologies)* by Leah Buechly, Kylie Peppler, and Michael Eisenberg (Peter Lang Publishing Inc.)

- Project Jacquard: `www.google.com/atap/project-jacquard/`

- Intel's Smart Fashion: `http://iq.intel.com/?_topic=fashion`

Chapter 4: Cutting and Sewing

- Sewing basics: `http://howtosew.com/`

- Beginner sewing projects: `http://sewingforbeginners.info/`

- Patternmaking: `www.craftsy.com/article/guide-to-patternmaking-tools`

- PatternMaker software: `www.patternmakerusa.com/`

- Fashion design: `https://fuel4fashion.wordpress.com/2013/10/11/the-fashion-design-process/`

Chapter 5: Making Electronics Sewable

- Great intro to circuits: *Getting Started in Electronics* by Forrest Mims (Master Publishing)
- Fabrickit: `www.fabrick.it/`
- Aniomagic: `www.aniomagic.com/`
- LilyPad: `www.lilypadarduino.org`
- *Fashioning Technology: A DIY Intro to Smart Crafting* by Syuzi Pakhchyan (O'Reilly)

Chapter 6: Soft Circuits

- Kobakant, DIY soft circuits: `www.kobakant.at/DIY/`
- Adafruit wearable projects: `https://learn.adafruit.com/category/wearables`
- Teknikio project tutorials: `www.teknikio.com/learn`
- SparkFun e-textiles tutorials: `https://learn.sparkfun.com/tutorials/tags/e-textiles?page=all`
- Instructables e-textiles tutorials: `www.instructables.com/howto/e-textiles/`

Chapter 7: Materials That Matter

- Library of smart materials: `www.openmaterials.org`
- Shape-memory polymer: `https://en.wikipedia.org/wiki/Shape-memory_polymer`
- *Photochromia* project: `www.madisonmaxey.com/photochromia/`
- Harry Wainwright: `www.hleewainwright.com/`
- X-Bionic textiles: `www.x-bionic.com/`
- Gore fabrics: `www.gore.com/en_xx/products/fabrics/index.html`
- Schoeller Textiles: `www.schoeller-textiles.com/`
- Online sources for conductive materials: `www.plugandwear.com` (Europe) and `www.lessemf.com` (United States)

Chapter 8: Digital Design for Wearables

- OpenSCAD, free solid-modeling software: `www.openscad.org/`
- Blender, free 3D-modeling software: `www.blender.org/`
- Autodesk 123D Catch software: `www.123dapp.com/catch`
- Tutorial for structured light scanning: `http://fab.cba.mit.edu/content/processes/structured_light/`
- Open Fit Lab: `http://openfitlab.com/`
- Tutorial for designing 3D-printed bracelets using Processing: `https://github.com/madelinegannon/BodyArchitectures`

Chapter 9: Digital Fabrication for Wearables

- Kate Goldsworthy: www.kategoldsworthy.co.uk/

- Laser-cutting services: www.ponoko.com/

- 3D-printing services: www.shapeways.com/ and www.3dhubs.com/

- Formlabs jewelry: http://formlabs.com/applications/jewelry/

- Digital sewing machine: www.softwearautomation.com/

Chapter 10: Designing for the Body, on the Body

- Tactum: www.madlab.cc/tactum/

- "Skinput: Appropriating the Body as an Input Surface," by Chris Harrison: www.chrisharrison.net/index.php/Research/Skinput

- Sean Gustafson's project *Imaginary Interfaces*: www.seangustafson.com/Projects/ImaginaryInterfaces

- "OmniTouch: Wearable Multitouch Interaction Everywhere," by Chris Harrison: http://chrisharrison.net/index.php/Research/OmniTouch

Chapter 11: Wearable Wellness

- Jawbone fitness tracker: www.jawbone.com

- Fitbit fitness tracker: www.fitbit.com

- Garmin fitness tracker: www.garmin.com

- Hexoskin: www.hexoskin.com/

- Clothing+: www.clothingplus.com

- Owlet baby monitor: www.owletcare.com

- Lumo Lift posture sensor: www.lumobodytech.com

- Like a Glove: www.likeaglove.me/

- Enable Foundation: www.enablecommunityfoundation.org/

- Google smart contact lenses: https://googleblog.blogspot.com/2014/01/introducing-our-smart-contact-lens.html

Chapter 12: Beauty Tech

- Katia Vega, beauty technologist: http://katiavega.com/

- TheLaserGirls 3D-printed nails: www.thelasergirlsstudio.com/

- MC10 BioStamp: www.mc10inc.com/our-products/biostamprc

Chapter 13: Superhumans and Cyborgs

- Cyborg Foundation: www.facebook.com/cyborgfoundation/
- Neil Harbisson: http://cyborgproject.com/
- Kevin Warwick, Project Cyborg: www.kevinwarwick.com/
- Wafaa Bilal 3rdi: http://wafaabilal.com/thirdi/
- Stelarc: http://stelarc.org/?catID=20247
- Prosthetics: https://en.wikipedia.org/wiki/Prosthesis
- OpenBionics: www.openbionics.org/
- Brain-computer interfaces: https://en.wikipedia.org/wiki/Brain%E2%80%93computer_interface

Chapter 14: Activated Garments

- CuteCircuit: www.cutecircuit.com
- Studio XO: www.studio-xo.com
- *XOX* project from Studio XO: www.xoxemotionaltech.com/
- Chromat: www.chromat.co/
- Hövding inflatable helmet: www.hovding.com
- Social Body Lab: http://research.ocadu.ca/socialbody/home
- Ying Gao: http://yinggao.ca/eng/interactifs
- Pauline van Dongen: www.paulinevandongen.nl/
- The Unseen Emporium: www.theunseenemporium.co.uk/
- The Crated: www.experiments.thecrated.com/
- Wearable Experiments: www.wearableexperiments.com/
- Anouk Wipprecht: www.anoukwipprecht.nl/
- Vega Wang: www.vegazaishiwang.com/

Chapter 15: Wearable Costumes

- Troika Ranch, *Midi Dancer*: http://troikaranch.org
- Prue Lang, energy harvesting: www.pruelang.com/2011/un-reseau-translucide/
- Imogen Heap's gloves: www.imogenheap.co.uk/thegloves/
- Hacking the Body (biosensing): https://hackingthebody.wordpress.com
- iLuminate LEDs and El wire: www.facebook.com/iLuminatedance

Chapter 16: Speculations on Wearable Futures

- Wearable technology news: www.wareable.com/

- *Wearable Technologies* magazine and conference: https://www.wearable-technologies.com/

- Fashioning Tech blog: http://fashioningtech.com/

- Biofabricate: www.biofabricate.co/

- Fabrican: www.fabricanltd.com/

- Iris van Herpen: www.irisvanherpen.com/

- Hussein Chalayan: www.chalayan.com

Index

A

Adrenaline dress, 168
Aniomagic, 56
Apple Watch, 18
Arduino Flora, 55
Artificial hair, 134
Arts and wearables
    batteries, 6
    Body Covering, 7
    camera, 7
    cost, 6
    electric ballet, 6
    Electric Girl Lighting Company, 6
    electric headband, La Farandole, 6

B

Baby monitors
    babywear, 124
    Mimo, 124
    MonBaby, 124
    Owlet and smartphone, 125
    Owlet Smart Sock, 124
Bag of Tricks, 17
    Bond's mission, 18
    camera, 19
    Digital Angel chip, 18
    Evena Eyes-On glasses, 18
    polarizing glasses, 18
    radio transmitter, 18
    smart watches, 18
Beauty technology
    and dermatology (*see* Dermatology and
        technology)
    electronics and digital devices, 133, 143
    fashion, 133
    hairware, 133
    human-computer interaction (HCI), 133
    living makeup, 137
    makeup, 134–136
    medicine, 133
    nails, 136–137
    Omote mask, 138
    research, 143
    tattoos (*see* Tattoos)
    technologist, 133
    wearables, 133
BioCouture, 188–189
Biomimetics, 12
Bionic engineering, 12
Biophysical sensing, 177
Bracing, 125–126
Brain-computer interface (BCI), 154

C

Cannabis plant, 23
Catalytic clothing, 187
Chromat, 167–169
Chromatic materials
    hypercolor fabric changing color, 79
    interactions, 78
    photochromatic, 79–80
    thermochromatic, 79
Circuits
    basic light circuit, 47
    components, 47
    conductors and insulators, 46
    current, 46
    definition, 45
    designing and troubleshooting, 48
    light circuit, 50–53
    polarity, LED, 48
    power sources
        batteries, 49
        datasheet, 49
        factors, choosing power source, 49
        LED, 49
        types of batteries, 49
    resistance, 46
    series *vs.* parallel, 50

© Sibel Deren Guler, Madeline Gannon, and Kate Sicchio 2016
S. D. Guler et al., *Crafting Wearables*, DOI 10.1007/978-1-4842-1808-2

Circuits (*cont.*)
    short circuit, 47
    soft, 45
    source, 45
    testing, LED, 48
    voltage, 46
    wearables, 45
Costume housing biosensors, 175
Crafting circuits
    art of, 59
    collection, 59
    comprehensive and whimsical approach, 61
    electronics store, 59
    function and materials, 60
    interdisciplinary practices, 59
    Kobakant, 59
    nonconventional materials, 59
    online, 59
    raw material, 59
    sewing and electronics, 59
    textile sensor database, 60
Culture and society
    costs and benefits, 193
    new trends and materials, 193
    privacy, 193–194
    robotics, 194–195
Cyborg
    fingercaps
        building circuits and painting, 201
        circuits, 200
        3D Hubs, 199
        different modeling programs, 199
        3D printing, 198–199
        effects, 202
        embedded with magnet, 201
        Harbisson, 198
        LED lights, 202
        lighting, 202
        materials, 198
        measures, 198
        paints, 200
        planning, 200
        printer quality, 200
        and resources, 203
        tools, 198
        Ultimaker, 199–200
Cyborgs and bionics
    artists
        Moon Ribas, 147
        Neil Harbisson, 146–147
        Stelarc, 146
        Wafaa Bilal, 147
    bodyhackers, 149
    cyborgism, 145
    definition, 145

foundation, 148
    LEDs, 151
    magnetic implants, 150–151
    NFC chips, 150
    research (*see* Research, cyborgs)
Cyborg-themed products
    devices, vision development
        and correction, 152
    earwear, 153
    eyewear (*see* Eidos eyewear)
    headphones, 153
    night vision, 152
    VibeAttire, 154

■ D

Dermatology and technology
    applications, 138
    dermoPatch, Feeligreen company, 139
    dermo-therapy, 138
    MC10 BioStamp, 138
    transient electronics, 139
Digital design
    complexity, 97
    designers, 97
    handcrafted design processes, 85
    human body, 111
        depth cameras, 90–91
        3D-scanning, 88–89
        Open Fit workflow, 93
        parametric (*see* Parametric modeling)
        photogrammetry, 89–90
        software, 88
    software
        choosing model, 86
        2D design tools, 85–86
        3D design tools, 86
        3D modeling, printing, 86–88
    structured light scanning, 92–93
    Tactum (*see* Tactum)
Digital embroidery, 108
3D-printed wax ring, 106–107
3D printers, 103
4D printing, 105–106
    casting, lost-wax, 106–107
    CNC machine, 102
    design file and material
        specification, 103
    developments, 102
    flexible filaments, 103–104
    printers types, 103
    process and applications, 103
    skirt and shoes, 104
    textile structures, 104
    wearable, 103

E

Education, textiles
  engineers, 30
  higher, tech *vs.* textiles, 29
  sewing class, 28–29
Eidos eyewear
  camera, 152
  earmask, 153
  eyemask, 153
  perception, 152
Electric Girl Lighting Company, 6
Electroencephalography (EEG), 155
Electroluminescent (EL) wire, 82
Electronics in clothing
  fabric, 30
  fibers, 30
  Intel's Smart Fashion, 32
  processes and tools, 30
  Project Jacquard, 30–31
  weaving, 30
Electronics sewable
  circuits (*see* Circuits)
  custom-made kits, 54–58
  e-textiles, 45, 58
  techniques, 45
Emotional Style
  Cardinal, 165
  Chromat, 167–168
  HugShirt, 165–166
  muscle-activated wearable, 164
  social body lab, 164–165
  studio XO, 167
E-textiles
  circuits soft (*see* Soft circuits)
  electronics (*see* Electronics sewable materials;
    Smart materials)
E-textiles toolkit assembly, 66–72
Eyewear
  analog tools, 7
  camera, 8
  computer inventions, 8
  design, 7
  fiber optic LED, 7
  Private Eye wearable headset, 9
  Reflection Technology, 8
  video capability, 8

F

Fabric
  analog methods, 192
  app-based services, 189
  BioCouture, 188–189
  catalytic clothing, 188
  color of, 189
  conductive materials and electronics, 186
  consumer preference, 190
  digital, 186, 192
  lifestyles, 190
  marketing strategy, 192
  materials, 189
  mediated matter design, 189
  retail displays, 192–193
  spray-on clothes, 187
  t-shirt vending machine store, 191
  virtual dressing rooms, 192
Fabrication
  application, 99
  digitized machines
    barriers, 109
    design process, 109
    embroidery, 108
    knitting, 107–108
    SoftWear Automation, 108–109
  3D printing, 102–104
  fashion designers, 99
  lasering (*see* Lasering)
  sensors and tools, 110
  techniques, 99
Fabrickit modules, 56–57
Fabtronic Sewing Set, 58
Farenheit 451, 11
Fashion design
  accessories, 25
  apparel design, 25
  application, 25
  conceptualization, 25
  designers, 25
  forecast, 25
  patterns, 26–27
  process, 25
  selection, color, fabric and trim, 26
  silhouettes, 26
  style selection and feasibility, 28
  technical sketch, 26
FashionLike, 192
Fashion pioneers
  Chalayan
    LED dresses, 185
    Remote Control Dress, 184
    technology and new materials, 183
    theatrical performances, 183
    transformer dress, 185
    Turkish-Cypriot designer, 183
  van Herpen, 185–186
Fashion safety
  haptic shoes, 162
  In&motion system, 162
  inflatable helmet, 161
  no contact jacket, 163
  USB necklace, safety, 163–164

Fitness trackers
    data, 122
    Fitbit, 122
    Jawbone, 123
    measurable, 121
    motivational tools, 121
    style, 121
    testing, 122
    Vivosmart, 122
Flax plant, 23

G

Garments
    Chromat's, 167–169
    environmentally reactive
        dissolving clothes, 170
        sparkle booties, 169
        wearable façade, 170
    interfaces
        digitizing shoes, 170–171
        illuminated clothing, 172–173
        mirror handbag, 172
        mobile dress, 172
        Nudgeables accessory kit, 171
        t-shirt OS, 171–172
Gearbox, 43
Geordi's VISOR, 16
Gestures and precise geometry
    control, 115
    3D model, 115
    intelligent geometry, 116
    intuitive and expressive, 115
    intuitive interactions, 116
    Motorola 360 smartwatch, 116
    traditional CAD program, 115
    touch and poke/pinch, 115
    user-manipulation, 116
    watch-band design, 115
Glowing materials
    EL wire, 82
    LEDs, 82
    optical fibers, 82–83

H

Hairware, 133–134
Harbisson, Neil
    awareness, cyborgism, 147
    British artist, 146
    eyeborg, 146
    treatment, color-blindness, 147
Hemp, 23
Homemade bend sensor
    assembling, 77
    conductive thread, 77–78

materials and tools, 77
neoprene/nonconductive fabric, 77–78
pressure sensor, 77
testing, 78
velostat, 77
Hook mechanism, 43

I

Intel Curie Compute Module, 32
INZECTIC, 83

J, K

Jute, 23

L

Laser
    components, 99
    computer, 99
    cutter, 99
    cutting
        fabrics, 100
        forms and patterns, 100
        leather samples, 100
        material, 100
        natural fabrics, 100
        templates and shapes, textiles, 100
    textures, 101
    welding, 101–102
Laser chakra dress, 169
Light Amplification by Stimulated
        Emission of Radiation, 99
Light circuit
    conductive thread, 51
    curling, leg of LED, 51
    lightband, 53
    light-up wristband, 51
    materials, 50
    negative loop, 53
    positive loop, 52
    sewing from positive to positive, 52
    wristband, 52
LilyPad Arduino, 54–55

M

Macrotermes, 84
Magnet implants
    awareness, 150
    interaction, objects, 151
    lifting paperclips, 150
    neodymium, 150
    power transformers and microwaves, 150
    sound-transmitting, 151

Makeup product
    Blinkifier, 135
    conductive ink, 134
    e-makeup circuit, 135
    fake eyelashes, 134
    FX e-makeup application, 135
    Kinisi model with LEDs, 135–136
    metalizing process, 134
Mann, S., 148
Manufacturing, textiles
    artists, 24
    cotton, 23
    crocheting, 25
    cultivation of fiber, 23
    economic and social implications, 25
    fabric, 23–25
    felting, 25
    fibers, 24–25
    knitting, 25
    knotting, 25
    large-scale mechanical machines, 25
    materials, 23–24
    natural/artificial fibers, 23
    tablecloth, 23
    weaving process, 24
Medical and wellness wearables
    bracing, 125–126
    challenges, 131
    clothing (*see* Smart clothing)
    concept products, 127
    fitness (*see* Fitness trackers)
    fitness trackers, 121–123
    posture (*see* Posture)
    quality of life, 121
    technologies and products, 131
Medical bionics
    BCI, 154
    noninvasive BCIs, 155–156
    open, 158
    prosthetic (*see* Prosthetics)
    restorative and enhanced, 154
    retinal implants, 155
    superhuman, 158–159
Muslins, 42

N

Nails
    Beauty Tech Nails, 137
    conductive nail polish, 136
    fake fingernails, 136
    RFID glass capsules, 136
NanoSphere, 83
Nautilus, 165
Near-field communication (NFC) microchips, 150

Nike's Power Lace shoes lacing, 15
Nitinol, 81
Noninvasive BCIs, 155–156
Nudgeables accessory kit, 171

O

Optical fibers, 82–83

P

Parametric modeling
    bracelet, 94–95
    features, tools, 97
    iterating, customizing
        and personalizing, 94
    limitation, 94
    object, 94
    personalize design, 96
Photochromatism, 79–80
Polarizing glasses, 18
Polymorphic materials, 81
Posture
    JINS MEME, 127
    Lumo Lift, 126
    Prana, 127
    products, 126
    sensor, 126
    suspenders project
        alligator clips, 130
        attachment, bend sensors, 129
        circuit, 129
        completion, 131
        curled legs, resistors, 130
        DIY bend sensors, 128
        fabric patch, 130
        materials, 128
        measurement, values, 129
        microcontroller, 129
        outputs and output patterns, 130
        sensors, 127
        sewing, 130
        threshold value, 129
    UPRIGHT posture, 127
Printed Circuit Shirt, 65–66
Prosthetics, 156–157
    artificial device, 156
    cable-operated limbs, 156
    customized racer cover, 158
    customized synthetic materials, 157
    early developments, 156
    materials and technologies, 156
    myoelectric limb, 156
    robotic, 156
Protein fibers, 24

Q

Quantum tunneling composite (QTC) materials, 83

R

Research, cyborg
    Mann, 148
    Warwick, 148–149
Retinal implants, 155
Robotic prosthetics, 157
Robotics, 194–195

S

Schoeller textiles, 83
Sci-fi prophecies
    cyberpunk, 11
    flatscreen TVs, 11
    gadgets and devices, 11
    Neuromancer, 11
Selective-laser sintering (SLS) 3D printer, 116
Sewing
    button, 39–40
    cutting fabric
        guidelines, 40
        smooth edge, 40
    hand stitches, 36
    hobby, 35
    interfacing, 36
    learning, 42
    machines, 43
    muslin, 42
    pillow making, 40–41
    projects and techniques, 36
    running stitch, 37–38
    scrap fabric, 36
    skills, 44
    starters, 36
    techniques, 36
    threading, 36–37
    toolKit, 33
    whipstitch, 36, 38–39
Shape-changing materials
    polymorph, 81
    SMA, 81
    SMP, 81
    types, 80
Shape memory alloys (SMAs), 81
Shape memory polymer (SMP)
    changes, 81
    electro-active, 81
    light-induced, 81
    plastic, 81
    returning, 80
    thermoactive, 81

Silkworms, 23
Skin centric interfaces
    3D-model, 112
    human-computer interaction, 112
    interactions, 112
    mobile computing, 112
    natural gestures, 112
    proprioceptive qualities, 112
    sensors and projectors, 112
Smart clothing
    e-textiles, 123
    glove, 124
    sensors, babies
        (see Baby monitors)
    techstyles
        Clothing⁺, 123
        fashion designers, 123
        Hexoskin's biometric shirt, 123
        iTBra, 123
Smart materials
    bend sensor, homemade, 77–78
    categories, 73
    chromatic, 78–80
    designers and engineers, 73
    e-textiles, 73
    fabrication techniques, 84
    glowing
        EL wire, 82
        optical fibers, 82–83
    piezoelectric, 73
    protective
        BIONIC Aramid, 84
        C_change, 83
        GORE, 84
        INZECTIC, 83
        macotermes, 84
        NanoSphere, 83
        Schoeller Textiles, 83
        X-Bionic, 84
        Xitanit, 84
    QTC, 83
    shape changing, 80–81
    thread
        choosing, 73
        conductive fabrics, 75–76
        conductiveness, common metals, 74
        conductive yarn, 74
        durable connection, 73
        Electrolycra, 76
        iron-on coating, 76
        ribbons and tapes, 74–75
        soft circuit, 73
        super-light mesh, 76
        tin/copper/cobalt plate, 76
        types, 73
        velostat, 77

Smart watches, 18
Social robotics, 194–195
Soft circuits
    crafting, 59–61
    designing, soft switch, 61–65
    e-textiles, 59
    fabrics and threads, 59
    materials, 59
    printed circuit shirt, 65–66
    projects, 72
    sewing skills, 72
    toolkit assembling, 66–72
Soft switch design
    assembling and closing, button, 64
    conductive fabric, 63
    construction, button, 63
    fabric enclosures, 61
    felt, 63
    foam with holes, 63
    momentary switch, 62
    nonconductive thread, 64
    push-button test circuit, 65
    sandwich, 64
    square piece of foam, 64
    square pieces of scrap fabric, 63
    testing with multimeter, 64
    textile closures, 61
    textile push-button, 63
    toggle, 61
    variations, 61
SoftWear automation's LOWRY, 109
Spray-on clothes, 187
Star Trek
    communicators, 15
    Geordi's VISOR, 16
    sci-fi TV and movie series, 15
    tricorders, 16
Stereolithography (SLA) 3D printer, 116
Stitching mechanism, 43
Structured light scanning works
    benefits and tradeoffs, 93
    3D scanning, 91–92
    DSLR cameras and LED lights, 92
    high-resolution, 92
Studio XO, 167
Superhuman bionics, 158–159
Synthetic fibers, 24

■ **T**

Tactum
    applications, 117
    computer interfaces, 111
    designer's, 117
    3D modeling back end

animated digital geometry, 114
    digital geometry, 111
    3D printing, 114
    fabrication-aware design, 114
    forearm, 114
    projected, 114
    wearable design, tactile interactions, 114
3D-modeling tool, 111
gesture-based interface, 111
gestures (*see* Gestures and precise geometry)
physical artifacts, 116–117
sensing
    detection, tactile interaction, 113
    range of natural gestures, 113
    single depth sensor, 113
    tracking, 113
    workstation, 113
skin interactions (*see* Skin centric interfaces)
Tattoos
    conductive, 140
    LEDs lights
        battery, 142
        circuit, 140
        circuit traces with conductive ink, 142
        design and sketch, 141
        glue dots, 143
        marker, 142
        materials, 140–141
        stickers, 142
        surface area, 142
        tapes, 143
        test circuit, hand, 143
Textiles
    artists, 24
    education, 28–30
    electronic devices, 23, 30–32
    exporters, 23
    fashion design (*see* Fashion design)
    industry, 23
    process manufacturing (*see* Manufacturing, textiles)
Textile companies, 32
Textiles social and economic impacts, 32
Tricorders, 16
TshirtOS, 171–172

■ **U**

U.S. army's Tactical Assault Light Operator Suit, 17

■ **V**

Van Herpen I., 185–186
Velostat, 77
VibeAttire, 154

■ W

Warwick, K., 148
Wearable costumes
  actuation, 178
  energy harvesting, 180
  haptic devices, 179
  performance and haptics
    custom-made fabric
     capacitance sensors, 179
    haptic feedback, 179
    LED sneakers, hip-hop
     dance performance, 178
    small motors, 178
  sensing performers
    Arduino LilyPad, 178
    DIY breath sensor, 177
    heap sings, 177
    Midi Dancer system, 176
    sensor system, gloves, 177
    skin-tone cuffs, 176
  sensors, performance, 180
  technology *vs.* performance, 181
Wearable designmaterials. *See* Smart materials
Wearable Façade, 170
Wearable Motherboard, 10
Wearables
  abacus, 4
  arts (*see* Arts and wearables)
  body architecture, 195
  clock-watch, 4
  computational device, 4
  culture (*see* Culture and society)
  designing and making, 3, 5
  developments, 10
  digital fabrication (*see* Fabrication)
  digital watch, 4
  electric shock, 6
  Eudaumons' shoe computer, 5

  eyewear (*see* Eyewear)
  fabric (*see* Fabric and fabrication)
  fashion (*see* Fashion pioneers)
  fiction
    Bag of Tricks, 17
    Batsuit, 16
    bionics and biomimetics, 12
    concept, 19
    diegetic prototypes, 12
    evolution of technology, 19
    Exoskeleton, 17
    minority report, 12–13
    power laces, 14
    Sci-fi (*see* Sci-fi prophecies)
    smart watches, 14
    speculative, 11
    Star Trek (*see* Star Trek)
    TV glasses, 14
    weapons-based martial
     arts fighters, 16
    women bracelets, 17
  hardware problems, 6
  hearing aid, 5
  history of, 3
  radio waves, 5
  research, 9
  ring, watch, 4
  technology, 195
  textile (*see* Textiles)
  timing device, 5
  tools, 7
  wearer, 3
  wristwatch, 4
Weaving, 24
Wool, 23

■ X, Y, Z

Xitanit, 84

Get the eBook for only $5!

Why limit yourself?

Now you can take the weightless companion with you wherever you go and access your content on your PC, phone, tablet, or reader.

Since you've purchased this print book, we're happy to offer you the eBook in all 3 formats for just $5.

Convenient and fully searchable, the PDF version enables you to easily find and copy code—or perform examples by quickly toggling between instructions and applications. The MOBI format is ideal for your Kindle, while the ePUB can be utilized on a variety of mobile devices.

To learn more, go to www.apress.com/companion or contact support@apress.com.

Printed in the United States
By Bookmasters